Data Visualization with Excel® Dashboards and Reports

Data Visualization with Excel® Dashboards and Reports

Dick Kusleika

WILEY

to Butters

About the Author

Dick Kusleika has been working with Microsoft Office for more than 20 years. He was formerly a Microsoft MVP, having been awarded 12 consecutive years. Dick has written several books about Excel and Access.

About the Technical Editor

Doug Holland is a software engineer and architect at Microsoft Corporation and holds a master's degree in Software Engineering from the University of Oxford. Before joining Microsoft, he was awarded the Microsoft MVP and Intel Black Belt Developer awards.

Acknowledgments

My sincere thanks to Kelly Talbot for helping me navigate the writing process and keeping me on track. I'd also like to thank Pete Gaughan for spending a little extra time at the beginning—it was a great help.

Thanks also to Judy Flynn and Doug Holland for catching my mistakes and providing comments that simply made the book better. It was a pleasure working with such a professional team.

— Dick Kusleika

Contents at a Glance

Contents

Introduction

Businesses are collecting and storing more data than ever before. It's not just very large businesses either. Small and medium-sized businesses have unprecedented access to data and storage. It's management's job to use that data in decision making, but they simply can't consume all of it in its raw form. Business intelligence (BI) is the process of turning raw data into useful information.

BI has been around in some form for a long time. But recently the increase in quality and accessibility of BI tools have increased its popularity. These tools, coupled with a new widespread availability of data, have fueled an environment where it seems that everyone is creating dashboards.

Excel is becoming the standard for BI tools (if it's not already). Microsoft has invested heavily in the BI tools built in to Excel and some that are outside Excel. They have created the PowerBI family of tools (PowerQuery, PowerPivot, and PowerBI) and have added many more chart types than were available just a few versions ago.

What was once highly specialized software soon became a feature in Excel and available to anyone. In the past, you may have needed an IT project to get the data and the tools to create a dashboard. Now, you likely have it all on your computer already. And at the center of those tools is Excel, a program you probably already have regardless of the size of your business.

Maybe you've been wanting to create a dashboard but never thought you had the skills. Or maybe management has asked you to create one. This book will guide you through Excel's data visualization features from shapes to conditional formatting to charts. I include several realistic case studies so you can see how a business question can turn into a chart or dashboard.

What Does This Book Cover?

The chapters in this book are divided into three parts. In Part I, I discuss dash-boards as a whole, including three case studies that result in a full dashboard. Part II focuses on how to get the most of out of the individual elements that make up a dashboard and introduces you to some non-chart data visualization elements. In Part III, I discuss individual charts in detail and provide case studies for many different chart types.

Chapter 1: Dashboard Basics   This chapter covers the very basics of dash-boarding, including when a dashboard is appropriate and the big-picture steps for building and formatting a dashboard.

Chapter 2: Dashboard Case Studies   This chapter includes three case studies. Each case study provides background for the business need, the details around the request for a dashboard, and the construction of the dashboard elements.

Chapter 3: Organizing Data for Dashboards   This chapter is all about data. It covers best practices for organizing your data into layers. I also discuss several external data sources and how to get them into Excel.

Chapter 4: The Fundamentals of Effective Visualization   This chapter is for users who are new to creating visualizations. In it, I cover what makes an effective visualization, how to use elements like color and text, and how to choose a chart type for the data you want to present.

Chapter 5: Non-chart Visualizations   Not all dashboard elements are charts. In this chapter, I discuss visualization features in Excel, and dive deeply into custom number formatting.

Chapter 6: Using Shapes to Create Infographics   This chapter covers the basics of shapes in Excel. It also covers how you can use shapes to frame your data in interesting ways.

Chapter 7: Visualizing Performance Comparisons   This chapter discusses all the chart types that are appropriate for comparing performance data, including case studies for many of the chart types.

Chapter 8: Visualizing Parts of a Whole   This chapter includes sections for chart types that you use when you want to tell a story about how com-ponent parts make up a whole. It also includes several case studies with step-by-step instructions.

Chapter 9: Visualizing Changes over Time   This chapter reviews the chart types for displaying data that changes over time. In addition to the case studies, it includes a section on how to control charts with the Visual Basic for Applications programming language.

Companion Download Files

As you work through the examples in this book, the workbooks and supporting files you need are all available for download from `www.wiley.com/go/ datavizwithexcel/`.

How to Contact the Publisher

If you believe you've found a mistake in this book, please bring it to our attention. At John Wiley & Sons, we understand how important it is to provide our customers with accurate content, but even with our best efforts an error may occur.

In order to submit your possible errata, please email it to our Customer Service Team at wileysupport@wiley.com with the subject line "Possible Book Errata Submission."

Display Data on a Dashboard

Dashboard Basics

In This Chapter

- Determining When to Use a Dashboard
- Establishing User Requirements
- Assembling the Data
- Building the Dashboard
- Formatting the Dashboard

Dashboards have never been more popular. We have more data available to us all the time and better visualization tools than ever before. At its core, a dashboard is a collection of charts. But it's much more than that. If you put some charts on a page, you would technically have a dashboard, but perhaps not a very good one. Creating a good dashboard takes some preparation, knowledge, and skill. In this chapter, I introduce you to dashboards and the concepts, skills, and best practices you'll need to create them.

Determining When to Use a Dashboard

Dashboards are used to present data. Data can be thought to be at various stages: raw, aggregated, analyzed, and presented. The stage your data is in depends on where it comes from and what you plan to do with it. There are many levels of aggregation and an infinite number of ways to analyze or present data. For example, an invoice is an aggregation of invoice lines and a sales report is an aggregation of invoices. Relative to an invoice, the invoice lines are raw data but relative to the sales report, the invoices are the raw data. Figure 1.1 shows data in its various stages.

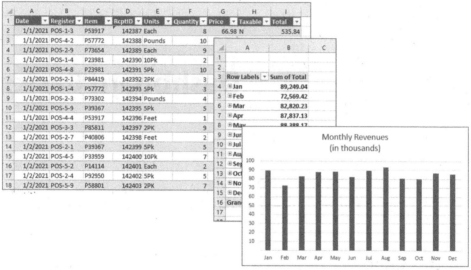

Figure 1.1: Data shown raw, aggregated, and analyzed and presented

Raw data is data that hasn't been processed. It can be transactions that come out of an accounting system, sales information from a point of sale, or readings from a measuring device like tank levels or temperatures. If you're starting with raw data, you will have to do some aggregating and possibly some analyzing before it's ready for a dashboard.

> **NOTE**   A workbook containing the charts in the figures for this chapter is named `Chapter1Figures.xlsx` and can be found on this book's companion website at www.wiley.com/go/datavizwithexcel/.

Aggregated data has been grouped and summarized in some way. A report of units produced by month sums the units produced each week or each day. And that may be a sum of units produced by shifts for a day. In many cases, dashboard builders start with aggregated data.

Dashboards tell a story about the underlying data. Analyzing data is determining what stories the data tells and which of those stories is worth telling. Analyzing is more than just drawing conclusions from the data. It's also understanding the nature of the data and what questions the data raises. It's common during data analysis to have to take a step back and aggregate the data in a different way.

Finally, there's the presentation stage, where dashboards live. The dashboard building process can start at any stage. If you get the source data from a data analyst, the story to tell may have already been determined and it's just a matter of presenting that story in an effective way. Conversely, if you start with raw data, you'll need to first aggregate and then analyze the data to make those determinations.

Dashboards are constantly evolving. At one time they were only static visuals telling one story. Now, dashboards include self-service business intelligence (BI) tools that either tell multiple stories or allow the users to find the meaning in the data themselves. With Microsoft's Power BI tool and its integration into Excel with Power Pivot and Power Query, self-service BI is becoming more mainstream and accessible.

CROSS-REFERENCE   Power Pivot, Power Query, and Power BI are introduced in Chapter 3, "Organizing Data for Dashboards."

What Is a Dashboard?

A dashboard is one or more visual elements that tell a story about related data. A report that aggregates data isn't a dashboard because it's not telling a story. That's typically called a report or table, although these terms are often used to mean the same thing. For our purposes, a dashboard must contain visual elements and not just a list of data.

The story is the most important aspect of a dashboard. It comes from analyzing the data to determine what's important about it. Key performance indicators (KPIs) are commonly displayed on dashboards. KPIs are ready-made stories for your dashboard to tell. I briefly discuss KPIs in the next section. A common pitfall in dashboard building is to start with a conclusion. The person requesting the dashboard may have an agenda or preconceived notion of what that data should say. But the data should drive the story, not the other way around. Try to reframe the conclusion as a question. If someone wants you to create a dashboard that shows that sales decreased because of bad weather, you can turn that into a question like "How does average daily temperature correlate with daily sales?" or "How much do we sell on rainy days vs. sunny days?"

The underlying data on a dashboard is related, but how it's related depends on who's looking at it. A member of the Human Resources department's dashboard might use data related to employee retention like hiring rate, firing rate, layoffs, voluntary terminations, and retirements. The human resources manager may have a dashboard that's a level above, such as more aggregated employee retention data along with payroll costs and benefit engagement. The person in charge of all administration in a company would look at human resources data next to finance, accounting, and legal data. At the top level of a company, data from administration, operations, and research and development is related.

Key Performance Indicators

How KPIs are determined and what makes a good one is well beyond the scope of this book. An organization's leaders will develop KPIs based on what they know about the organization. If you're running a for-profit business, net income is an important measurement and you don't have to analyze the data to know that it's something you'll want to look at. KPIs are unique to each organization, but similar organizations will have similar KPIs. Finance departments are interested in net income, free cash flow, and working capital. And manufacturers are interested in units produced and line utilization.

Establishing User Requirements

Don't start building a dashboard until you have a plan. Just like building a house, if you start without a plan, you may have to tear it down and start over. To make your plan, start by finding out what the end users need. There are at least three users you'll want to talk to before you begin: the person requesting the dashboard, the person providing the data, and the end user. All these users may be one person, and that person may even be you.

Get as much detail as you can from the person requesting the dashboard. If they have a general idea of what they want, now is the time to probe for details to get a clear picture. As I mentioned in the previous section, the requester might be starting with a conclusion in mind. Try to turn that conclusion into a question or series of questions so you're on the same page.

Questions about the source data are sometimes overlooked but shouldn't be. Find out where the data is coming from and if it's already been aggregated or analyzed. Depending on your project, you may want to try to get the data in as raw a form as possible in case you have to change direction once you get started. It's a lot easier to aggregate raw data in a different way but almost impossible to disaggregate it.

Determine if the data is coming from inside or outside of the organization, who maintains it, and how often it's updated. Financial data from an accounting system may only be available monthly or quarterly. Other types of data, like data from a point of sale, may be able to be queried in real time.

If you don't have the data you need, your dashboard project might turn into two projects: a data-collection project and a dashboard project. You may find that not only is the data not readily available, it doesn't exist at all. If the organization doesn't track defects from the production line, there may be no way to get historical data. In that case, you could set up a system to start tracking the data you need, which would delay how quickly a dashboard could be created. Having this conversation early in the project helps set the expectations of all the stakeholders.

Types of End Users

You can divide end users by how they intend to use the dashboard to get a better understanding of how to construct it. Monitors use dashboards to see the state of an organization or project at a given time. You use your car's dashboard to monitor speed, fuel levels, and trouble alerts. Deciders use dashboards to determine if they should take one action, another action, or no action at all. A production manager might use a dashboard of sales and line utilization data to determine if a third shift is necessary.

Planners are people at the highest levels of an organization that determine the direction of the organization. They are looking at broader trends, and the actions they take are more policy based. Planners might look at operating results by division to determine how to allocate resources for the next five years. Presenters use dashboards to present information. A dashboard presented at a shareholder meeting may be used to simply give shareholders information they don't see day to day.

There is a lot of overlap in these categories of users. Someone monitoring a project, for example, will certainly take action if the information dictates it. And shareholders might change the direction of a company by changing management if they don't like the information presented. Know your audience, and in some cases your audience's audience, so you can provide the right level of information.

Determine how often the dashboard will be created. If you're creating a dashboard to show the effects of the Olympics on a city's finances, you'll probably only do that one time. For one-off dashboards, you don't have to be as concerned about data maintenance and how efficiently you can build it.

For periodic or real-time dashboards, make sure the data availability lines up with how often you will be publishing. Also, invest more of your time in automation for dashboards you will be publishing more. Real-time dashboards have to be fully automated. Dashboards you publish annually can be less so.

Document the dashboard-building process from the start. You don't need fancy software for this, just a text document or a spreadsheet. Record the information about the users and the data that you've already discovered. Also document how the data moves through the process from raw, possibly through a database, and into a spreadsheet. Even if it's a dashboard that will be created often, or fully automated, document the data flow so you or someone else can troubleshoot problems when they arise. Imagine yourself re-creating the dashboard a year from now, after you've forgotten all the details, and try to provide answers to the questions you would have.

Plan on iterating through the dashboard design process. When you get a usable draft, send it to the stakeholders for input. Continue to send iterations for input throughout the process. You can continue to work on the next stage while you wait for input, but if there are problems, you'll save yourself a lot of rework compared to handing over a final design that's not right.

Finally, plan to review the results after the dashboard is complete. If you email a dashboard weekly, set up a reminder to check back with the end users in a few months to make sure it's still meeting their needs. This is particularly important if you are spending time creating the ongoing dashboard. In one case, I was creating a monthly dashboard and the publishing mechanism had failed. I didn't realize that it didn't get published for several weeks, but nobody asked where it was. It turned out that the needs of the end users had changed, and we stopped publishing that dashboard, saving time every month.

Assembling the Data

For Excel users, working with data is the best part of dashboard building. As you are no doubt aware, Excel provides great tools for data aggregation and manipulation, including hundreds of formulas and data tables and tools for sorting data, splitting data, and removing duplicates. In the following sections, I discuss some of Excel's tools for manipulating data.

REFERENCE   If the data driving your dashboard originates outside Excel, the first task will be to import the data. I discuss working with external data in Chapter 3.

PivotTables

One of Excel's most powerful tools is the *PivotTable*. A PivotTable is a report that filters, sorts, and summarizes your data based on conditions that you set. PivotTables are interactive in that you can drag and drop fields into the appropriate PivotTable Fields areas to quickly change how your data is summarized.

REFERENCE   Charts made from PivotTables are called PivotCharts. PivotCharts have interactive functions that other charts don't have. I discuss PivotCharts in more detail in Chapter 9, "Visualizing Changes over Time."

Anything you can do with a PivotTable you can do with worksheet formulas. A PivotTable will summarize your data in much less time than it takes to write the formulas to do the same thing. If you want to make changes to a PivotTable by adding, removing, or rearranging fields, it updates in a fraction of a second. Rewriting formulas for changes takes much longer. Figure 1.2 shows a portion of some raw data and Figure 1.3 shows one possible PivotTable you can create from the data.

▲	A	B	C	D	E
1	State	Region	Month	Qtr	Sales
2	California	West	Jan	Qtr-1	1,118
3	California	West	Feb	Qtr-1	1,960
4	California	West	Mar	Qtr-1	1,252
5	California	West	Apr	Qtr-2	1,271
6	California	West	May	Qtr-2	1,557
7	California	West	Jun	Qtr-2	1,679
8	Washington	West	Jan	Qtr-1	1,247
9	Washington	West	Feb	Qtr-1	1,238
10	Washington	West	Mar	Qtr-1	1,028
11	Washington	West	Apr	Qtr-2	1,345
12	Washington	West	May	Qtr-2	1,784
13	Washington	West	Jun	Qtr-2	1,574
14	Oregon	West	Jan	Qtr-1	1,460
15	Oregon	West	Feb	Qtr-1	1,954
16	Oregon	West	Mar	Qtr-1	1,726
17	Oregon	West	Apr	Qtr-2	1,461
18	Oregon	West	May	Qtr-2	1,764
19	Oregon	West	Jun	Qtr-2	1,144

Figure 1.2: Raw data for a PivotTable

Sum of Sales	Column Labels ▼		
Row Labels ▼	Qtr-1	Qtr-2	Grand Total
⊟ Central	21,025	22,176	43,201
Illinois	4,243	3,623	7,866
Kansas	4,776	4,007	8,783
Kentucky	3,342	4,626	7,968
Missouri	4,669	4,556	9,225
Oklahoma	3,995	5,364	9,359
⊟ East	17,267	17,864	35,131
Florida	4,722	4,630	9,352
Massachusetts	3,442	4,155	7,597
New Jersey	4,365	4,316	8,681
New York	4,738	4,763	9,501
⊟ West	16,778	18,242	35,020
Arizona	3,795	4,663	8,458
California	4,330	4,507	8,837
Oregon	5,140	4,369	9,509
Washington	3,513	4,703	8,216
Grand Total	55,070	58,282	113,352

Figure 1.3: A PivotTable

The PivotTable in Figure 1.3 was made by dragging the Qtr field to the Columns area, the Region and State fields to the Rows area, and the Sales field to the Values area. By default, Excel sums the Sales field because its data is numeric. For non-numeric data, Excel defaults to counting the data. Figure 1.4 shows the PivotTable Fields task pane with these conditions.

Figure 1.4: The PivotTable Fields task pane

The areas of the PivotTable Fields task pane are as follows:

- **Tools (represented by the gear icon)**: This section allows you to change the layout of the task pane and sort the field names. If you have a lot of fields, you may prefer a layout that shows more fields.

- **Search**: By typing in this text box, you limit the field list to only those fields that match or partially match the text you type.

- **Filters**: If you drag a field into this area, Excel places a drop-down box above your PivotTable. You can select one or more values from the drop-down to limit what data the PivotTable displays.

- **Columns**: Fields in this area are displayed across the top of the PivotTable. You can put multiple fields in the Columns area to nest them. That is, fields that are higher up in the Columns area will span multiple columns and the cells below it will only show values that are related to the higher fields. Figure 1.5 shows the Month field nested below the Qtr field. The values Jan, Feb, and Mar are the only values related to Qtr-1, so they're the only values shown nested beneath it.

Column Labels ▼								
⊟Qtr-1			Qtr-1 Total	⊟Qtr-2			Qtr-2 Total	Grand Total
Jan	Feb	Mar		Apr	May	Jun		
Sum of Sales 18,579	19,194	17,297	55,070	20,754	18,771	18,757	58,282	113,352

Figure 1.5: Nested fields in the Columns area

- **Rows**: Fields in this area are displayed down the left side of the PivotTable. As with the Columns area, you can nest fields to display them in a hierarchy. The PivotTable shown in Figure 1.3 shows the State field nested beneath the Region field.

- **Values**: Fields in this area are aggregated in the body of the PivotTable. Sum and Count are the most commonly used aggregators. But there are several more ways to aggregate, including Average, Min, and Max. The aggregation occurs at the intersection of the Column and Row fields. For example, where Qtr-1 and Missouri intersect, the PivotTable in Figure 1.3 sums the sales for only those rows that contain a State of Missouri and a Qtr of Qtr-1.

Excel adds grand totals and, if there are nested fields in the Columns or Rows areas, subtotals. These totals can be shown or hidden depending on how you want to display the data. To turn off the grand totals, select any part of the PivotTable and choose Options from the PivotTable Tools Analyze tab of the Ribbon to show the PivotTable Options dialog box shown in Figure 1.6. Uncheck the check boxes labeled Show Grand Totals For Rows and Show Grand Totals For Columns.

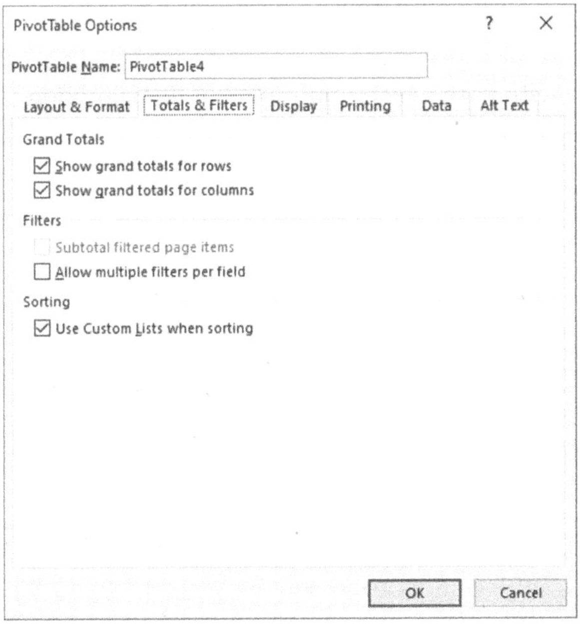

Figure 1.6: The PivotTable Options dialog box

To hide the subtotals for nested fields, right-click one of the values in the field and choose Field Settings from the context menu. On the Field Settings dialog box, shown in Figure 1.7, choose one of the following option buttons.

- **Automatic:** Displays subtotals with the same aggregation (sum, count, etc.) as the child field.

- **None:** Hides subtotals for the field.

- **Custom:** Displays subtotals with the same or a different aggregation than the Child field.

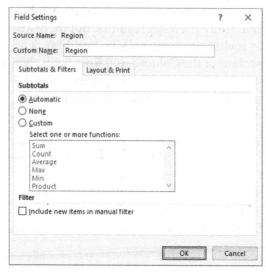

Figure 1.7: The Field Settings dialog box

Figure 1.8 shows a PivotTable with both grand totals and subtotals hidden.

Sum of Sales	Column Labels	
Row Labels	Qtr-1	Qtr-2
⊟ Central		
Illinois	4,243	3,623
Kansas	4,776	4,007
Kentucky	3,342	4,626
Missouri	4,669	4,556
Oklahoma	3,995	5,364
⊟ East		
Florida	4,722	4,630
Massachusetts	3,442	4,155
New Jersey	4,365	4,316
New York	4,738	4,763
⊟ West		
Arizona	3,795	4,663
California	4,330	4,507
Oregon	5,140	4,369
Washington	3,513	4,703

Figure 1.8: A PivotTable with no grand totals or subtotals

The GETPIVOTDATA Worksheet Function

PivotTables are dynamic by nature. That means they can change size and the location of the data you want, making it difficult to refer to their cells in formulas. Fortunately, Excel provides the GETPIVOTDATA worksheet function so that you can be sure you always point to the correct data.

For example, if you wanted to use California's first quarter sales in a formula, you can use this GETPIVOTDATA function:

```
=GETPIVOTDATA("Sales",$I$3,"State","California","Region","West","Qtr","
Qtr-1")
```

If more data is added to the source data and the PivotTable is refreshed so the cell that contains California's first quarter sales moves, the formula still points to the right place. The first argument of the function refers to the field in the Values area that you want to return. The next argument, I3, is the top-left cell of the PivotTable that contains the data. The last six arguments are pairs of values that determine what intersection of columns and rows to use.

The argument pairs can be in any order, but within the pairs, the field name must come first followed by the value for that field. The pair of arguments "State" and "California" tell the function to use the row where California appears on the State field. As the function evaluates the remaining pairs of arguments, it narrows down to the value to return.

You can also use GETPIVOTDATA to return totals. For example, to return the grand total of the Qtr-1 column, use this function:

```
=GETPIVOTDATA("Sales",$I$3,"Qtr","Qtr-1")
```

Or to return the grand total of the entire PivotTable, use this function:

```
=GETPIVOTDATA("Sales",$I$3)
```

The GETPIVOTDATA function is tedious to create manually. Fortunately, Excel will build the function for you when you click inside a PivotTable. Simply type an equal sign and click a cell inside the body of the PivotTable to have Excel build the function with all the proper arguments. If you want to refer to a cell in a PivotTable and avoid the GETPIVOTDATA function, you can simply type the cell address in your formula. To turn off the default behavior of using GETPIVOTDATA, go to File ⇨ Options ⇨ Formulas and uncheck the Use GetPivotData Functions For PivotTable References check box.

WARNING   Unlike formulas, a PivotTable does not automatically display changes made to data after the PivotTable is created. Click the Refresh button on the PivotTable Tools Analyze tab of the Ribbon to update the PivotTable for any changes.

Worksheet Functions

Excel has hundreds of worksheet functions to help you manipulate and stage data for a dashboard. In practice, you won't use most of them. But there are some worksheet functions that show up more often than not in dashboarding projects. In the following sections, I'll discuss some of the more common ones.

The VLOOKUP Function

The VLOOKUP function finds a value in the first column of a range and returns a value in another column on the same row as the found value. The syntax for VLOOKUP is as follows:

```
VLOOKUP(lookup_value, table_array, col_index_num, range_lookup)
```

Figure 1.9 shows an example of the VLOOKUP function.

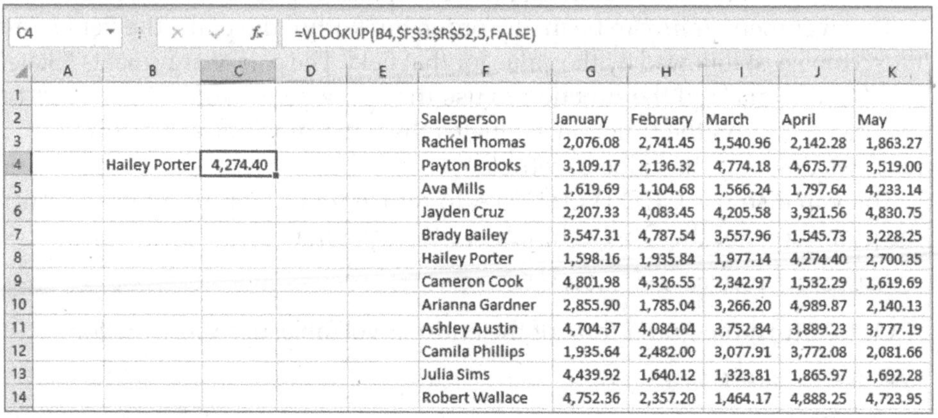

C4		▼	:	×	✓	*fx*	=VLOOKUP(B4,$F$3:$R$52,5,FALSE)				
▲	A	B	C	D	E	F	G	H	I	J	K
1											
2						Salesperson	January	February	March	April	May
3						Rachel Thomas	2,076.08	2,741.45	1,540.96	2,142.28	1,863.27
4		Hailey Porter	4,274.40			Payton Brooks	3,109.17	2,136.32	4,774.18	4,675.77	3,519.00
5						Ava Mills	1,619.69	1,104.68	1,566.24	1,797.64	4,233.14
6						Jayden Cruz	2,207.33	4,083.45	4,205.58	3,921.56	4,830.75
7						Brady Bailey	3,547.31	4,787.54	3,557.96	1,545.73	3,228.25
8						Hailey Porter	1,598.16	1,935.84	1,977.14	4,274.40	2,700.35
9						Cameron Cook	4,801.98	4,326.55	2,342.97	1,532.29	1,619.69
10						Arianna Gardner	2,855.90	1,785.04	3,266.20	4,989.87	2,140.13
11						Ashley Austin	4,704.37	4,084.04	3,752.84	3,889.23	3,777.19
12						Camila Phillips	1,935.64	2,482.00	3,077.91	3,772.08	2,081.66
13						Julia Sims	4,439.92	1,640.12	1,323.81	1,865.97	1,692.28
14						Robert Wallace	4,752.36	2,357.20	1,464.17	4,888.25	4,723.95

Figure 1.9: The VLOOKUP function

In this example, there is a table of commissions by salesperson and month in the range F3:R52. The formula finds the April commission for the salesperson in cell B4. The salesperson's name must be in the first column of the range. The formula looks down column F until it finds the salesperson's name, then returns the value in the fifth column.

The range_lookup argument is set to FALSE in this example because you want the formula to only return a value if it finds an exact match. If you set range_lookup to TRUE, Excel expects the data in the first column to be sorted and will return a close match if there isn't an exact one. There are situations where returning an approximate match is useful, but they are rare, and most of the time you'll want the last argument to be FALSE.

The XLOOKUP Function

The XLOOKUP function is a relatively new addition to the Excel worksheet function lineup. It works like VLOOKUP but doesn't require the value to find to be in the first column. Here is the syntax for XLOOKUP:

```
XLOOKUP(lookup_value, lookup_array, return_array, if_not_found,
match_mode, search_mode)
```

The first argument is the same for XLOOKUP and VLOOKUP. Instead of supplying the entire range and assuming the lookup value is in the first column, you supply a lookup_array (the column to search) and a return_array (the column with the value to return).

The XLOOKUP function also includes the if_not_found argument that lets you specify a value to return if the lookup value isn't in the list. If you don't specify this argument and the value isn't found, XLOOKUP returns the #N/A error value just like VLOOKUP.

The match_mode argument is like the range_lookup argument in VLOOKUP. Instead of TRUE or FALSE, you supply a number to tell Excel whether you want an exact match or one of the approximate match options. The exact match option, 0, is the default.

The last argument, search_mode, allows you to tell Excel how to search for the value. If you have a large data set, the search_mode argument can help speed up the search. For most data sets, it can be ignored.

Figure 1.10 shows an XLOOKUP formula to find the name of the salesperson with the highest commission in April.

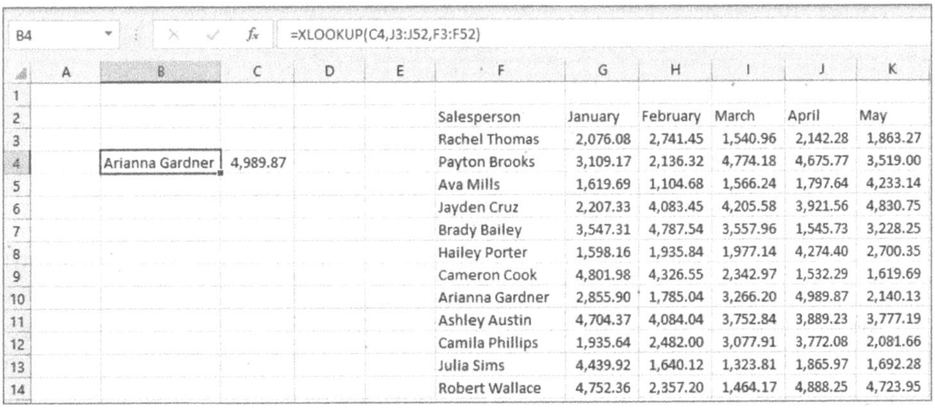

B4			f_x	=XLOOKUP(C4,J3:J52,F3:F52)						
	A	B	C	D	E	F	G	H	I	J	K
1											
2						Salesperson	January	February	March	April	May
3						Rachel Thomas	2,076.08	2,741.45	1,540.96	2,142.28	1,863.27
4		Arianna Gardner	4,989.87			Payton Brooks	3,109.17	2,136.32	4,774.18	4,675.77	3,519.00
5						Ava Mills	1,619.69	1,104.68	1,566.24	1,797.64	4,233.14
6						Jayden Cruz	2,207.33	4,083.45	4,205.58	3,921.56	4,830.75
7						Brady Bailey	3,547.31	4,787.54	3,557.96	1,545.73	3,228.25
8						Hailey Porter	1,598.16	1,935.84	1,977.14	4,274.40	2,700.35
9						Cameron Cook	4,801.98	4,326.55	2,342.97	1,532.29	1,619.69
10						Arianna Gardner	2,855.90	1,785.04	3,266.20	4,989.87	2,140.13
11						Ashley Austin	4,704.37	4,084.04	3,752.84	3,889.23	3,777.19
12						Camila Phillips	1,935.64	2,482.00	3,077.91	3,772.08	2,081.66
13						Julia Sims	4,439.92	1,640.12	1,323.81	1,865.97	1,692.28
14						Robert Wallace	4,752.36	2,357.20	1,464.17	4,888.25	4,723.95

Figure 1.10: The XLOOKUP function

Instead of looking for a value in the first column, this formula looks for a value in the fifth column and returns the corresponding value from the first column. The formula in cell C4, =MAX(J3:J52), finds the largest value in column J. The XLOOKUP function looks down column J for that value and returns the value in column F on the same row. Because you know the value exists and you want an exact match, you don't need to supply any of the other arguments to the function.

The INDEX and MATCH Functions

If you're using a version of Excel that doesn't include XLOOKUP, you can create the same result using a combination of the INDEX function and the MATCH function. The INDEX function returns a value from a range based on the row number and column number you provide. For a single column range, you only have to provide the row number. The MATCH function part of the formula computes which row INDEX uses. Figure 1.11 shows a formula to return the same values as the XLOOKUP function in the previous example.

B4		✕	✓	*fx*	=INDEX(F3:F52,MATCH(C4,J3:J52,0))					
	A	B	C	D	E	F	G	H	I	J	K
1											
2						Salesperson	January	February	March	April	May
3						Rachel Thomas	2,076.08	2,741.45	1,540.96	2,142.28	1,863.27
4		Arianna Gardner	4,989.87			Payton Brooks	3,109.17	2,136.32	4,774.18	4,675.77	3,519.00
5						Ava Mills	1,619.69	1,104.68	1,566.24	1,797.64	4,233.14
6						Jayden Cruz	2,207.33	4,083.45	4,205.58	3,921.56	4,830.75
7						Brady Bailey	3,547.31	4,787.54	3,557.96	1,545.73	3,228.25
8						Hailey Porter	1,598.16	1,935.84	1,977.14	4,274.40	2,700.35
9						Cameron Cook	4,801.98	4,326.55	2,342.97	1,532.29	1,619.69
10						Arianna Gardner	2,855.90	1,785.04	3,266.20	4,989.87	2,140.13
11						Ashley Austin	4,704.37	4,084.04	3,752.84	3,889.23	3,777.19
12						Camila Phillips	1,935.64	2,482.00	3,077.91	3,772.08	2,081.66
13						Julia Sims	4,439.92	1,640.12	1,323.81	1,865.97	1,692.28
14						Robert Wallace	4,752.36	2,357.20	1,464.17	4,888.25	4,723.95

Figure 1.11: The INDEX and MATCH functions

The syntax for the MATCH function is

```
MATCH(lookup_value, lookup_array, match_type)
```

The MATCH function works like VLOOKUP except that there is no column to return. It simply returns the position of lookup_value in the lookup_array list of values. The last argument of MATCH, 0, looks for an exact match like when the last argument of VLOOKUP is FALSE. In this example, MATCH returns the value 8 because the value in C4 is the eighth value in the range J3:J52.

Once Excel computes the value returned by MATCH, the INDEX function is evaluated like

```
=INDEX(F3:F52,8)
```

The syntax for the INDEX function is

```
INDEX(reference, row_number, column_number)
```

Because the reference argument is a single column, F3:F52 in this example, you only need to supply the row_number argument.

The SUMPRODUCT Function

The SUMPRODUCT function is one of Excel's most powerful worksheet functions. It's designed to multiply two or more ranges together and sum the results to a single number. A simple example of SUMPRODUCT is shown in Figure 1.12.

	A	B	C	D	E	F	G
			=SUMPRODUCT(A2:A5,B2:B5)				
1	Quantity	Price					
2	2	9.07					
3	3	4.46					
4	10	8.43					
5	9	4.53					
6							
7		Invoice Total:	156.59				
8							

Figure 1.12: The SUMPRODUCT function

In this example there are quantities, and for each quantity, a price. SUMPRODUCT multiplies each quantity by its corresponding price and sums all of the results. It's the same as putting in the formula =A2*B2 and filling down in column C and then using =SUM(C2:C5), but it does it in one formula.

The SUMPRODUCT function works like an array formula, discussed in the next section, and that's where its real power lies. With SUMPRODUCT, you can filter out values by multiplying them by 0, so they have no effect on the final sum. Figure 1.13 shows an example of using SUMPRODUCT to only sum totals for one product in one month.

L6   =SUMPRODUCT(($C$2:$C$3651=K6)*(MONTH($A$2:$A$3651)=4)*($I$2:$I$3651))

	A	B	C	D	E	F	G	H	I	J	K	L
1	Date	Register	Item	RcptID	Units	Quantity	Price	Taxable	Total			
2	1/1/2021	POS-1-3	P53917	142387	Each	8	66.98	N	535.84			
3	1/1/2021	POS-4-2	P57772	142388	Pounds	10	75.43	N	754.30			
4	1/1/2021	POS-2-9	P73654	142389	Each	9	93.00	Y	837.00			
5	1/1/2021	POS-1-4	P23981	142390	10Pk	2	51.03	N	102.06			
6	1/1/2021	POS-4-8	P23981	142391	5Pk	10	57.56	N	575.60		P23981	5,000.32
7	1/1/2021	POS-2-1	P84419	142392	2PK	3	44.53	N	133.59			
8	1/1/2021	POS-1-4	P57772	142393	5Pk	3	59.39	Y	178.17			
9	1/1/2021	POS-2-3	P73302	142394	Pounds	4	69.06	N	276.24			
10	1/1/2021	POS-5-9	P39367	142395	5Pk	5	61.18	N	305.90			
11	1/1/2021	POS-4-4	P53917	142396	Feet	1	19.67	N	19.67			

Figure 1.13: Filter values with SUMPRODUCT

This SUMPRODUCT example consists of three sections: two comparison sections and one result section. The magic of SUMPRODUCT is that when a comparison returns TRUE, multiplying it treats TRUE as the number 1, and when a comparison returns FALSE, multiplying it treats FALSE as the number 0. The first section, ($C$2:$C$3651=K6), compares every value in column C to the value in cell K6 and returns a TRUE or FALSE. The second section, (MONTH($A$2:$A$3651)=4), compares the month of every date in column A to 4 and returns a TRUE or FALSE.

The last section, ($I$2:$I$3651), doesn't do any comparison. Instead, it simply returns the long list of numbers from column I. Each of these sections is evaluated to an array of 3,650 values. The values in the arrays for the first two sections are either TRUE or FALSE and the values in the array of the last section are the values in column I.

Next, SUMPRODUCT multiplies each line of the arrays together. For the first items in the arrays, which correspond to row 2 of the data, SUMPRODUCT multiplies FALSE * FALSE * 535.84 because the value in C2 is not equal to the value in K6 and the month in A2 isn't 4. Since FALSE evaluates to 0 and multiplying any number by 0 equals 0, the total for that item is 0.

For the data in row 6, the item does match, but the month still does not. SUMPRODUCT evaluates that row as TRUE * FALSE * 575.60. The TRUE value is evaluated as a 1, but since the second section is FALSE, thus 0, the whole row still evaluates to 0. Only when the formula gets down to row 924 do both the item and the month match. When it evaluates that row, it multiplies TRUE * TRUE * 47.12. The TRUE values evaluate to 1 and that row adds 47.12 to the final sum.

You can see that if any condition is FALSE, Excel inserts a 0 into the multiplication and makes the whole row 0. Only if every condition is TRUE is a value other than 0 added to the total. It doesn't matter if you have 2 conditions or 20, if they're all TRUE, Excel keeps multiplying by 1, which has no effect on the final section.

In this way, SUMPRODUCT is like a PivotTable. In a PivotTable, Excel aggregates the values where all the row fields intersect all the column fields. The value of a PivotTable over SUMPRODUCT is that it's far easier to change a PivotTable than to rewrite a bunch of SUMPRODUCT formulas. But the value of formulas is that they recalculate instantly when the data changes, whereas you must refresh a PivotTable.

Another similarity between SUMPRODUCT and PivotTables is that you can aggregate values by counting them instead of summing them. To count values using SUMPRODUCT, only include comparison sections in the formulas. For example, to count all the rows with a specific product in April, use the following formula:

```
=SUMPRODUCT(($C$2:$C$3651=K7)*(MONTH($A$2:$A$3651)=4))
```

This formula is like the preceding example except that the section representing column I is omitted. Now when both conditions are TRUE, Excel multiplies 1 * 1, and the result, 1, is included in the sum. There are 18 rows in the example data that have P23981 as the item and the date is in April. For each of those rows, 1 is added to the total and the formula returns 18.

Another technique you can use with SUMPRODUCT is adding comparison sections together that refer to the same column. For example, if you want to sum the total for two products, P23981 and P73302, that occur in April, use the following formula:

```
=SUMPRODUCT((($C$2:$C$3651="P23981")+($C$2:$C$3651="P73302"))
* (MONTH($A$2:$A$3651)=4)*($I$2:$I$3651))
```

In this example, there are two conditional sections that refer to column C. They can never both be TRUE because any row in column C can only contain one item. By adding them together, Excel will add 0 + 0, 0 + 1, or 1 + 0 and will return the total if column C is either product (or 0 if it's neither). Because Excel multiplies before it adds, you have to enclose these conditional sections in their own sets of parentheses to force Excel to perform that evaluation first. Only use this technique when the comparison sections refer to the same column. If you add together comparisons for different columns, and they're both TRUE, it would return a 2 and your result would be wrong.

Array Formulas

The SUMPRODUCT function in the previous section is a special kind of array function. It only sums the results and can't aggregate them in any other way. Array formulas use the exact same calculation as SUMPRODUCT but you can choose how to aggregate the filtered values. With array formulas, you have to commit the formula after you enter it using Ctrl+Shift+Enter, not just Enter as you do with SUMPRODUCT or other worksheet functions.

Using the same data set from the SUMPRODUCT examples, if you want to return the largest total for product P23981 in April, you would use an array formula and the MAX function, as shown below and in Figure 1.14:

```
=MAX(($C$2:$C$3651=K6)*(MONTH($A$2:$A$3651)=4)*($I$2:$I$3651))
```

The formula bar in Figure 1.14 shows curly braces around the formula. You don't type those curly braces. Excel inserts them automatically when you commit the formula using Ctrl+Shift+Enter instead of just Enter. If your array formula isn't returning the correct result, the first thing to check is that the curly braces are there. If they are not, press F2 to edit the cell and recommit it with Ctrl+Shift+Enter.

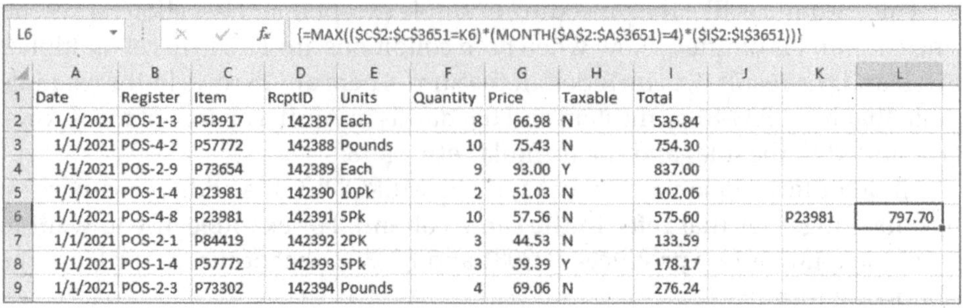

| L6 | | | ✕ | ✓ | fx | {=MAX(($C$2:$C$3651=K6)*(MONTH($A$2:$A$3651)=4)*($I$2:$I$3651))} | | | | | |

	A	B	C	D	E	F	G	H	I	J	K	L
1	Date	Register	Item	RcptID	Units	Quantity	Price	Taxable	Total			
2	1/1/2021	POS-1-3	P53917	142387	Each	8	66.98	N	535.84			
3	1/1/2021	POS-4-2	P57772	142388	Pounds	10	75.43	N	754.30			
4	1/1/2021	POS-2-9	P73654	142389	Each	9	93.00	Y	837.00			
5	1/1/2021	POS-1-4	P23981	142390	10Pk	2	51.03	N	102.06			
6	1/1/2021	POS-4-8	P23981	142391	5Pk	10	57.56	N	575.60		P23981	797.70
7	1/1/2021	POS-2-1	P84419	142392	2PK	3	44.53	N	133.59			
8	1/1/2021	POS-1-4	P57772	142393	5Pk	3	59.39	Y	178.17			
9	1/1/2021	POS-2-3	P73302	142394	Pounds	4	69.06	N	276.24			

Figure 1.14: An array formula to find the largest value

Just like SUMPRODUCT, this array formula contains two conditional sections and one values section. After Excel multiplies the three sections together, again treating TRUE as 1 and FALSE as 0, instead of summing the result, it finds the maximum value of the results. In fact, if you were to change the MAX to SUM in that formula, you would get the same result as the SUMPRODUCT formula.

To find the smallest value from a list of filtered values requires a slightly different technique. Since the values that you filter out evaluate to 0 prior to being aggregated, the smallest value from a list of positive values would always equal 0. Fortunately, the MIN function ignores text values and we can use that to only include nonzero values. The following formula returns the smallest value for item P23981 in April:

```
=MIN(IF(($C$2:$C$3651=K15)*(MONTH($A$2:$A$3651)=4)=0,"",$I$2:$I$3651))
```

The two conditional sections are places in the conditional argument of an IF function. If when multiplied together they equal 0, an empty string (two double quotes) is inserted in the filtered values, otherwise the value from column I is inserted. Since MIN ignores strings, it will ignore all the empty string values and only return the smallest value where the conditions are TRUE.

Tables

Tables are special areas in a spreadsheet that hold data. They're meant to be like database tables, but they only share some of the same properties. The two main advantages to using tables are that cell formats and formulas are consistent for all the rows, and references to the table grow and shrink automatically as the table grows and shrinks. Figure 1.15 shows a small table and a column chart created from that table.

If you change the number of rows or columns in the table, the chart will adjust automatically. The chart isn't simply referencing the range A1:C6, it's referencing the special area with a name like Table1 and is aware when that area grows or shrinks.

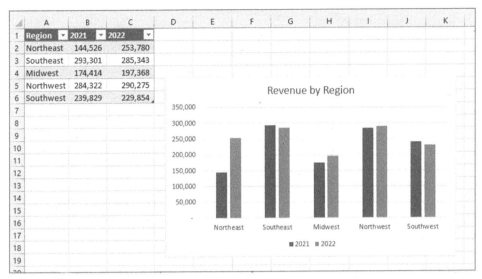

Figure 1.15: A column chart based on a table

The first step is to convert a normal Excel range into a table. To do that, select the range and choose Insert ➪ Table from the Ribbon to show the Create Table dialog in Figure 1.16.

Figure 1.16: The Create Table dialog

This dialog confirms the range you want to convert and lets you specify if the first row of your range contains headers. Click OK to finish creating the table. Next, select the table and choose Insert ➪ Recommended Charts from the Ribbon and choose the Clustered Column option to insert the chart. You can change the chart's title as I have, but it's not necessary for this example.

Now imagine a scenario where you want to add the next year to this chart and you want to split Texas out of the Southwest region and make it its own region. With a normal Excel range, you would add a new series for the new year and adjust the existing series to point to the larger range. But because you're using a table, you can simply add the data and the chart will adjust.

To add the new year, enter **2023** in cell D1. Figure 1.17 shows that Excel has increased the table columns for the new range and has already added a new series to the chart.

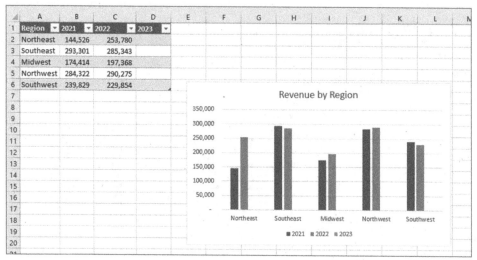

Figure 1.17: The table expands for new data.

Next, enter **Texas** into cell A7. Excel will increase the table rows and you can enter values for the new year and split the Southwest region. Figure 1.18 shows the new table size and the resulting chart.

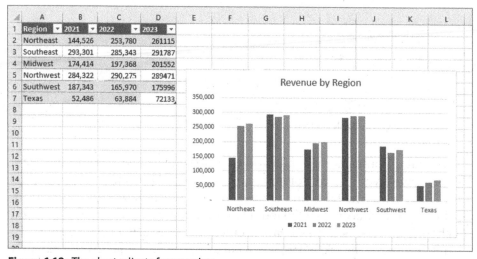

Figure 1.18: The chart adjusts for new data.

Excel has automatically added a new clustered column to the chart for the new region and the 2023 series is populated with the data entered in the table. The new data entered for Texas for existing years is automatically formatted with the same number format as the other data in those columns. Because 2023 is a new column, it does not have existing formatting to apply and you must format that column separately. Nothing on the chart was changed. You only have to add new data to the table to achieve these results.

Structured Table Referencing

The chart in the previous example adjusted as the data in the table changed. When you refer to tables in formulas using *structured table referencing*, your formulas will automatically account for changes in the table too. For these examples, the name of the table was changed to tblRevenue from Excel's default table name. To change the name of a table, select any part of the table and choose Table Tools Design ⇨ Table Name from the Ribbon and type the table's new name.

To create a formula using structured table referencing, select an unused cell in the worksheet, enter the start of a formula like **=SUM(**, and point to the range B2:B7. If you enter data in a cell that's adjacent to the table, Excel will assume you want to expand the table, so choose a cell away from the table. By default, Excel will convert your formula to structured table referencing like the formula below:

```
=SUM(tblRevenue[2021])
```

Instead of referring to the range B2:B7, Excel converted the argument to tblRevenue[2021], referring to the column labeled 2021 in the table named tblRevenue. If you're staging data for a dashboard, you can use structured table referencing to make sure your formulas always cover all the data.

You don't have to point to the data to get structured table referencing. You can enter that same formula manually. Start entering a formula by typing **=SUM(tbl** into a cell. Figure 1.19 shows the drop-down box Excel displays showing all your choices that contain those letters.

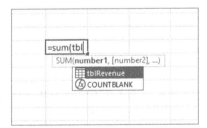

Figure 1.19: Excel's formula entry drop-down

If you have more than one table in your workbook and you choose to name them all starting with the same letters, like *tbl*, this method gives you a handy list of tables to choose from. In this example, there is only one table and it is selected because it's the first one on the list. From here, you can press the Tab key to complete the table name without having to type it all. After the table name, type an open bracket, [, to see a list of options related to that table. Figure 1.20 shows the list of options for tblRevenue.

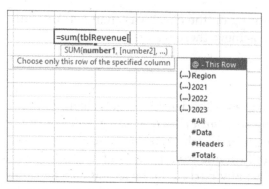

Figure 1.20: Options for table formula completion

The first option is the @ symbol. When you're using formulas from within a table, the @ symbol tells Excel to return the value from the same row as the formula. The reference [@2021] returns the value from the column named 2021 and that's on the same row. Contrast that to the reference [2021], which returns the entire column.

The next four options are the column names in the table. Excel is aware of the structure of the table and autogenerates named ranges for the columns. The last four options are references to special areas in the table. The #All reference refers to the entire table including headers and totals. The #Data reference is the same as #All except it excludes headers and totals. The #Headers and #Totals references refer only to their respective areas. You can arrow down to the option you want and press Tab to complete the entry.

For example, if you arrow down to the #Data reference, press Tab, and enter a closing bracket and closing parenthesis, you would get the following formula that sums all the data in the table:

```
=SUM(tblRevenue[#Data])
```

Text to Columns

When you're dealing with data that originated outside of Excel, sometimes the data is all lumped together instead of nicely laid out in columns. Excel's Text to Columns feature can help you manipulate data into a usable format. Figure 1.21 shows data pasted into column A of a worksheet. It is columnar data separated by commas but is all in one cell.

To separate the data, follow these steps:

1. Select the data and choose Data ⇨ Text to Columns from the Ribbon.

2. From the Convert Text to Columns Wizard, shown in Figure 1.22, select the Delimited option and click Next.

3. Unselect the Tab delimiter and select the Comma delimiter. Excel shows a preview of how it split the data, as shown in Figure 1.23. Click Next.

4. On the last step, you can format each column. Excel will generally convert dates and numbers successfully. If you have text that contains numbers with leading zeros, Excel will remove the zeros unless you format that column as Text. Figure 1.24 shows the data split into separate columns.

◢	A
1	January,69,47,38,97,36
2	February,14,47,62,90,67
3	March,42,78,83,94,82
4	April,72,15,65,61,21
5	May,56,70,84,22,33
6	June,37,38,97,39,34
7	July,18,96,76,91,88
8	August,13,59,79,43,80
9	September,70,36,33,77,69
10	October,29,58,25,99,87
11	November,56,83,88,39,24
12	December,93,99,52,33,97

Figure 1.21: Data that is lumped together in a cell

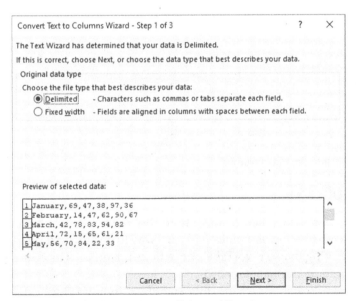

Figure 1.22: The Convert Text to Columns Wizard

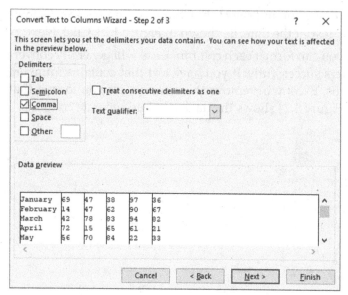

Figure 1.23: Excel splits the data on the delimiter.

▲	A	B	C	D	E	F
1	January	69	47	38	97	36
2	February	14	47	62	90	67
3	March	42	78	83	94	82
4	April	72	15	65	61	21
5	May	56	70	84	22	33
6	June	37	38	97	39	34
7	July	18	96	76	91	88
8	August	13	59	79	43	80
9	September	70	36	33	77	69
10	October	29	58	25	99	87
11	November	56	83	88	39	24
12	December	93	99	52	33	97

Figure 1.24: Data split into separate columns

Removing Duplicates

Another common problem when dealing with raw data is duplicate records. Excel's Remove Duplicates tool is a quick and easy way to delete duplicate records in place without having to use PivotTables or tedious formulas. The data shown in Figure 1.25 has some duplicate records.

To remove the duplicates, select the data and click Remove Duplicates from the Data tab on the Ribbon. This will show the Remove Duplicates dialog, shown in Figure 1.26.

⊿	A	B	C	D
1	Invoice	Date	Customer	Amount
2	IN001000	12/1/2021	Atlantic Northern	847.97
3	IN001000	12/1/2021	Atlantic Northern	847.97
4	IN001003	12/21/2021	Big T Burgers and Fries	763.62
5	IN001003	12/21/2021	Big T Burgers and Fries	763.62
6	IN001006	12/25/2021	Sixty Second Avenue	516.08
7	IN001007	12/4/2021	Mainway Toys	706.85
8	IN001008	12/19/2021	Carrys Candles	726.68
9	IN001013	12/2/2021	The Legitimate Businessmens Club	666.51
10	IN001014	12/14/2021	Zevo Toys	780.58
11	IN001016	12/15/2021	North Central Positronics	370.02
12	IN001022	12/25/2021	Fake Brothers	142.65
13	IN001022	12/25/2021	Fake Brothers	142.65
14	IN001022	12/25/2021	Fake Brothers	142.65
15	IN001023	12/14/2021	General Services Corporation	931.21
16	IN001024	12/3/2021	General Products	918.33
17	IN001026	12/6/2021	Taco Grande	303.72
18	IN001032	12/10/2021	Videlectrix	939.56
19	IN001036	12/15/2021	Wernham Hogg	909.72
20	IN001037	12/30/2021	Sample, inc	563.13
21	IN001040	12/24/2021	Taco Grande	472.36
22	IN001040	12/24/2021	Taco Grande	472.36
23	IN001042	12/7/2021	Roxxon	909.71
24	IN001046	12/1/2021	LuthorCorp	121.00
25	IN001048	12/15/2021	Videlectrix	897.77

Figure 1.25: Data with duplicate records

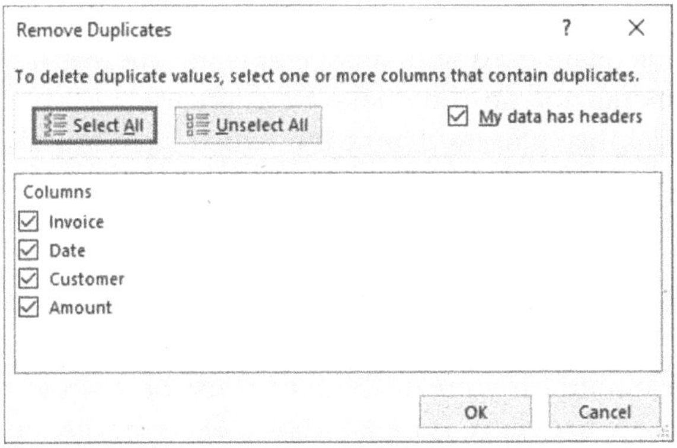

Figure 1.26: The Remove Duplicates dialog

The dialog shows all the columns from the data, and you can select which of those columns will determine what's a duplicate. With invoices, like in this example, all the data will be duplicated, so choose all the columns. For other types of data, maybe only one or two of the columns will determine a duplicate. To avoid deleting data you shouldn't, try to use as many columns as possible. When you click OK, Excel displays the message box in Figure 1.27 showing how many rows will be deleted.

Figure 1.27: Excel displays the number of deleted values.

Click OK to dismiss the message box and you're left with only unique records. You can undo this action if you determine you made a mistake.

Building the Dashboard

If you're a typical Excel user, like me, you probably relish working with numbers, tables, and PivotTables. You may not be as comfortable designing visual elements. Fortunately, there are lot of great examples to draw from, and you probably already see them in news articles or on the websites you visit. Dashboarding has been around long enough that the community has developed some visualization principles to help you create great dashboards. Once you learn these principles, you'll likely become a critic of every dashboard you see!

The first rule is to stay on message. If you've done the planning steps, you already have a good idea of what data you have available and what the end user's needs are. Make every element of your dashboard further the story your dashboard tells. Can you tell the story and meet the user's needs with one simple chart? If so, don't clutter the dashboard with other elements. There is no minimum number of visual elements you need to make a dashboard.

To that end, don't let the availability of data determine which elements to include on the dashboard. It's very likely you'll have more data available than you need. When you have a data set that's perfectly aggregated and requires almost no work to drive a chart, it's tempting to include it because of the low cost of creation. But there's an even greater cost if it detracts from the dashboard's overall message.

That's not to say that every element on your dashboard must be a showstopper. On every dashboard there are more important and less important elements. Elements that support the story, but aren't necessarily critical, can still be included if they don't add clutter. There's a balance between providing as much information as possible and keeping the dashboard clean and simple that you will learn with experience.

Organizing Elements

There's a lot of information and opinions about how to design for documents with multiple elements, particularly in the area of web page design. I think there are three main principles that cover most of it: size, color, and placement.

The largest element will get the most attention. Make the element with most important information larger than the others. It doesn't have to be so large that it dominates the page, but its size should be an indication of its importance. Consider the white space around an element as part of its size. Figure 1.28 shows a dashboard with three elements, one of which is larger to indicate its importance over the others.

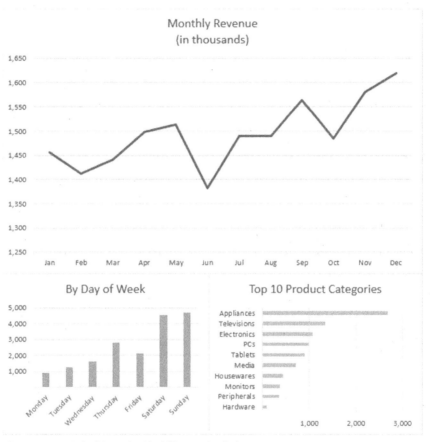

Figure 1.28: A dashboard with different sized elements

Elements with bright and contrasting colors will be perceived as more important than light, consistently colored elements. If every element on your dashboard has bright, contrasting colors, it will look more cluttered than the same layout with only one such element. I'm not advocating one garishly colored chart with a bunch of gray ones. It only takes a subtle difference in color to draw a reader's attention. In every case, you'll want to limit the total number of colors you use and the ones that are there should complement each other. But a slight variation can make an element stand out.

Generally, the most important element should be at the top left of the page and the least important at the bottom right. Think of someone reading a few lines of text. They start at the top left and read across, then drop down to the next line and read across from there. Whatever's at the top left will get the reader's attention first. Another design pattern is to place the most important element in the center and surround it with less important elements. This pattern seems most effective when one element is overwhelmingly more important than the others.

Varying Elements

A dashboard typically contains several different chart types. If every element is a line chart, the reader has to work harder to interpret the information. There is a case for having the same chart type for all the elements. If the data is the same for every element except for one dimension, like sales over time, but each chart is for a different region, then using the same chart type will help the reader make the connection that the data is similar. However, when the data varies by more dimensions, like units vs. dollars and time scale, different chart types are warranted. Figure 1.29 shows a dashboard where all eight charts are the same type, indicating that the data is the same except for one dimension.

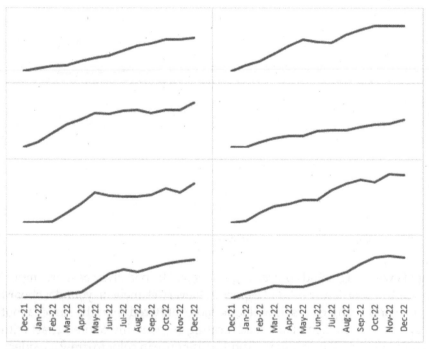

Figure 1.29: A dashboard of the same chart type

As you'll see in Part III, "Tell a Story with Visualization," the chart type you select should match the data and the story you're telling. But there is some overlap. Line charts are great for showing changes over time, but a column chart can be just as effective if the time is broken into discrete periods, like months.

That doesn't mean that every element has to be a different chart type. It just means that if you do use the same chart type for different data, don't place them right next to each other and make them the same size and color. And like the warning against including data simply because it's available, don't include a chart type because it's the hot, new thing or you just learned how to make it. Ensure that the chart types fit the data and further the story.

Showing Trends

If you want to show a trend, you can add a trendline to a chart. Some charts already show the trend and the trendline doesn't add any information. Figure 1.30 shows a line chart with a dashed trendline. The trend is easy to see without the added trendline, so it should be omitted.

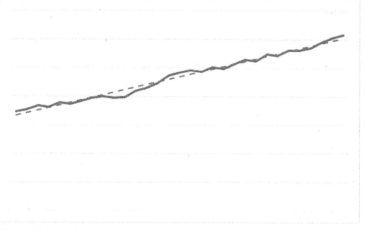

Figure 1.30: A trendline that adds little information

In other cases, the trendline is helpful. If the data has variations that make the trend hard to see, and showing the trend is part of the story you're telling, then include a trendline. Figure 1.31 shows a line chart of daily sales. The periodic dips for the decreased sales over the weekends make it harder to spot the trend. In this case, a trendline helps the reader interpret the data more easily.

To add a trendline, right-click on a series and choose Add Trendline. By default, a linear trendline is added to the chart and the Format Trendline task pane is displayed, as shown in Figure 1.32.

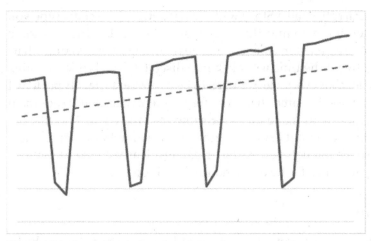

Figure 1.31: A trendline helps when data varies.

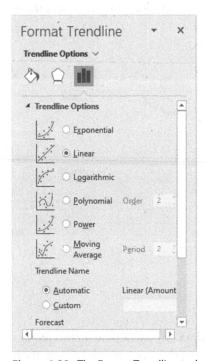

Figure 1.32: The Format Trendline task pane

There are several options for the type of trendline to display. Choose a trendline type that fits your data:

- **Exponential:** Best for data sets that rise or fall at increasingly higher rates.
- **Linear:** Best for simple, linear data sets.

- **Logarithmic:** Best for data sets that rise or fall quickly, then level out.

- **Polynomial:** Best for data sets that fluctuate.

- **Power:** Best for data sets that rise or fall at a constant rate.

- **Moving Average:** Best for data sets that have regular fluctuations that you want to smooth out.

Formatting the Dashboard

Formatting can be the difference between a good dashboard and a great one. Fortunately, Excel provides a lot of formatting options for most of the chart types it offers. Excel also provides formatting options that don't add much value and can take away from the message of the chart.

As with overall dashboard design, keep your formatting clean and simple. Overformatting distracts the user from interpreting the data and leads to less effective charts. Figure 1.33 shows a chart with a lot of formatting. Figure 1.34 shows the same chart with a clean and simple design. While the first chart shows how powerful Excel's charting engine is, the second chart showcases the data and the message.

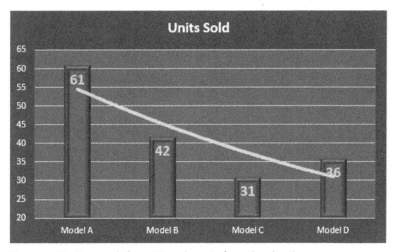

Figure 1.33: Too much formatting detracts from the chart's message.

The worst offender of Excel's formatting options is 3D. Applying 3D formatting almost always distorts the visual elements so they no longer represent the underlying data. With 3D column charts, the front row of columns has a larger area and the back row is partially obscured. 3D charts look cool, but they make it difficult for the reader to interpret the data accurately and the message may be lost.

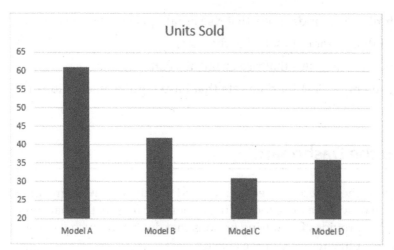

Figure 1.34: Clean and simple formatting keeps the message front and center.

Here are some other chart formatting options to avoid or use with caution:

▪ **Background color:** White or very light colors are acceptable backgrounds. Black and other dark colors lessen the contrast between the chart elements that represent data and the background. The background never represents data and should not be emphasized.

▪ **Foreground color:** Don't include too many colors in your chart elements. Use color for a specific purpose, like to call attention to an important data point. Excel's color pallet, shown in Figure 1.35, makes it easy to keep your colors consistent by offering different levels of light and dark. Excel's theme gallery, shown in Figure 1.36, provides different pallets of colors that are complementary.

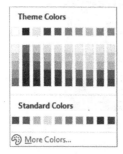

Figure 1.35: Excel's color pallet

▪ **Gradients:** Gradient fills change the color of a chart element from very dark to very light. This offers no value and should be avoided.

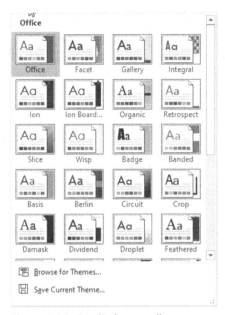

Figure 1.36: Excel's theme gallery

- **Pictures:** Picture fill colors a chart element with a repeating image. It not only adds no value but is distracting and decreases the effectiveness of the chart. Picture fill should also be avoided.

- **Effects:** The Format Data Series task pane has an Effects tab for most chart elements. It includes formatting options like Shadow, Glow, and Bevels. If used judiciously, some of these options can add depth to a chart that can be visually appealing. But there is a tendency to overuse these options and distract from the chart's message. Generally, you should avoid this tab unless you have a compelling reason to use it.

- **Borders:** Borders are lines that surround the plot area of a chart. They are almost never necessary. The axes already provide a visual boundary for the plot area. If you hide the axes because they aren't necessary, the border probably isn't necessary either. If you decide to use a border, make the color lighter so the data elements stand out.

- **Gridlines:** Excel includes gridlines by default on most chart types. Often, they don't add any value to the chart. If there is an important data point that you want to draw attention to and it's not near the axis, consider using a data label or color for that data point. If you choose to use gridlines, make sure they are light enough that they don't draw attention from the data elements.

▪ **Data labels:** If every data point has a data label, then you've created a table of data that's hard to read. Use data labels to highlight important data points, like the minimum or maximum value. Data labels can also be used to explain unexpected values. Figure 1.37 shows a chart that uses a data label to explain an unusual dip in the output for a manufacturing plant.

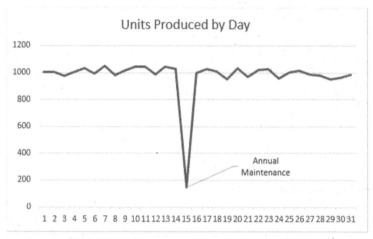

Figure 1.37: Data labels can be used to highlight unusual variations.

▪ **Axes:** In most cases, the axes provide context and scale to the chart. In some cases, such as variance charts, the value of the axes is diminished. Don't include an axis just because Excel adds them by default. Think about how they contribute to the message and help the reader interpret the data when you choose to show or hide them.

Avoid adding clip art to your charts. Your chart is already a picture. You don't need to add another picture to it. It can only detract from the data and message.

Number Formats

Your charts will almost always contain numbers, either in the axes or in data labels. Excel will use the formatting of the source data by default and that may not be what you want. Always use commas to make the numbers easier to read.

Format the numbers in your chart to the proper level of significance. If you're showing revenue numbers in the tens of millions, you don't need to show the pennies. Excel provides a robust number formatting system that allows you to format almost any way you want. Try to show the lowest number of digits possible without losing any data. For example, show the number 17,483,262 as 17.4 and use the title or axis label to tell the user that the numbers are in millions. The chart shown in Figure 1.38 uses this technique in the value axis.

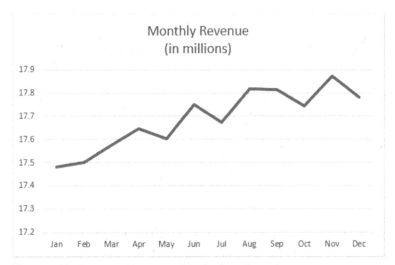

Figure 1.38: Formatted large numbers in the value axis

To format large numbers in an axis, use the Number section of the Format Axis task pane, shown in Figure 1.39. The zeros indicate where a digit is displayed. Where there are no digits to the right of a comma, the triplet representing hundreds or thousands is completely hidden.

Figure 1.39: The Number section of the Format Axis task pane

Table 1.1 shows some ways that you can format large numbers.

Table 1.1: Custom formats for large numbers

TO DISPLAY THIS NUMBER...	USE THIS CUSTOM FORMAT
17.5	0,,.0
17	0,,
$17.5	$0.0,,
$17	$0,,

Continues

Table 1-1 (*continued*)

TO DISPLAY THIS NUMBER...	USE THIS CUSTOM FORMAT
17.5M	0.0,,"M"
17M	0,,"M"
$17.5M	$0,,,.0"M"
$17M	$0,,"M"
17,483K	0,000,"K"
$17,483K	$0,000,"K"

You can use dollar signs for money and letters, like K for thousands, M for millions, and B for billions, to show the scale of the numbers. Only use these options if you have a few numbers on your chart, like if you've highlighted a couple of important data points. For axes, don't use dollar signs or letters. Instead, use the axis label or the chart's title to show the scale.

CHAPTER 2

Dashboard Case Studies

In This Chapter

- Monitoring Progress
- Displaying Key Performance Indicators
- Reporting Financial Information

Dashboards can be used to display information for a wide variety of purposes. In this chapter, I discuss three common uses of dashboards: monitoring the progress of a project or goal, displaying data to determine the performance or health of an entity (like a company or department), and reporting common financial data. I present a case study for each dashboard type including instructions on how to plan, collect, and manipulate data and construct the dashboard.

Monitoring Progress

A dashboard to monitor progress presents the user with information about the current status of a project or goal. It implies that whatever is being monitored has an end. That may be, for example, a project to produce a product or a financial or operational goal. When the project is complete and the product delivered, the resources for that project are put to use elsewhere. Or when the goal is achieved, a new goal is set.

What you measure to determine where you are in a project, or how close you are to your goal, varies greatly. You may have a time-based budget, a financial budget, or intermediate deliverables to gauge progress. And sometimes you have all three.

Case Study: Monitoring a Software Project

Your company is developing time clock software for internal use and has assigned developers to complete the project. The IT department has developed a budget for the number of developer hours it needs for the project and a list of tasks it will perform. They have asked you to help design and create a dashboard so that stakeholders in the organization can monitor the progress of the project.

> **NOTE**   The workbook for this case study is `SoftwareProject.xlsx` and can be found at www.wiley.com/go/datavizwithexcel/.

Planning and Layout

You start with a brainstorming session with the IT department and the people in the organization who will use the dashboard. The purpose of the meeting is to determine what information the dashboard will display and how often it will be updated. Write down every idea, even the bad ones. In the next step, you can determine what's important and will end up in the final product. The brainstorming session yields the following list:

- Hours compared to budget
- Tasks completed compared to budget
- The next milestones to hit
- Features that have stalled or are taking longer than expected
- The amount of code that has been written
- Features or tasks that have not been assigned resources
- The number of days until the software launch
- The amount of code that has been tested
- The current phase of the project
- The amount of time until the next phase starts
- The tasks that have not started, are in progress, have been completed, or are overdue

The group takes some time to consider the list and reconvenes to determine what should make it on to the dashboard. After some debate and discussion, they agree on the following information:

- Something to show the overall status of the project. The CEO and CIO don't necessarily want to dig into the detail unless there's a problem. They want something like a green-yellow-red indicator and ask you to work with IT to develop the conditions for each status.

- Something that shows how many hours have been spent compared to the total hours budgeted.

- Something that shows how many tasks are completed compared to the total number of tasks.

- They determine that code commits, when a developer puts code into the repository, will be good indicator of whether work is progressing. They ask you to include something that shows code commits.

- Something that shows what phase they're in, how far along in that phase they are, and what the next phase is.

The development team divides the project into phases (major features or infrastructure) and sprints (two-week periods where specific tasks are completed). They think showing code commitment in the context of sprints will be most useful. Your next step is to design an initial layout, sometimes called wireframing, shown in Figure 2.1.

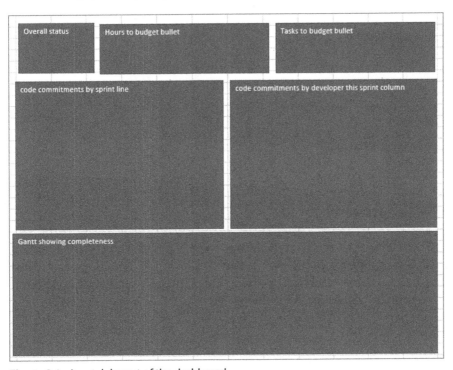

Figure 2.1: A rough layout of the dashboard

As you can see from Figure 2.1, the layout doesn't need to be pretty or all lined up at this stage. It includes some initial determinations of what type of visuals to use for some of the areas. For hours and tasks, you decide to use a bullet chart. For code commits, you decide on a line chart for commits by sprint and a column chart for commits by developer for the current sprint. To show progress through the phases, you suggest a Gantt chart. Everyone agrees that the layout is a good start, and it's on to the next step: collecting the data.

Collecting the Data

For hours and tasks, the development team agrees to provide a summary of actual and budgeted numbers. You provide them with a template, and they return it with the current numbers, as shown in Figure 2.2.

	A	B	C
1	Metric	Hours	Tasks
2	Actual	744	306
3	Budget Project to Date	750	294
4	Total	2,250	814
5			

Figure 2.2: Collecting data for hours and tasks

The code repository produces a report of commits as a comma-separated values (CSV) file. Figure 2.3 shows part of an Excel table with the data pasted into it.

	A	B	C
1	Sprint	Developer	Commits
2	1	Rachel	7
3	1	Andrew	5
4	1	Payton	7
5	1	Carlos	9
6	1	Ava	5
7	2	Rachel	4
8	2	Andrew	10
9	2	Payton	4
10	2	Carlos	10
11	2	Ava	10
12	3	Rachel	4
13	3	Andrew	4
14	3	Payton	6

Figure 2.3: Collecting data for code commits

The development team assigns labels to the 15 sprints, shown in Figure 2.4. They use far more detailed descriptions and tasks lists to develop the software, but they believe these labels will provide the right level of detail for someone evaluating the overall progress of the project.

▲	A	B	C
1	Feature	Start	End
2	Database	1	2
3	User Login	3	3
4	User Maintenance	4	6
5	Time Entry	7	9
6	Time Edit	10	12
7	Review	13	13
8	Submit	14	15

Figure 2.4: Collecting data for overall progress

Finally, you and the development team devise the criteria for the green-yellow-red status indicator. Your initial suggestion follows:

- **Green:** At or under budget for hours and tasks
- **Yellow:** Over budget by not more than 10%
- **Red:** Over budget by more than 10%

You send the criteria to the broader group for approval. While you wait for the response, you start building the visual elements.

Building the Visual Elements

In the following subsections, you'll walk through building the visual elements. Start by creating a worksheet named **Dashboards** where you'll place the final elements.

Hours and Tasks Bullet Charts

For hours and tasks, you decide to create bullet charts. Bullet charts are a great way to show progress toward a goal in a relatively small space. Select the table containing the hours and tasks data and follow these steps to create the first bullet chart:

1. From the Insert tab on the Ribbon, select Recommended Charts and choose the Clustered Bar option.
2. Right-click the chart and choose Select Data.
3. Click the Switch Row/Column button to move Hours to the Category axis.
4. Select the Total series and click the Remove button. Figure 2.5 shows the Select Data Source dialog after these changes and Figure 2.6 shows the chart at this stage.
5. Right-click the Actual series and choose Change Series Chart Type.
6. On the Change Chart Type dialog, move the Actual series to the secondary axis. Figure 2.7 shows the Change Chart Type dialog.

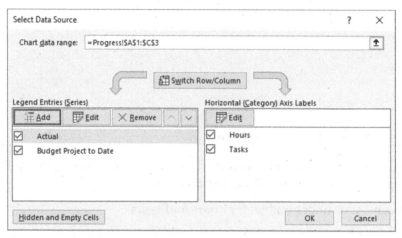

Figure 2.5: The Select Data Source dialog

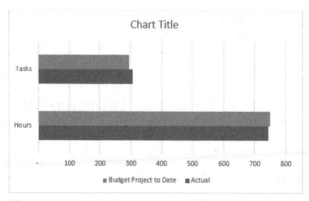

Figure 2.6: An intermediate hours bar chart

7. Right-click the Actual series and choose Format Data Series to show the Format Data Series task pane.

8. Change the Gap Width value to **400%**.

9. On the Fill & Line tab of the task pane, change Fill to Solid and set the color to a dark orange.

10. Click the Budget series and change Gap Width to **90%**, change Fill for the Budget series to Solid, and set the color to a light orange. Figure 2.8 shows the chart after these changes have been made.

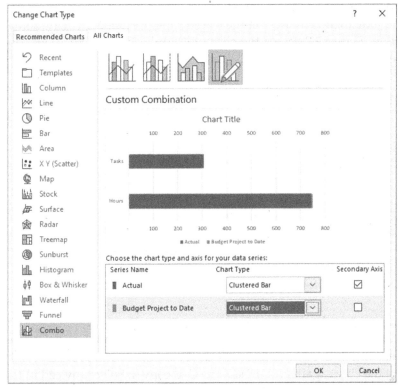

Figure 2.7: Move the Actual series to the secondary axis.

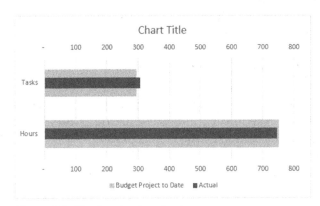

Figure 2.8: Overlapping bar charts

Before you split this chart into two separate charts, clean it up. From the Chart Elements button, uncheck the Primary Vertical axis and Secondary Horizontal axis check boxes to remove them. Next, uncheck the Gridlines and Legend check boxes to hide them. Finally, change the Number format of the Horizontal Axis to **Number**. Figure 2.9 shows the chart with only the elements you want for the final chart.

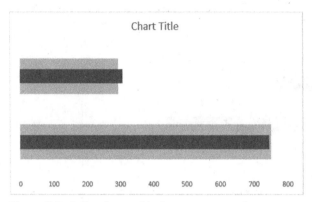

Figure 2.9: Bullet charts with elements removed

The next step is to split the chart into two separate charts and place them on the dashboard. Insert a new worksheet and name it **Dashboard**. Select the chart and press Ctrl+X to cut it. Select the Dashboard sheet and press Ctrl+V to paste it. Select the chart again and press Ctrl+C to copy it. Select any cell in the worksheet and press Ctrl+V to paste the copy of the chart.

Right-click one of the charts and choose Select Data. Uncheck the Tasks category and click OK. Change the chart's title to **Actual Hours vs. Budget**. Remove the Hours category from the other chart and change its name to **Tasks Completed vs. Budget**.

By building one chart and splitting it, you only have to apply the formatting once. However, removing categories will change the scale of the axis. Set the Minimum value of each axis to zero by right-clicking and choosing Format Axis.

Resize both charts by dragging the lower-right sizing handle. Don't spend a lot of time getting the size and position of the charts perfect. When other visual elements are added to the dashboard, you will have to adjust them to fit. Figure 2.10 shows the two bullet charts positioned on the Dashboard worksheet.

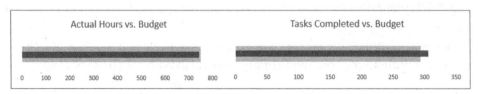

Figure 2.10: Two bullet charts positioned on the dashboard

Code Commits Line Chart

The next visual element you'll create is a line chart that shows the code commits by sprint. The code commit data isn't staged properly for a line chart, so you decide to create a PivotChart to manipulate the data. To create the PivotChart, follow these steps:

1. Turn the code commits data into a table by selecting it and pressing Ctrl+T.

2. On the Table Tools Design tab of the Ribbon, change the name of the table to **tblCommits**.

3. Select the table and choose Insert ➪ PivotChart ➪ PivotChart from the Ribbon to show the Create PivotChart dialog.

4. Choose Existing Worksheet and select a cell on the Dashboard worksheet. It doesn't matter which cell you select as you will move the chart later. Figure 2.11 shows the Create PivotChart dialog.

Figure 2.11: Create a PivotChart on the Dashboard worksheet.

5. Click OK and Excel will place a PivotChart outline on the sheet and show the PivotChart Fields task pane.

To populate the PivotChart, drag the Sprint field to the Axis (Categories) box and the Commits field to the Values box. The resulting PivotTable and Pivot-Chart are shown in Figure 2.12.

To format the PivotChart, follow these steps:

1. Right-click the series on the chart and choose Change Series Chart Type.

2. Select the Line option and click OK.

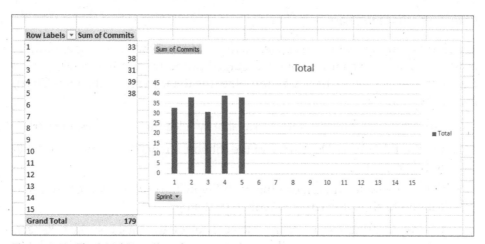

Figure 2.12: The initial PivotChart for commits by sprint

3. Select the Row Labels drop-down on the PivotTable and choose Value Filters to show the Value Filter (Sprint) dialog.

4. Filter the data for Sum Of Commits ⇨ Does Not Equal ⇨ **0** as shown in Figure 2.13.

Figure 2.13: Filter the PivotTable to hide zeros.

5. Delete the legend by selecting it and pressing Delete.

6. Change the title to **Code Commits by Sprint**.

7. On the PivotChart Analyze tab of the Ribbon, choose Hide All from the Field Buttons drop-down.

8. Right-click the line and choose Format Series and change the fill to solid fill and dark blue.

9. Position the chart over the PivotTable. Figure 2.14 shows the final PivotChart.

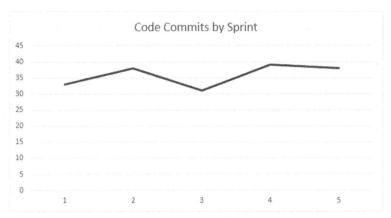

Figure 2.14: The completed Code Commits by Sprint line chart

Code Commits by Developer Bar Chart

The next visual element is a bar chart to show the code commits by developer for the current sprint. Creating PivotCharts from the Commits table saves you from having to write formulas to stage the data for different types of charts. Positioning PivotCharts on a dashboard is a little more difficult than simply moving charts around, but the cost is worth it.

Create another PivotChart from the Commits table and place it to the right of the line chart you just created. For this chart, drag the Sprint field to the Filters box, the Developer field to the Axis (Categories) box, and the Commits field to the Values box on the PivotChart Fields task pane, as shown in Figure 2.15.

Filter the PivotChart by selecting **5** from the Sprint drop-down on the chart. Figure 2.16 shows the filter box from the Sprint drop-down.

Next, right-click the chart, choose Change Chart Type, and change the chart to a bar chart. Hide the field buttons, delete the legend, change the chart title, and change the series color to match the color of the line chart from the previous section. Figure 2.17 shows the four visual elements of the dashboard. They are in the right positions relative to each other but wait until you have all the elements created to put them in their final position.

Project Progress Chart

To show the progress of the project, you choose to simulate a Gantt chart for the labels the development team assigned to the sprints. You can simulate a Gantt chart by creating a stacked bar chart where some of the data points are invisible.

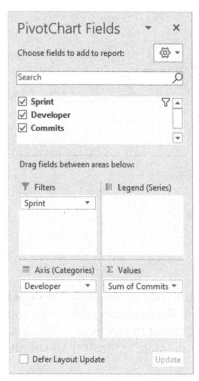

Figure 2.15: Create the PivotTable data for the Commits by Developer chart.

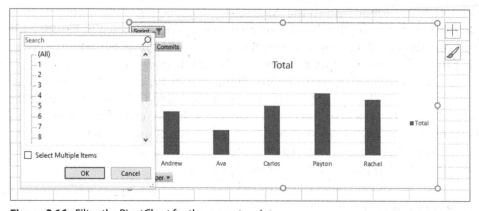

Figure 2.16: Filter the PivotChart for the current sprint.

Start by converting the phase data into a table and name it **tblPhases**. Add a new column to the table named **Blank** and enter the formula =C1 into the first cell of the new column. This will represent the blank space before the bar for each phase will begin.

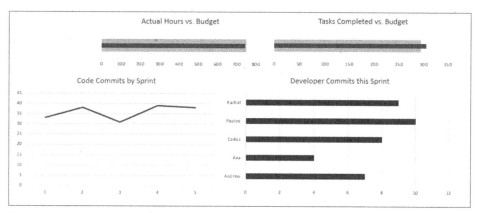

Figure 2.17: The first four visual elements

Add two new columns named **Complete** and **Future**. These will drive the length of each bar for completed and future phases. Enter the following formula in the Completed column:

```
=MAX(MAX((tblCommits[Developer]<>"")*(tblCommits[Sprint]>=[@Start])
*(tblCommits[Sprint]<=[@End])*(tblCommits[Sprint]))-[@Start]+1,0)
```

This formula finds the largest sprint that has code commits in the range of sprints for the row. Then it subtracts the first sprint for the phase. Finally, it is surrounded by a MAX function to make sure the value isn't negative for sprints not started. Enter the following formula in the Future column to compute the duration of sprints not yet started:

```
=[@End]-[@Start]+1-[@Complete]
```

Select the table and insert a stacked bar chart. The table and initial chart are shown in Figure 2.18.

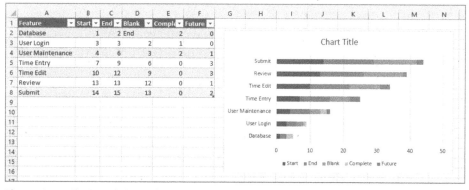

Figure 2.18: The initial phases bar chart and table

Next, right-click the chart and choose Select Data. Remove the Start and End series leaving only the Blank, Complete, and Future series. Right-click the vertical axis, choose Format Axis, and check the Categories In Reverse Order check box as shown in Figure 2.19.

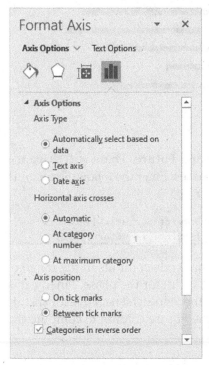

Figure 2.19: Reverse the order of the categories.

Format the Blank series to No Fill and No Line to hide the series. The chart in Figure 2.20 shows empty space for the Blank series.

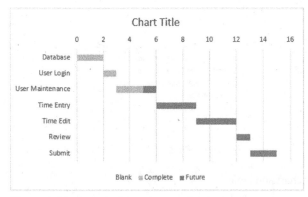

Figure 2.20: A stacked bar chart to simulate a Gantt chart

Remove the legend, gridlines, and horizontal axis by selecting them and pressing Delete. Format the vertical axis and set the line to No Line. Change the chart title to **Overall Project Progress**. Now cut the chart and paste it onto the Dashboard worksheet.

Project Status Indicator

The last visual element will be a green-yellow-red status indicator. For this element, you'll create a linked picture pointing to a conditionally formatted cell. Start by adding a new row to the Progress table. In the Metric column, enter **Status**; in the Hours column, enter the formula `=(B3-B2)/B3`; and in the Tasks column, enter the formula `=-(C3-C2)/C3`.

Add another new row to the table. In the Metric column, enter **Color**. In the Hours column, enter the formula `=IF(B5>=0,"Green",IF(B5<-0.1,"Red","Yellow"))` and copy that formula to the Tasks column.

Create a new worksheet named **Status** in the workbook. Resize cell B2 to be close to the size you want the status indicator to be. It doesn't have to be perfect as you can change it later. Change the fill color for the cell to yellow. This will be the default color, and you'll use conditional formatting to change it to green or red as necessary.

With cell B2 selected, choose Conditional Formatting ➪ New Rule from the Home tab of the Ribbon. Choose "Use a formula to determine which cells to format" from the Select A Rule Type list. Enter the following formula:

```
=AND(Progress!$B$6="Green",Progress!$C$6="Green")
```

Click the Format button and change the fill color to green. Figure 2.21 shows the Formatting Rule dialog.

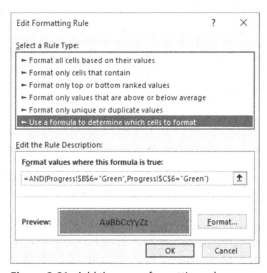

Figure 2.21: Add the green formatting rule.

Open the Conditional Formatting dialog again from the Ribbon by choosing Manage Rules. Check the Stop If True check box next to the rule you just created. Click the New Rule button to create a new rule, again selecting the formula option. Use the following formula for the new rule:

```
=OR(Progress!$B$6="Red",Progress!$C$6="Red")
```

Format the new rule to a fill color of red (the rule whose formula starts with =OR). Click OK to return to the Conditional Formatting Rules Manager and reorder the rules so the green rule (the rule whose formula starts with =AND) is first. Figure 2.22 shows the Conditional Formatting Rules Manager.

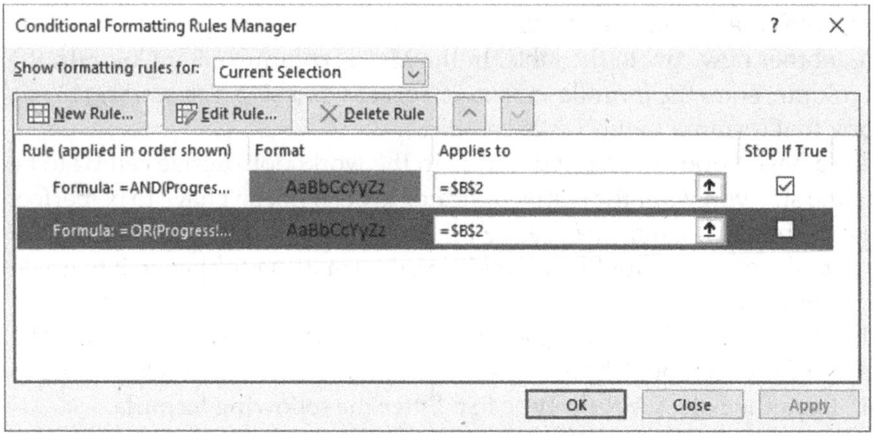

Figure 2.22: Conditionally formatting a cell for green or red

The first rule makes the cell green if both cells in the progress table say green. If that rule is true, no further rules are processed. The second rule makes the cell red if either cell in the progress table says red. If neither rule is true, the cell defaults to yellow.

Right-click cell B2 and choose Copy. Right-click anywhere on the Dashboard worksheet and choose the Linked Picture option from the Paste Special menu. If the cell on the Status worksheet changes color, the linked picture will also change.

Laying Out the Dashboard

With all six visual elements created and on the Dashboard worksheet, you can now position and resize the elements. The PivotCharts are the most tedious to move because you want them to cover the PivotTable data that drives them. Start by lining up the PivotCharts where you want them.

To make lining up the charts easier, select each chart, and in the Format Chart Area task pane, set the border to No Line. If you prefer lines, you'll have to take a little extra time to get everything lined up. Fortunately, you should only have to do it once. With no lines, you can be a pixel or two off and it won't be obvious.

Finally, resize or delete rows or columns to move the dashboard closer to the top-left corner of the page. If the dashboard will be viewed in Excel, make sure all the elements are on the screen. If the dashboard will be printed, resize the elements so they fit on one page. Use the Print Preview function to see where the page breaks are. If you're close to one page, consider using the Scaling option rather than resizing all the elements. The final dashboard is shown in Figure 2.23.

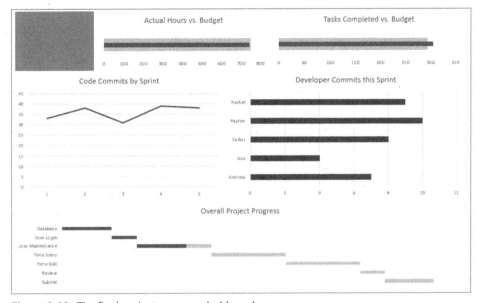

Figure 2.23: The final project progress dashboard

Displaying Key Performance Indicators

Displaying key performance indicators (KPIs) is a common use of dashboards. KPIs are metrics that an organization, like a company or department, has identified as important to measuring its performance. There is no standard set of KPIs, but there are so many examples available on the Internet that you would have no shortage of ideas if you're tasked with developing them.

KPIs can be financial, operational, or both. They can also range from a high level that pertains to the entire company to a low level that might pertain to one subset of a department. KPIs can and do change as the business evolves.

Case Study: Human Resources KPIs

The Human Resources (HR) department has developed a set of metrics around hiring and employee retention that it believes are key indicators of its ability to achieve its business objectives. They are asking you to create a dashboard to display the data.

NOTE   The workbook for this case study is `HumanResources.xlsm` and can be found at www.wiley.com/go/datavizwithexcel/.

Planning and Layout

HR presents you with the following list of KPIs:

- **Recruiting Costs by Year:** The total dollars spent on recruiting
- **Recruiting Cost by Applicant:** The average dollars spent on recruiting per applicant and per successful applicant
- **Diversity Hires:** The number of hires split between gender and race
- **90-Day Quit Rate:** The number of vacancies that occur within 90 days of hire
- **Reasons for Voluntary Separations:** The number of voluntary separations in a predefined set of categories
- **Average Time to Fill Vacancies:** How long, in days, it takes to fill a vacancy

They want to see the recruiting cost, quit rate, and time to fill vacancies metrics for each of the last five years. For diversity hires and voluntary separation, they'd like to see data from the most recent year. The data will be compiled and presented once per year.

You create a rough layout of the visual elements and, after further discussion on the order in which they should appear, settle on the layout shown in Figure 2.24.

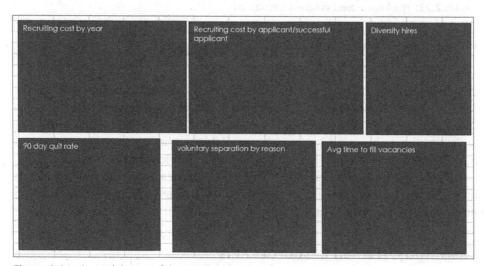

Figure 2.24: A rough layout of the HR dashboard

Collecting the Data

The HR department tracks recruiting expenses by year and by type of expense. They divide expenses into salaries for in-house recruiters, fees for external recruiters, and other expenses such as the cost of attending job fairs. While they haven't asked for any visualizations by expense type, you ask them to provide the data in as raw a form as they have it. If they decide to add a KPI that uses that information later, you'll have the historical data already. Figure 2.25 shows the data they provide.

⊿	A	B	C	D
1	Year	Recruiter Salary	Recruiter Fees	Other
2	2017	78,500	109,250	24,003
3	2018	70,542	99,900	17,503
4	2019	72,271	183,000	13,615
5	2020	70,825	94,800	33,228
6	2021	78,201	143,550	28,938

Figure 2.25: Recruiting cost Data provided by HR

Next, they provide you with a modified employee list. They've deleted some information that was confidential or not relevant. The list includes the employee's identification number and start date. If there was a separation, the end date and reason is recorded. A portion of the data is shown in Figure 2.26.

⊿	A	B	C	D
1	EmployeeID	StartDate	EndDate	Reason
2	1002	10/4/2020		
3	1021	8/28/2004		
4	1022	3/3/2019		
5	1024	9/17/2014		
6	1029	2/5/2015		
7	1034	12/12/2004		
8	1035	10/10/2002		
9	1036	9/26/2006		
10	1045	11/6/2005		
11	1070	7/11/2016		
12	1080	3/28/2018		
13	1084	7/3/2006		
14	1092	12/17/2005	44300	Salary
15	1115	3/13/2020	44271	Involuntary
16	1122	8/13/2016		
17	1127	2/20/2010		
18	1131	6/21/2017		
19	1140	7/1/2002		
20	1141	9/13/2020		
21	1145	12/30/2020		
22	1146	7/16/2005		
23	1152	11/22/2009		
24	1159	11/1/2008		
25	1168	7/24/2010	40708	Retired
26	1169	9/19/2011	43731	Retired

Figure 2.26: An employee list with separation reasons

Whenever a new hire is made, the HR department logs the date the job became available, the date it was filled, the number of applicants, and the gender and race of the successful candidate. Figure 2.27 shows a portion of that data.

	A	B	C	D	E	F	G
1	Job	Department	Vacant	Filled	Gender	Race	Applicants
2	Cashier	Store	1/11/2017	1/22/2017	Male	White	60
3	Cashier	Store	1/7/2017	1/28/2017	Male	Black	80
4	Maintenance	Backoffice	1/4/2017	2/1/2017	Female	Black	69
5	Bookkeeper	Backoffice	3/16/2017	4/13/2017	Male	Black	44
6	Controller	Corporate	4/24/2017	5/13/2017	Male	Black	14
7	Cashier	Store	4/15/2017	5/15/2017	Male	White	74
8	Cashier	Store	6/7/2017	6/25/2017	Female	White	66
9	Cashier	Store	5/26/2017	7/14/2017	Female	White	66
10	Cashier	Store	5/29/2017	7/18/2017	Female	Hispanic	69
11	Maintenance	Backoffice	6/26/2017	7/21/2017	Female	White	64
12	Cashier	Store	8/8/2017	8/29/2017	Male	White	65
13	Maintenance	Backoffice	8/4/2017	9/8/2017	Male	Black	65
14	Accountant	Corporate	8/25/2017	10/4/2017	Female	White	22
15	Billing Clerk	Backoffice	9/27/2017	10/20/2017	Female	White	48
16	Maintenance	Backoffice	9/27/2017	10/27/2017	Female	Other	58
17	Cashier	Store	10/18/2017	11/11/2017	Female	Black	70
18	Cashier	Store	11/8/2017	12/6/2017	Male	Asian	73
19	Cashier	Store	10/28/2017	12/8/2017	Male	White	68
20	Cashier	Store	11/2/2017	12/15/2017	Female	Other	78

Figure 2.27: The new hire log

Building the Visual Elements

Each visual element is discussed in one of the following subsections. Create a worksheet named **Dashboard** to hold these elements.

Recruiting Costs by Year

For the recruiting costs by year element, you decide to create a simple column chart. Start by converting the data to a table by selecting the data and choosing Table from the Insert menu on the Ribbon. On the Table Tools Design tab of the Ribbon, change the name of the table to **tblCosts**. Add a column named **Total** to the table and enter the following formula:

```
=SUM(tblCosts[@[Recruiter Salary]:[Other]])
```

To create the column chart, select the table and choose Recommended Charts from the Insert tab on the Ribbon. The initial chart, shown next to the table in Figure 2.28, includes series that you don't want, but it's easier to delete them than to try to exclude them from the initial chart.

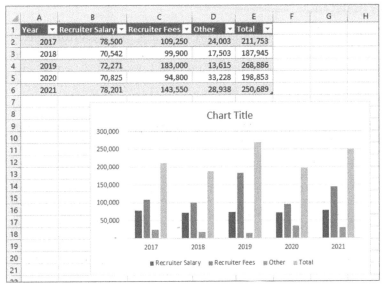

	A	B	C	D	E	F	G	H
1	Year	Recruiter Salary	Recruiter Fees	Other	Total			
2	2017	78,500	109,250	24,003	211,753			
3	2018	70,542	99,900	17,503	187,945			
4	2019	72,271	183,000	13,615	268,886			
5	2020	70,825	94,800	33,228	198,853			
6	2021	78,201	143,550	28,938	250,689			

Figure 2.28: The initial recruiting cost column chart and data

Right-click the chart and choose Select Data. In the Select Data Source dialog, remove all the series except the Total series. Create a new worksheet called **Dashboard** in the workbook. Cut the chart (Ctrl+X) and paste it onto the Dashboard sheet (Ctrl+V).

To complete the formatting of the chart, follow these steps:

1. Delete the legend.
2. Change the title to **Recruiting Costs (in thousands)**.
3. Right-click the vertical axis and choose Format Axis. Change the number format to 0,;;.
4. Choose Page Layout ⇨ Themes from the Ribbon and choose the Ion theme.

The final chart is shown in Figure 2.29. Don't worry about resizing or positioning the chart until all the elements are on the Dashboard worksheet.

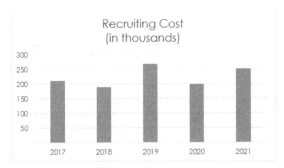

Figure 2.29: The final recruiting cost column chart

Recruiting Cost by Applicant

For this visual element, you'll need to add more columns to the recruiting cost table. First, convert the vacancy data to a table and name it **tblVacancy**. Add four new columns to the recruiting cost table. Use the information in Table 2.1.

Table 2.1: New recruiting cost columns

COLUMN NAME	FORMULA
Applicants	=SUMPRODUCT((YEAR(tblVacancy[Filled])=[@Year])* (tblVacancy[Applicants]))
Success	=SUMPRODUCT(--(YEAR(tblVacancy[Filled])=[@Year]))
Cost per Applicant	=[@Total]/[@Applicants]
Cost per Success	=[@Total]/[@Success]

Select the table and choose Insert ➪ Insert Column Or Bar Chart ➪ More Column Charts from the Ribbon. Choose the clustered column chart with the year in the category axis as shown in Figure 2.30.

Right-click the chart, choose Select Data, and delete all the series except Cost per Applicant and Cost per Success. Figure 2.31 shows the chart at this stage.

Change the Cost per Applicant series to a line chart and move it to its own axis. Right-click on either series and choose Change Series Chart Type. On the Change Chart Type dialog, change the Cost per Applicant chart type to Line and check the Secondary Axis check box. Figure 2.32 shows the Change Chart Type dialog.

Change the chart title to **Recruiting Cost per Applicant**. Cut and paste the chart to the Dashboard worksheet. Change the column series fill color to match the other recruiting cost chart and the line series fill color to something complementary. The two completed elements on the Dashboard worksheet are shown in Figure 2.33.

Diversity Hires

You decide to split the diversity hire element into two doughnut charts. The vacancy data isn't in a form to support a doughnut chart, so you will need to create PivotCharts to manipulate the data first. To create the first doughnut chart, follow these steps:

1. Add a new column to the vacancy table named **CurrentYear** and enter the formula =YEAR([@Filled])=MAX(YEAR([Filled])).

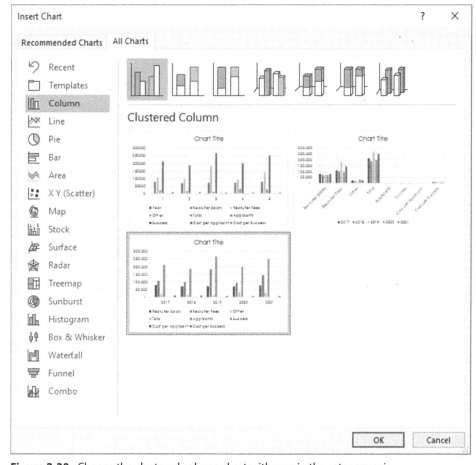

Figure 2.30: Choose the clustered column chart with year in the category axis.

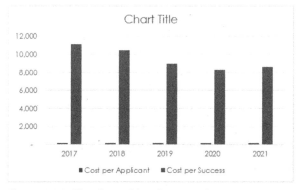

Figure 2.31: The chart with only two series

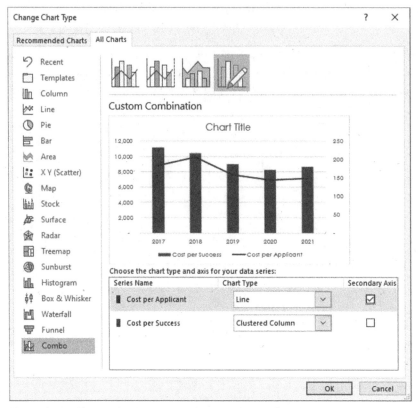

Figure 2.32: Change the Cost per Applicant series to a line chart.

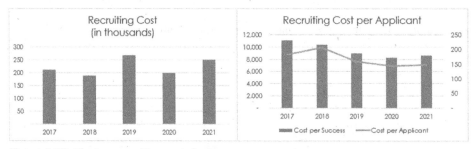

Figure 2.33: The two recruiting cost charts

2. Select the vacancy table and choose Insert ➪ PivotChart ➪ PivotChart from the Ribbon.

3. On the Create PivotChart dialog, choose Existing Worksheet and select a cell on the Dashboard worksheet. Click OK.

4. Drag the CurrentYear field to the Filters box, the Gender field to the Axis (Categories) box, and the Job field to the Values box. Figure 2.34 shows the PivotTable Fields task pane.

Figure 2.34: The PivotTable Fields task pane for the Gender chart

5. On the PivotChart, filter the CurrentYear field to TRUE to show only the current year's data.

6. Choose PivotChart Tools Analyze ⇨ Field Buttons ⇨ Hide All.

7. Delete the legend.

8. Add data labels, choose Percentage, and format the font to stand out against the series.

9. Change the chart title to **Gender** and drag it to the top right of the doughnut.

Follow the same steps to create a Race doughnut chart. Instead of the Gender field, drag the Race field to the Axis (Categories) box. Select each data point and format the fill color to be similar to the fill colors of the Gender chart. Figure 2.35 shows both doughnut charts.

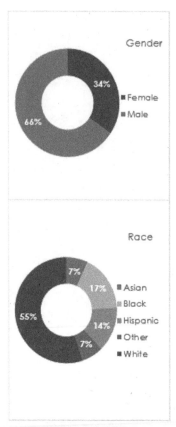

Figure 2.35: Doughnut charts for the diversity hire KPIs

90-Day Quit Rate

To identify vacancies that occur within 90 days, convert the employee data to a table named **tblEmployee**. Add a new column to the table named **90Days** and enter the following formula:

```
=NOT(OR(ISBLANK([@EndDate]),[@EndDate]-[@StartDate]>90))
```

This formula will return TRUE if the StartDate and EndDate values are within 90 days and FALSE if they are outside 90 days or the EndDate column is blank.

Create a PivotChart from the table and place it on the Dashboard worksheet. In the PivotTable Fields task pane, drag the 90Days field to the Filters box, the EndDate field to the Axis (Categories) box, and the EmployeeID field to the Values box as shown in Figure 2.36.

Next, change the aggregate for the EmployeeID field by right-clicking on the field in the PivotTable and choosing Summarize Values By ➪ Count as shown in Figure 2.37.

Figure 2.36: Building the PivotChart for the 90-Day Quit Rate chart

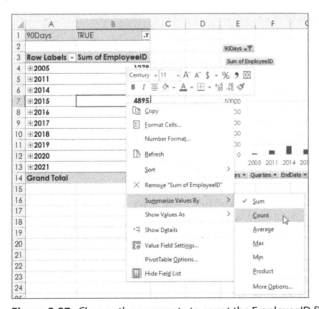

Figure 2.37: Change the aggregate to count the EmployeeID field.

Pull down the 90Days field button and filter to TRUE. Pull down on the Years field button and select only the last five years. To finish formatting the chart, follow these steps:

1. Hide the field buttons by selecting PivotChart Tools ⇨ Analyze ⇨ Field Buttons ⇨ Hide All from the Ribbon.

2. Right-click the chart and select Change Chart Type. Choose the Line With Markers option.

3. Delete the legend.

4. Change the title to **90-day Quit Rate**.

This chart would work equally well as a column or bar chart. However, a line chart creates a visual distinction from the recruiting costs charts on the dashboard. The final chart is shown in Figure 2.38.

Figure 2.38: The final 90-Day Quit Rate chart

Voluntary Separation by Reason

For this element, you choose a bar chart because it provides more space for category labels. Create another PivotChart from the employee table and place it on the Dashboard worksheet.

To filter the chart for only the current year, start by dragging the EndDate to the Axis (Categories) box. This will create three fields in that box: Years, Quarters, and EndDate. Next, drag the Years field from the Axis (Categories) box to the Filters box. Finally, drag the Quarters and EndDate fields out of the Axis (Categories) box and drop them back up in the fields area. If you were to drag EndDate directly to Filters, you wouldn't get the Years aggregate field.

Finish constructing the data by dragging the Reason field to the Axis (Categories) box and the EmployeeID to the Values box. Change the aggregate for EmployeeID from sum to count.

Filter the PivotChart by selecting only the current year from the Years field button. Now select the Reason field button and uncheck the Involuntary entry. Figure 2.39 shows the chart after filtering on year and reason.

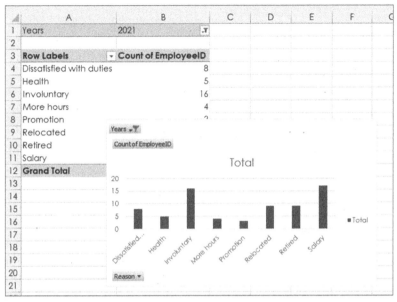

Figure 2.39: The voluntary separation chart filtered

Right-click on the chart and choose Change Chart Type. Select the Clustered Bar option. Hide the field buttons and delete the legend to clean up the chart.

Next, sort the reasons by count. Click the Row Labels filter on the PivotTable and choose More Sort Options. On the Sort dialog, shown in Figure 2.40, choose Descending and Count of EmployeeID and click OK.

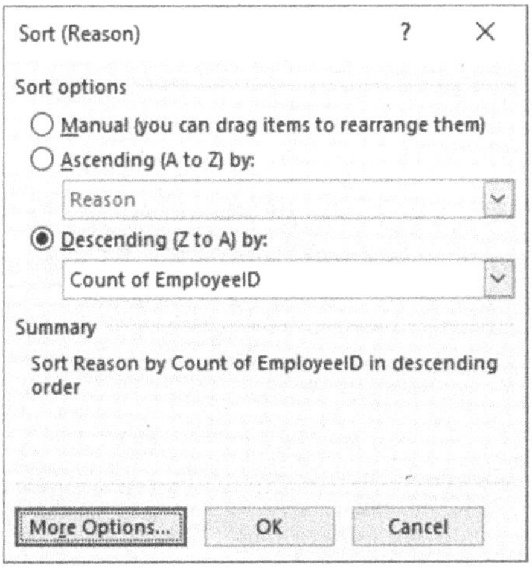

Figure 2.40: Sort the PivotChart by Count of EmployeeID.

Finally, change the chart title to **Voluntary Separations**. The final chart is shown in Figure 2.41.

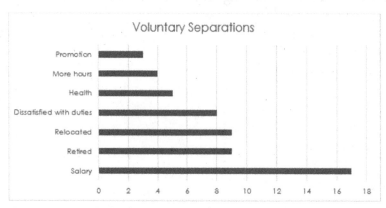

Figure 2.41: The final Voluntary Separations bar chart

Average Time to Fill Vacancies

To create the final dashboard element, start by adding a new column to the vacancy table named **Days**. Enter the formula `=[@Filled]-[@Vacant]` to count the days the vacancy was open. Create another PivotChart from the table and place it on the Dashboard worksheet.

To construct the chart, drag the Filled field to the Axis (Categories) box and the Days field to the Values box. If the Days field doesn't appear in the field list, it's because you already have a PivotTable made from that table and this Pivot-Table is using the same cache as the previous one. Right-click on the PivotTable and choose Refresh to see the Days field. Change the aggregate for Days from sum to average.

Follow these steps to complete the formatting of the chart:

1. Hide the field buttons.
2. Delete the legend.
3. Change the chart type to Line With Markers.
4. Change the chart title to **Average Days to Fill Vacancies**.
5. Right-click the vertical axis, choose Format Axis, and change the minimum to zero.

The final chart is shown in Figure 2.42.

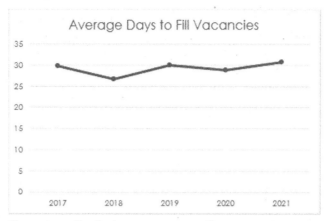

Figure 2.42: The final Average Days to Fill Vacancies chart

Laying Out the Dashboard

Because you split the diversity hire charts into two doughnut charts, the layout will be different than the original rough layout. Instead of one chart in the top right, extend both doughnut charts down the entire right side of the dashboard.

You can use the fill and size handles for each chart to move and resize them. For this dashboard, however, you choose to use Visual Basic for Applications (VBA) to position the charts. Start by naming each chart. Select the recruiting costs chart and enter **RecCost** in the Name box (to the left of the Formula Bar) to rename the chart as shown in Figure 2.43. You'll use this name in the VBA code to refer to the chart.

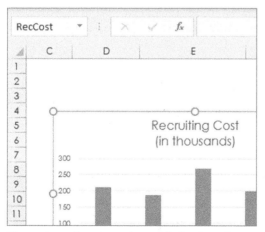

Figure 2.43: Rename a chart with the Name box.

Rename the other charts by selecting them and entering a new name in the Name box. Manually move and resize the recruiting cost chart to the position and size you want. Press Alt+F11 to open the Visual Basic Editor (VBE). Press Ctrl+R to show the Project Explorer. Find the `HumanResources.xlsm` project, right-click the project, and choose Insert ⇨ Module as shown in Figure 2.44.

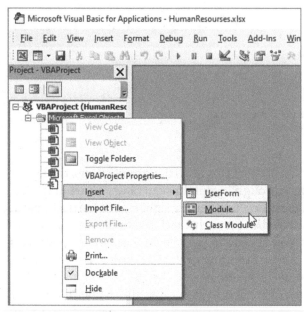

Figure 2.44: Insert a module into the project.

In the resulting code pane, enter the following code:

```
Sub MoveCharts()

    With ActiveSheet
        .Shapes("PerApp").Top = .Shapes("RecCost").Top
        .Shapes("PerApp").Height = .Shapes("RecCost").Height
        .Shapes("PerApp").Width = .Shapes("RecCost").Width
        .Shapes("PerApp").Left = .Shapes("RecCost").Left _
            + .Shapes("RecCost").Width

        .Shapes("QuitRate").Top = .Shapes("RecCost").Top _
            + .Shapes("RecCost").Height
        .Shapes("QuitRate").Left = .Shapes("RecCost").Left
        .Shapes("QuitRate").Width = .Shapes("RecCost").Width * 2 / 3

        .Shapes("VolSep").Top = .Shapes("QuitRate").Top
        .Shapes("VolSep").Height = .Shapes("QuitRate").Height
        .Shapes("VolSep").Width = .Shapes("QuitRate").Width
        .Shapes("VolSep").Left = .Shapes("QuitRate").Left _
            + .Shapes("QuitRate").Width
```

```
            .Shapes("Vacancy").Top = .Shapes("VolSep").Top
            .Shapes("Vacancy").Height = .Shapes("VolSep").Height
            .Shapes("Vacancy").Width = .Shapes("VolSep").Width
            .Shapes("Vacancy").Left = .Shapes("VolSep").Left _
                + .Shapes("VolSep").Width

            .Shapes("Gender").Top = .Shapes("PerApp").Top
            .Shapes("Gender").Height = .Shapes("PerApp").Height
            .Shapes("Gender").Width = .Shapes("PerApp").Width / 2
            .Shapes("Gender").Left = .Shapes("PerApp").Left _
                + .Shapes("PerApp").Width

            .Shapes("Race").Top = .Shapes("Vacancy").Top
            .Shapes("Race").Height = .Shapes("Vacancy").Height
            .Shapes("Race").Width = .Shapes("Gender").Width
            .Shapes("Race").Left = .Shapes("Vacancy").Left _
                + .Shapes("Vacancy").Width
        End With

    End Sub
```

Each chart on the dashboard is a Shape object. This code sets the Top, Height, Width, and Left properties of each object relative to another chart. This ensures that the charts line up perfectly. Close the VBE and return to Excel. Press Alt+F8 to show the Macro dialog and run the MoveCharts macro you just created.

If any of the PivotTables are showing, you can hide the columns and rerun the macro to reposition the charts. To change the overall size or position of the dashboard, simply manually adjust the top-left chart and rerun the macro. The final dashboard is shown in Figure 2.45.

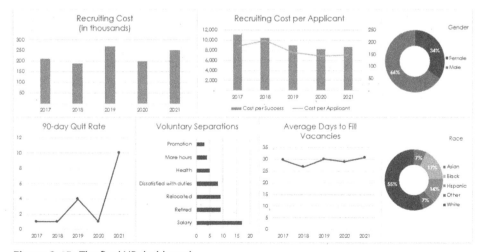

Figure 2.45: The final HR dashboard

The macro will be saved with the workbook. Save the workbook as a Macro-enabled workbook (.xlsm) if it isn't already to ensure you don't lose the macro.

Reporting Financial Information

Financial data is the lifeblood of business. Almost all business dashboards contain some financial data. While operations drive the finances, the financial data is the primary measuring stick for how a business is doing. Knowing what data to monitor and what to do with it is not an easy task. But it all starts with monitoring, and dashboards are the perfect tool for that.

Case Study: Financial Information and Ratios

Your company has asked you to create a financial dashboard for the Finance and Accounting department. They'd like to see current year data as well as trends over the last five years.

NOTE   The workbook for this case study is `FinancialInformation.xlsm` and can be found at www.wiley.com/go/datavizwithexcel/.

Planning and Layout

The Finance department has identified metrics it believes are key to understanding the financial health of the business. In addition to these metrics, they'd like to see a summary of the current year's income statement and a five-year trend of revenue on the dashboard. The metrics and a brief description of each are as follows:

- **Current Ratio:** Current assets divided by current liabilities. This ratio helps users understand the company's ability to pay its obligations over the next year.

- **Quick Ratio:** Cash and receivables divided by current liabilities. This ratio is an indication of the company's ability to pay its obligations in the short term.

- **Debt-to-Equity:** Traditionally calculated as total liabilities divided by total equity. However, the company has modified the formula for internal reporting to only include interest-bearing debt.

- **Cash Conversion Cycle:** Days sales of inventory plus days sales outstanding less days payables outstanding. This measures the time it takes for the business to convert inventory to cash.

- **Gross Margin Percent:** Sales less cost of sales divided by sales.

- **Net Margin Percent:** Gross margin net of operating expenses and other expenses or income divided by sales.

For each of these metrics, they would like to see the current year value and the five-year trend. You submit the rough layout shown in Figure 2.46 for approval.

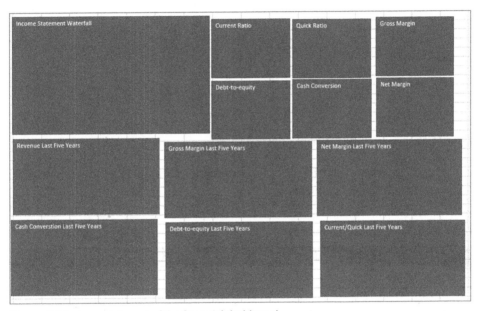

Figure 2.46: A rough layout of the financial dashboard

Collecting the Data

You are provided with the balance sheet and income data shown in Figure 2.47. You'll need to calculate the ratios to drive the charts.

⯅	A	B	C	D	E	F	G
1		2015	2016	2017	2018	2019	2020
2	Cash	683,994	1,453,502	1,443,111	1,897,996	2,418,683	2,546,219
3	Accounts Receivable	3,068,493	3,105,048	3,174,708	3,170,586	3,272,631	3,289,239
4	Inventory	1,523,461	1,464,310	1,448,988	1,512,308	1,493,221	1,547,914
5	Other Current Assets	621,453	618,731	610,613	635,064	620,823	628,673
6	Property	3,648,732	3,620,934	3,947,334	4,156,194	4,109,664	4,448,519
7	Other Long-term Assets	50,243	55,427	62,434	57,433	68,333	75,461
8	Accounts Payable	(2,836,512)	(2,738,809)	(2,663,304)	(2,560,968)	(2,507,282)	(2,544,193)
9	Accrued Expenses	(200,148)	(236,059)	(212,684)	(224,868)	(191,848)	(174,914)
10	Debt	(3,861,487)	(3,886,332)	(3,728,124)	(3,639,605)	(3,596,656)	(3,105,572)
11	Common Stock	(100,000)	(100,000)	(100,000)	(100,000)	(100,000)	(100,000)
12	Additional Paid-in Capital	(1,547,889)	(1,547,889)	(1,547,889)	(1,547,889)	(1,547,889)	(1,547,889)
13	Retained Earnings	(1,050,340)	(1,808,863)	(2,435,187)	(3,356,251)	(4,039,680)	(5,063,457)
14		-	-	-	-	-	-
15							
16	Sales		39,261,030	40,046,251	40,046,251	42,449,026	45,420,458
17	COGS		(25,990,802)	(27,311,543)	(27,151,358)	(28,525,745)	(31,612,639)
18	Margin		13,270,228	12,734,708	12,894,893	13,923,281	13,807,819
19	Overhead		(11,268,350)	(11,204,624)	(10,702,229)	(12,245,144)	(11,415,137)
20	Operating Profit		2,001,878	1,530,084	2,192,664	1,678,137	2,392,682
21	Interest Expense		(195,871)	(168,511)	(190,351)	(192,421)	(167,080)
22	Net Income		1,806,007	1,361,573	2,002,313	1,485,716	2,225,602
23	Budgeted Revenue		-	41,224,000	42,049,000	42,049,000	44,571,000

Figure 2.47: Balance sheet and income statement data

Create new lines under the provided financial data and use the formulas in Table 2.2 to calculate the metrics.

Table 2.2: Financial metric formulas

METRIC	FORMULA
Debt-to-Equity	=C10/SUM(C11:C13)
Days Sales of Inventory	=AVERAGE(B4:C4)/C17*365
Days Sales Outstanding	=AVERAGE(B3:C3)/-C16*365
Days Payables Outstanding	=-AVERAGE(B8:C8)/C17*365
Cash Conversion Cycle	=C25+C26-C27
Current Ratio	=-SUM(C2:C5)/SUM(C8:C9)
Quick Ratio	=-SUM(C2:C3)/SUM(C8:C9)
Gross Margin	=C18/C16
Net Margin	=C22/C16

Building the Visual Elements

Create a new worksheet named **Dashboard** and begin staging the data for each visual element.

Summary Income Statement

You choose to present the summary income statement as a waterfall chart. Fortunately, the source data is almost already well formatted for this chart. The accountants have presented credit balance accounts, like Sales, as negatives. For the waterfall chart, you'll need to reverse the signs by following these steps:

1. In an unused cell, enter **-1**.
2. Copy the cell by pressing Ctrl+C.
3. Select cells C16:G23.
4. From the Home tab on the Ribbon, select Paste ⇨ Paste Special to show the Paste Special dialog.
5. Select Multiply as shown in Figure 2.48 and click OK.
6. Delete the contents of the cell with -1 in it.

Figure 2.48: Reversing signs via Paste Special ⇨ Multiply

To create the waterfall chart, select cells A16:A22, hold down the Ctrl key and select G16:G22. From the Ribbon, choose Insert ⇨ Waterfall to create the initial chart shown in Figure 2.49.

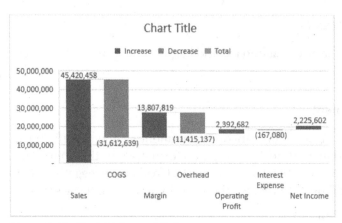

Figure 2.49: The initial waterfall chart

Cut the chart and paste it on to the Dashboard worksheet. Format the chart by following these steps:

1. Change the chart title to **Current Year Income Statement (in thousands)**.

2. Delete the legend.

3. Delete the vertical axis.

4. Click the Margin data point twice to select only that data point. Right-click on the data point and choose Format Data Point. Check the Set As Total check box.

5. Repeat that process for the Operating Profit and Net Income data points. Figure 2.50 shows the chart after checking Set As Total for those data points.

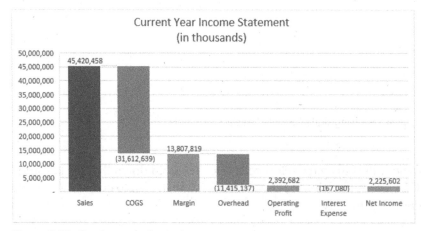

Figure 2.50: Set the totals data points.

6. Delete the gridlines.

7. Format the data labels to the custom number format * #,###,;* (#,###,).

8. Add line breaks to any axis labels that are too long, like Operating Profit and Interest Expense. In the source data cells, place your cursor where you want the line break and press Alt+Enter. The final waterfall chart is shown in Figure 2.51.

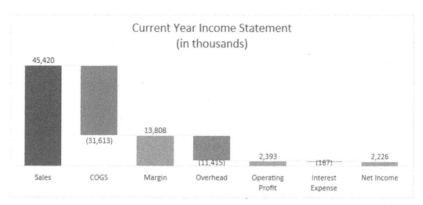

Figure 2.51: The Current Year Income Statement waterfall chart

Current Year Ratios

The current year ratio elements will be four equally sized charts showing the current ratio, quick ratio, debt-to-equity ratio, and cash conversion cycle. These will be simple numbers, but you decide to put a gauge-style chart behind them. You consult with the Finance department to determine a reasonable upper bound for each of the ratios. They tell you to use 4 for the current and quick ratios, 2 for the debt-to-equity ratio, and 30 for the cash conversion cycle.

Start by creating a table on the Data worksheet like the one shown in Figure 2.52. Enter the max value supplied for each metric. For the Value, point to the cell in column G for that metric. For example, the Current Value formula in cell B37 is =G30. For the Blank calculation, enter the formula =B40-B37 and fill across. The formula for the Bottom in cell B39 is =B40/0.8-B40 and fill it across to the other columns also.

		Current	Quick	Debt-to-equity	Cash Conv
35					
36		Current	Quick	Debt-to-equity	Cash Conv
37	Value	2.95	2.15	0.46	14.76
38	Blank	1.05	1.85	1.54	15.24
39	Bottom	1.00	1.00	0.50	7.50
40	Max	4.00	4.00	2.00	30.00

Figure 2.52: Stage the data for the gauge charts.

Select cells A37:B39 and from the Ribbon, choose Insert ⇨ Insert Pie Or Doughnut Chart ⇨ Doughnut to create the chart shown in Figure 2.53.

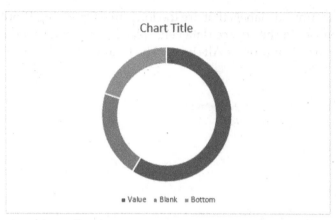

Figure 2.53: The initial current ratio doughnut chart

Cut the chart and paste it on to the Dashboard worksheet. Resize the chart to the approximate size of the final chart. Follow these steps to format the chart:

1. Delete the legend.
2. Change the chart title to **Current Ratio** and make its font size **10.5**.
3. Right-click the series and choose Format Data Series. Set the angle of the first slice to **216** and the doughnut hole size to **57**.
4. From the Ribbon, choose Chart Tools ⇨ Format and select Plot Area from the Chart Element drop-down to show the sizing handles of the plot area. Resize the plot area to fill more of the chart as shown in Figure 2.54.

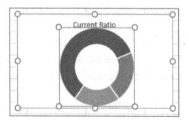

Figure 2.54: Resize the plot area to fill More of the chart area.

5. Select the Value data point by clicking it twice and change the fill color to **40% blue**.
6. Select the Blank data point and change the fill color to **15% white**.
7. Select the Bottom data point and change the fill to No Fill. Figure 2.55 shows the chart after these changes.

Figure 2.55: Set the fill colors for each data point.

8. Select the Value data point and choose Data Labels ⇨ Show from the Chart Element dialog.

9. Select the data label and move and resize it so that the data label is in the center of the gauge. Change the font size to **24** and the font color to dark blue. The final gauge chart is shown in Figure 2.56.

Figure 2.56: The Current Ratio gauge chart

To create the other three-gauge charts, copy the current ratio chart and paste it three times on to the worksheet. Change the chart titles for the new charts so you can keep track of which one you're working on. You may have to re-center the chart titles.

Select the series in the quick ratio chart and change the SERIES formula in the formula bar to `=SERIES(,Data!$A$37:$A$39,Data!$C$37:$C$39,1)` to point to the correct data. Excel keeps the chart's properties, like size, but unfortunately the series properties are lost. Repeat the step from the current ratio chart to format the quick ratio chart. Then repeat the process of changing the SERIES formula and formatting for the other three charts. The four-gauge charts are shown in Figure 2.57.

Figure 2.57: Four balance sheet ratio gauge charts

Current Year Margins

For the other two smaller charts in the top-right portion of the dashboard, you decide on gauges behind numbers similar to the balance sheet ratios. To distinguish them, you'll use a different color for the series. Add two columns to the table you created in the previous section.

Point to the proper cells for the Value formula. Use **40%** and **7%** for the Max value for gross and net margin, respectively. Fill the Blank and Bottom formulas to the right for the new columns. Figure 2.58 shows the updated table.

35							
36		Current	Quick	Debt-to-equity	Cash Conv	Gross Margin	Net Margin
37	Value	2.95	2.15	0.46	14.76	30.40%	4.90%
38	Blank	1.05	1.85	1.54	15.24	9.60%	2.10%
39	Bottom	1.00	1.00	0.50	7.50	10.00%	1.75%
40	Max	4.00	4.00	2.00	30.00	40.00%	7.00%

Figure 2.58: Gross and net margin calculations

Copy one of the other gauge charts and paste it on to the worksheet twice. Select one of the new charts, and from the Ribbon choose Chart Tools ➪ Format and select Series 1 from the Chart Elements drop-down. Edit the SERIES formula in the formula bar to point to column F for gross margin. Repeat the process for the other new chart except point to column G for net margin.

Change the fill color of the data points and add and format the data label as you did for the other gauge charts. The final six-chart panel is shown in Figure 2.59.

Current Ratio	Quick Ratio	Gross Margin
2.95	2.15	30.40%

Debt-to-equity Ratio	Cash Conversion Cycle	Net Margin
0.46	14.76	4.90%

Figure 2.59: The six-chart gauge panel

Five-Year Income Statement Metrics

The next three charts show five-year trends for three income statement metrics: revenue, gross margin, and net margin. You could create staging areas for these charts, but there are no additional formulas, so you may find it just as easy to keep the source data where it is.

To create the revenue chart, select cells C1:G1 on the Data worksheet. Hold down the Ctrl key and select cells C16:G16. From the Insert tab on the Ribbon, click Recommended Charts and choose the Clustered Column option. Cut the chart and paste it on to the Dashboard worksheet. Follow these steps to format the chart:

1. Change the chart title to **Revenue (in millions)**.

2. Format the vertical axis to start at zero, then delete it.

3. Delete the gridlines.

4. Change the fill color for the data series to match the income-statement-related gauge charts. As the gauge charts are meant to be in the background, choose a darker accent in the same color column.

5. Add data labels and change the number format to **0.00,,**. The revenue chart is shown in Figure 2.60.

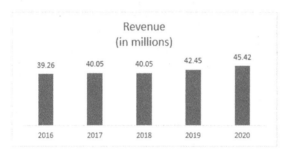

Figure 2.60: The five-year revenue chart

Copy the revenue chart and paste it twice on to the worksheet to make the gross and net margin charts. Change the titles of the charts to **Gross Margin** and **Net Margin**. Note on the Data worksheet that gross margin is on row 33 and net margin is on row 34. Select the data series on each chart and edit the series in the formula bar as follows:

▪ **Gross Margin**: =SERIES(,Data!$C$1:$G$1,Data!$C$33:$G$33,1)

▪ **Net Margin**: =SERIES(,Data!$C$1:$G$1,Data!$C$34:$G$34,1)

Change the fill colors to match the revenue chart. Add data labels, and if necessary, change the number format to Percentage with two decimals. The three five-year income statement charts are shown in Figure 2.61.

Figure 2.61: Three five-year income statement charts

Five-Year Balance Sheet Metrics

For the balance sheet trend charts, use a line chart to visually distinguish it from the income statement charts. Copy one of the income statement charts and paste it. Change the chart type to Line With Markers. Change the data labels to be above the markers by selecting Data Labels ⇨ Above from the Chart Element dialog. Now make two copies of that chart to complete the set.

Change the chart titles to **Cash Conversion Cycle, Debt-to-equity Ratio,** and delete the title from the third chart as you'll use the legend as the title. For the Cash Conversion chart, edit the SERIES formula to be `=SERIES(,Data!$C$1:$G$1,Data!$C$29:$G$29,1)`. Edit the SERIES formula for the debt-to-equity chart to be `=SERIES(,Data!$C$1:$G$1,Data!$C$25:$G$25,1)`. For the current/quick ratio chart, edit the SERIES formula to be `=SERIES(,Data!$C$1:$G$1,Data!$C$30:$G$30,1)`. Change the number format of the data labels on all three charts to Number with two decimals.

To add the quick ratio data to the last chart, select C31:G31 on the Data worksheet and press Ctrl+C to copy it. Select the current/quick ratio chart on the Dashboard worksheet and select Home ⇨ Paste ⇨ Paste Special on the Ribbon to add a new series. The Paste Special dialog is shown in Figure 2.62.

Figure 2.62: Pasting a new series to an existing chart

For each chart, change the line fill color and the marker fill and border colors to be a darker accent of the same color used in the balance sheet gauge charts. For the quick ratio series, choose a different color but don't use the same color as the income statement charts.

Add a legend to the top of the current/quick ratio chart using the Chart Element dialog. To change the series names in the legend, right-click the chart and choose Select Data. In the Select Data Source dialog, select Series 1 and click the Edit button to display the Edit Series dialog, shown in Figure 2.63. Change the Series name to `=Data!$A$30` and click OK.

Repeat the process to change Series 2 to point to the cell with the quick ratio label. Click OK to close the Select Data Source dialog. Select the legend and set the font size to be the same as the other two balance sheet trend charts. Figure 2.64 shows all six trend charts.

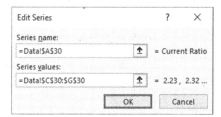

Figure 2.63: Point the series name to a cell.

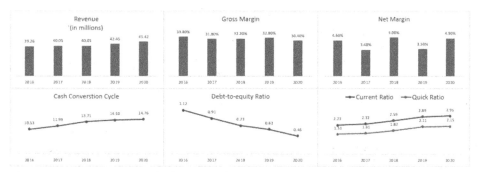

Figure 2.64: Six trend charts for financial data

Laying Out the Dashboard

With so many elements on this dashboard, it's best to use VBA to position and resize the charts. The gauge charts are the most finicky because of their small size and the placement of the data label in the center of the gauge, so use those as the anchor and adjust all the other charts relative to those.

Start by naming each chart so the VBA code is easier to read. Select each chart and type a new name in the Name box just to the left of the formula bar.

Press Alt+F11 to open the VBE. Press Ctrl+R to show the Project Explorer if it's not already showing. Find your project in the Project Explorer, right-click the project name, and choose Insert ⇨ Module from the context menu. This will open a new code pane for your VBA code. Enter the following code into the code pane:

```
Sub MoveCharts()

    With ActiveSheet

        'Top row of gauge charts
        MoveSingleChart chtDest:=.Shapes("QuickGauge"), _
            chtSource:=.Shapes("CurrentGauge"), _
            LeftAdd:=.Shapes("CurrentGauge").Width, TopAdd:=0, _
            WidthFactor:=1, HeightFactor:=1
        MoveSingleChart chtDest:=.Shapes("GrossGauge"), _
            chtSource:=.Shapes("QuickGauge"), _
```

Continues

(continued)

```
                LeftAdd:=.Shapes("QuickGauge").Width, TopAdd:=0, _
                WidthFactor:=1, HeightFactor:=1

        'Bottom row of gauge charts
        MoveSingleChart chtDest:=.Shapes("DtoEGauge"), _
            chtSource:=.Shapes("CurrentGauge"), _
            LeftAdd:=0, TopAdd:=.Shapes("CurrentGauge").Height, _
            WidthFactor:=1, HeightFactor:=1
        MoveSingleChart chtDest:=.Shapes("CCCGauge"), _
            chtSource:=.Shapes("DtoEGauge"), _
            LeftAdd:=.Shapes("DtoEGauge").Width, TopAdd:=0, _
            WidthFactor:=1, HeightFactor:=1
        MoveSingleChart chtDest:=.Shapes("NetGauge"), _
            chtSource:=.Shapes("CCCGauge"), _
            LeftAdd:=.Shapes("CCCGauge").Width, TopAdd:=0, _
            WidthFactor:=1, HeightFactor:=1

        'Waterfall. Set the width first since it's subtracting
        .Shapes("Water").Width = .Shapes("CurrentGauge").Width * 3
        MoveSingleChart chtDest:=.Shapes("Water"), _
            chtSource:=.Shapes("CurrentGauge"), _
            LeftAdd:=.Shapes("Water").Width * -1, TopAdd:=0, _
            WidthFactor:=3, HeightFactor:=2

        'Top row of trend charts, 75% of the height of the waterfall
        MoveSingleChart chtDest:=.Shapes("RevTrend"), _
            chtSource:=.Shapes("Water"), _
            LeftAdd:=0, TopAdd:=.Shapes("Water").Height, _
            WidthFactor:=2 / 3, HeightFactor:=0.75
        MoveSingleChart chtDest:=.Shapes("GrossTrend"), _
            chtSource:=.Shapes("RevTrend"), _
            LeftAdd:=.Shapes("RevTrend").Width, TopAdd:=0, _
            WidthFactor:=1, HeightFactor:=1
        MoveSingleChart chtDest:=.Shapes("NetTrend"), _
            chtSource:=.Shapes("GrossTrend"), _
            LeftAdd:=.Shapes("GrossTrend").Width, TopAdd:=0, _
            WidthFactor:=1, HeightFactor:=1

        'Bottom row of trend charts
        MoveSingleChart chtDest:=.Shapes("CCCTrend"), _
            chtSource:=.Shapes("RevTrend"), _
            LeftAdd:=0, TopAdd:=.Shapes("RevTrend").Height, _
            WidthFactor:=1, HeightFactor:=1
        MoveSingleChart chtDest:=.Shapes("DtoETrend"), _
            chtSource:=.Shapes("CCCTrend"), _
            LeftAdd:=.Shapes("CCCTrend").Width, TopAdd:=0, _
            WidthFactor:=1, HeightFactor:=1
        MoveSingleChart chtDest:=.Shapes("CurrentTrend"), _
            chtSource:=.Shapes("DtoETrend"), _
```

```
        LeftAdd:=.Shapes("DtoETrend").Width, TopAdd:=0, _
        WidthFactor:=1, HeightFactor:=1

    End With
End Sub

Sub MoveSingleChart(chtDest As Shape, chtSource As Shape, _
    LeftAdd As Double, _
    TopAdd As Double, _
    WidthFactor As Double, _
    HeightFactor As Double)

    chtDest.Top = chtSource.Top + TopAdd
    chtDest.Width = chtSource.Width * WidthFactor
    chtDest.Left = chtSource.Left + LeftAdd
    chtDest.Height = chtSource.Height * HeightFactor

End Sub
```

The first procedure calls the second procedure for each chart on the dashboard. It passes in the chart to change, the chart to change relative to, how much to add to the Top or Left properties, and how much to change the Height or Width properties relative to chtSource.

Close the VBE and return to Excel. Press Ctrl+F8 to show the Macros dialog box and run the MoveCharts macro. If you're not happy with the layout of the chart, simply manually resize the current ratio gauge chart and rerun the macro so all the other charts adjust relative to it. The final dashboard is shown in Figure 2.65.

Figure 2.65: The financial data dashboard

Organizing Data for Dashboards

In This Chapter

- Separating Data Layers
- Working with External Data
- Transforming Data in Power Query

In this chapter, I discuss separating your data layers as a practice to help you work with and update the various parts of your dashboard. I also provide several examples of getting external data into Excel from some of the more common sources. Finally, I give a brief introduction to transforming data with Power Query using examples.

Separating Data Layers

A best practice of dashboarding is to separate your data into layers. The most common separation is three layers: the source layer, the staging and analysis layer, and the presentation layer. Figure 3.1 shows a simple example of the three layers, each on its own worksheet.

Figure 3.1: The three data layers

Having separate layers allows you to change parts of the dashboard without having to change every aspect. If, for example, the format of your source data changes, you might have to change the formulas in the staging layer to accommodate it. But as long as the layout of the staging data stays the same, you don't have to touch the chart on the presentation layer. Similarly, if you decide to change a chart and it requires a different staging layout, the source data is untouched.

Another big advantage of separate layers is that it makes updating the dashboard more efficient. This is achieved by keeping the source data in whatever form you receive it. Imagine you receive a poorly formatted text file as your source data. You import it into Excel, move some columns and rows around, do some find-and-replace operations, and otherwise manipulate the data until it's ready to drive a chart. This is an example of merging the source and staging layers. The next time you're ready to update the chart, you have to import the updated file and do all those same data manipulation steps.

Now take that same scenario and import the text file into Excel. Instead of manipulating it in place, you write formulas on another sheet that form the data the way you want, leaving the source worksheet just as it was when you imported it. The next update is simply importing the new text file and letting the worksheet formulas calculate. It's a little more work up front, but well worth it when you need to update the dashboard.

Source Data Layer

The source data layer is the layer where you first start working with the data. It might not be the ultimate source of the data, but it is the source with respect to your project. When you're dealing with source data, you're concerned with the format of the data, where it comes from, how often it is updated, and what level of summarization has already been applied.

The data can come to you in many different formats. You might get it in a table in an Excel workbook. In that case, the data may already be in great shape to be staged. Other formats include text files, XML files, websites, or databases, all of which will require some work to get it into Excel.

How you get the data will also vary. Files may be emailed to you, available on a network share, available on an FTP server, or available on a web server, for example. You might be able to query data in a database directly. In some cases, the database administrator might be unwilling to give you permission to query the database directly and you'll have to settle for someone else extracting the data for you. However you get the data, try to automate getting it into Excel as much as you can. Querying from a database or files on a network share lends itself to automation pretty easily. FTP and email require more effort to get the data into the form you want.

How often the data is updated is usually only relevant when it's less frequently than you want to publish a dashboard. But keep in mind that the data for a dashboard often comes from more than one place. Your publishing schedule will be limited to the data with the least frequent updates. Some data needs to be reconciled before you can be comfortable using it. For example, you may have access to point-of-sale data in near real time, but the end-of-day process may alter that data enough that you should wait until the process is run before collecting the data.

As I said in the preceding chapter, you generally want to get the data in the rawest form possible, with some notable exceptions. The first exception is when there is simply too much raw data. For example, a meter that returns a measurement every five seconds throughout the day returns a lot of data. You have to strike a balance between the flexibility of very raw data and the amount of data storage you'll need. In some cases, you should accept some level of summarization before the data gets to you.

Another exception is poorly formatted data. The best data you can get is organized into rows and columns. Each column is a field that holds a single value relating to an object. Each row is a record, or a collection of fields that describe one object. This is known as normalization in the data world. Unfortunately, you will inevitably receive data that is not normalized. If you can get it properly formatted before it gets to you, all the better. If not, you'll have to spend some effort getting the data properly staged. The file in Figure 3.2 is nicely formatted into rows and columns and ready for Excel formulas or PivotTables. The file in Figure 3.3 will need more complex formulas or other data transformation techniques before it's ready to use.

	A	B	C	D	E
1	Product	Customer	Date	Category	Sales
2	1957	60871	8/13/2021	Women's Activewear	1,795.66
3	9994	40265	2/27/2021	Men's Outerwear	983.75
4	7085	60871	8/15/2021	Children's	214.3
5	1142	64637	2/12/2021	Children's	598.49
6	6176	60871	8/11/2021	Children's	981.46
7	1900	91416	6/3/2021	Men's Outerwear	985.28
8	1927	85150	1/4/2021	Men's Outerwear	785.38
9	8189	65296	2/3/2021	Men's Activewear	460.61
10	3560	31811	7/5/2021	Men's Outerwear	577.76
11	1410	64637	10/8/2021	Men's Outerwear	143.59
12	3661	64637	4/25/2021	Children's	925.25
13	4438	60871	6/18/2021	Children's	220.98
14	3708	65066	8/6/2021	Women's Activewear	385.61
15	9537	91416	2/5/2021	Women's Activewear	975.1
16	9818	85150	7/11/2021	Men's Outerwear	354.29
17	4612	60871	5/16/2021	Men's Activewear	961.36
18	3504	40265	8/23/2021	Children's	200.12
19	2443	40265	5/9/2021	Women's Outerwear	1,089.33
20	2465	31507	10/9/2021	Women's Outerwear	516.78
21	6819	91416	11/11/2021	Women's Activewear	1,212.56
22	4691	31507	12/2/2021	Men's Outerwear	276.86
23	4714	65296	1/14/2021	Women's Outerwear	383.66
24	7414	65296	6/4/2021	Women's Outerwear	1,209.41
25	3936	31507	5/5/2021	Men's Activewear	543.15

Figure 3.2: A well formatted data file

Staging and Analysis Layer

The staging and analysis layer is where you get the data ready for the presentation layer. While raw data is great for flexibility, it can be terrible for driving a chart. This layer allows you to summarize the source data in different ways for different visual elements. You might present a line chart showing how something changes over time and a column chart showing values by category and both charts have the same data source. In that case, you might summarize the data by date on one worksheet and by category on another.

	A	B	C	D	E	F	G	H	I
1	Customer		Category		Product			Date	ID	Sales
2										
3	31507									
4										
5			Children's							
6										
7				1452			8/15/2021	248	$369.94
8										
9										
10				1548			5/21/2021	56	$563.17
11										
12				3547			5/18/2021	426	$476.59
13										
14										
15				4575			12/27/2021	328	$229.43
16										
17				9459			8/28/2021	314	$363.82
18										
19										
20			Men's Activewear							
21										
22				1146			10/6/2021	264	$287.09
23										
24										
25				1203			4/10/2021	43	$463.02

Figure 3.3: A poorly formatted data file

For the simplest dashboards, this layer may contain only one worksheet. But for most dashboards, this layer and the source layer will consist of multiple worksheets. You don't need to try to jam all your staging areas onto one worksheet.

Some charts just work better when the data is in a certain form. If you change the chart type for a certain element, you may have to change how you stage the data on this layer too. The aggregation and analysis of the data on this layer is usually made up of either worksheet formulas or a PivotTable.

Presentation Layer

The presentation layer holds the visual elements. If you have interactive controls, those live on this layer too. Sometimes the staging layer and the presentation layer are on the same worksheet. If it works for the size of your data, you can hide the staging data directly behind the chart it drives. That doesn't always work, though, and it's best to keep them separate.

The presentation layer might consist of one or more worksheets in a workbook and another file format that's used to distribute the dashboard. There's nothing wrong with using Excel to hold the final dashboard, but some people prefer PowerPoint, a PDF file, or the body of an email. In those cases, the presentation layer consists of the worksheets where you build the elements and the format you use to distribute them.

Working with External Data

If your source data is not in Excel, the first step will be to import it. Excel can import many different data sources. And with the introduction of Power Query and Power Pivot in more recent versions, the number of sources that Excel can handle has greatly increased.

Power Query vs. Power Pivot

A few years ago, Microsoft brought business intelligence (BI) to a wider audience with a suite of tools. While they've evolved over time, the main tools related to Excel are Power Query and Power Pivot.

Power Query is an extract, transform, and load (ETL) engine. It's built into more modern versions of Excel and it's also built into other stand-alone BI applications like Microsoft's Power BI. Power Query has replaced the legacy import wizards from the Get External Data group on the Data tab of the Ribbon.

Those legacy wizards were the extract and load parts of ETL. There was some limited transformation that could be done, but mostly they read in external data and loaded it on a worksheet. Power Query has far more transform capabilities, and I'll discuss some of them later in this chapter. Whole books have been written on Power Query, so I'll only be scratching the surface here.

Power Pivot is an add-in for Excel that allows you to make more sophisticated data models than you can with Excel alone. You can define data hierarchies, write more advanced formulas using the DAX language, and define KPIs for your data, among other things. Power Pivot is beyond the scope of this book, but it often gets lumped together with Power Query so it's good to understand the distinction.

Text Files

Text files come in two main flavors: delimited and fixed width. Delimited files have a special character, like a comma or a tab, that separates each field in a row (the rows are separated by line breaks). Every row in a fixed-width file has the same number of characters. And every field in a row has the same number of characters as that field in another row. When the data doesn't fill up a field, spaces are used so that the next field starts in the same place for every row. Figure 3.4 shows the same data formatted as delimited and fixed width.

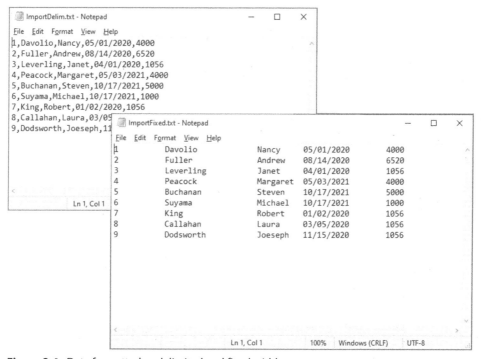

Figure 3.4: Data formatted as delimited and fixed width

Each format has its good and bad points. Fixed-width files are larger to hold the same amount of data due to all the whitespace. Even though you can't see them, nonprintable characters still have to be stored. The downside to delimited is that sometimes the special character exists in the data, creating confusion about what is data and what is a field separator. There are standards for dealing with the delimiting character in the data, but not every program uses the same standard. Generally, if you put double quotes around fields with a delimiting character in the data and use two double quotes when the double quote character is in the data, most programs will open them without issue.

NOTE   The text files for the examples in this section are named `ImportDelim` `.txt` and `ImportFixed.txt` and can be found at `www.wiley.com/go/` `datavizwithexcel/`.

To import a fixed-width file, follow these steps:

1. Create a blank workbook in Excel.

2. Choose Data ⇨ Get Data ⇨ From File ⇨ From Text/CSV from the Ribbon as shown in Figure 3.5.

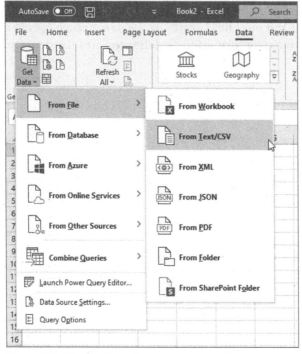

Figure 3.5: The Get Data drop-down on the Ribbon

3. Navigate to the file named `ImportFixed.txt` to import and open it. Excel displays how it interprets the file. In this case Excel reports that it's using a custom delimiter and there's nothing in the delimiter text box. I don't know why it doesn't choose the Fixed Width option that you can see in Figure 3.6, but I suspect that passing an empty string delimiter is the secret code for fixed width.

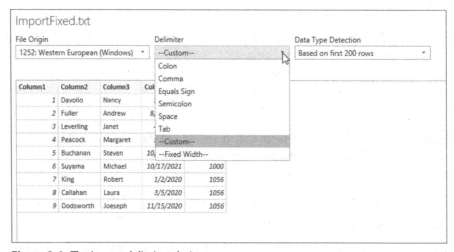

Figure 3.6: The import delimiter choices

4. Click the Load button to transfer the data into the worksheet. Figure 3.7 shows the table it creates and the Queries & Connections task pane.

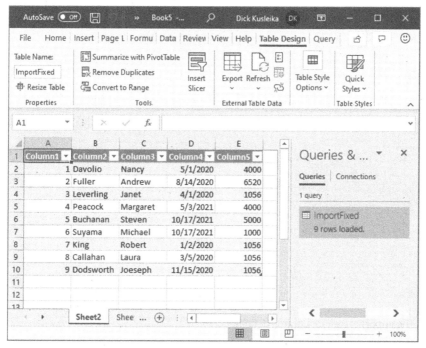

Figure 3.7: The text file in a table

The steps to open a delimited file are the same. Power Query will hopefully correctly guess that the delimiter is a comma, as it does in Figure 3.8.

You can import text files into Excel using File ⇨ Open from the Ribbon. This will start the legacy Text Import Wizard, shown in Figure 3.9. If you prefer the legacy wizards for text files or any other file types, you can add them back to the Ribbon. On the Ribbon, go to File ⇨ Options ⇨ Data and check next to any legacy import wizards you'd like to have access to. Figure 3.10 shows the Excel Options dialog where you can make these selections.

The Power Query imports have two big advantages over the legacy methods. First, you have a lot more options to transform the data during the import. I discuss transforming data in Power Query later in this chapter. The second advantage is that it creates an updatable table in Excel that's linked to the source.

With the legacy methods, you import the data and it is disconnected from the source file. If you replace the source file with an updated one, you have to reimport. With Power Query, you simply refresh the table and the data is updated. This makes updating a dashboard much simpler.

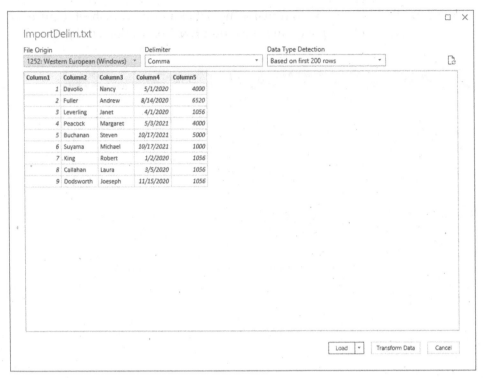

Figure 3.8: The import screen for comma delimited

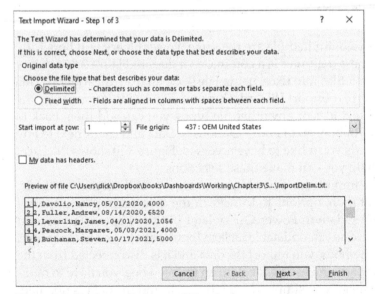

Figure 3.9: The legacy Text Import Wizard

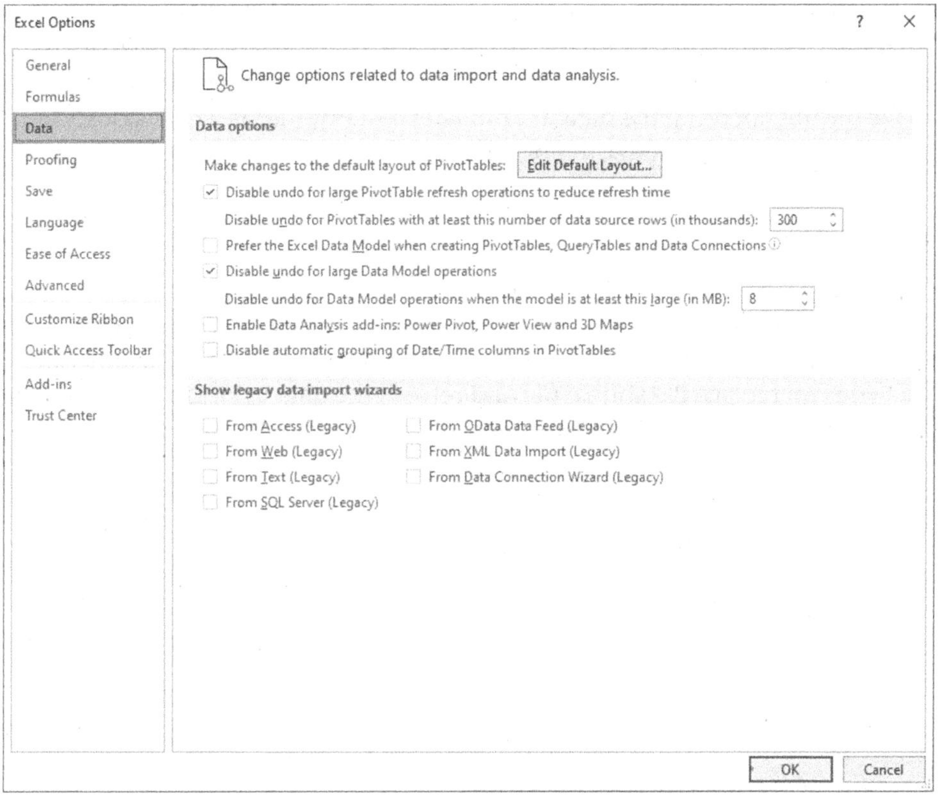

Figure 3.10: Include legacy import wizards on the Ribbon in Excel Options.

At the bottom of the import screen, you can click on the Transform Data button to open the Power Query Editor. Again, I'll discuss some transformation basics later in this chapter. The Load button is a drop-down that includes Load and Load To options. The Load option is the default and creates the table on a worksheet. The Load To option shows the Import Data dialog as shown in Figure 3.11.

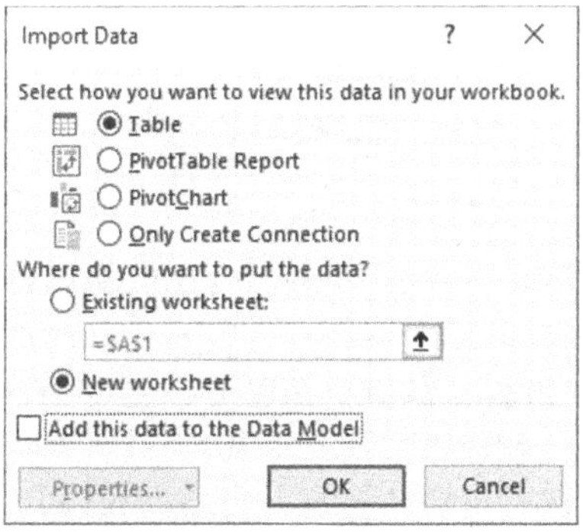

Figure 3.11: The Import Data dialog

The first option is to send the data to a table just as Load does. You can also send the data directly to a PivotTable or PivotChart, which is a good option if you intend to pivot the data anyway. Another option is to create the connection to the file but not bring the data in until later. Finally, there's a check box to add that data to the Data Model, a topic I'll discuss in the next section.

Excel Files

You can also import other Excel files using Power Query. The process is very similar to importing text files. Like with text files, importing Excel files instead of just opening them or copying and pasting the contents has the advantage that you can replace the source file and refresh the data to streamline updates. Figure 3.12 shows part of an Excel file with sales transaction data.

▲	A	B	C	D	E	F
1	TranID	TranDate	SalesPerson	ItemID	Quantity	Amount
2	10274	6/18/2020	2	P7672	39	1,092.00
3	18945	11/23/2020	8	P8311	75	3,675.00
4	12709	11/24/2020	7	P4268	4	148.00
5	18186	2/19/2020	1	P7783	90	1,080.00
6	11947	9/3/2020	5	P2534	95	3,040.00
7	19077	12/28/2020	2	P8906	25	1,175.00
8	16016	2/4/2020	4	P8116	10	470.00
9	12386	4/19/2020	9	P8419	84	1,764.00
10	18643	2/23/2020	1	P9271	69	1,518.00
11	15081	5/8/2020	4	P3936	73	2,044.00
12	12638	1/6/2020	3	P9016	87	1,914.00
13	19910	8/22/2020	6	P9156	24	936.00
14	11413	8/1/2020	8	P5772	14	350.00
15	10225	8/28/2020	9	P8903	14	504.00
16	13048	1/13/2020	2	P3853	27	972.00
17	19216	4/15/2020	7	P6526	3	72.00
18	19561	10/7/2020	9	P4351	77	1,309.00
19	18876	9/2/2020	6	P5189	44	924.00
20	17801	2/13/2020	7	P3969	68	748.00

Figure 3.12: Sales transaction data in an Excel file

NOTE   The files for the examples in this section are named `SalesTransactions` `.xlsx`, `SalesPersons.txt`, and `SalesByLastName.xlsx` and can be found at `www.wiley.com/go/datavizwithexcel/`.

To import an Excel file, choose Data ⇨ Get Data ⇨ From File ⇨ From Workbook from the Ribbon, as shown in Figure 3.13.

Navigate to and select the file to show the Power Query Navigator screen shown in Figure 3.14. The Navigator screen shows importable items in the file. In this example, the workbook has two worksheets, one Excel table, and one named range. Each importable item type has a distinct icon so you can tell what type it is. When an item is selected, preview data is shown on the right.

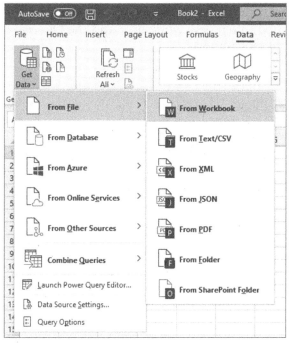

Figure 3.13: Import an Excel file from the Ribbon.

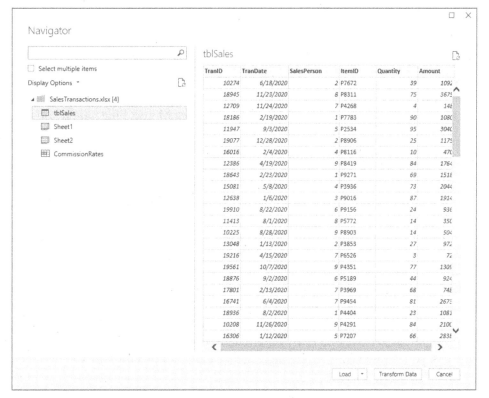

Figure 3.14: The Power Query Navigator window

Select the Excel table and click Load to import it into the active workbook. Figure 3.15 shows the data loaded into a new worksheet and the Queries & Connections task pane identifying the import.

	A	B	C	D	E	F	G
1	TranID	TranDate	SalesPerson	ItemID	Quantity	Amount	
2	10274	6/18/2020	2	P7672	39	1092	
3	18945	11/23/2020	8	P8!			
4	12709	11/24/2020	7	P4:			
5	18186	2/19/2020	1	P7			
6	11947	9/3/2020	5	P2!			
7	19077	12/28/2020	2	P8!			
8	16016	2/4/2020	4	P8:			
9	12386	4/19/2020	9	P8&			
10	18643	2/23/2020	1	P9:			
11	15081	5/8/2020	4	P3!			
12	12638	1/6/2020	3	P9(			
13	19910	8/22/2020	6	P9:			
14	11413	8/1/2020	8	P5			
15	10225	8/28/2020	9	P8!			
16	13048	1/13/2020	2	P3:			
17	19216	4/15/2020	7	P6:			
18	19561	10/7/2020	9	P4:			
19	18876	9/2/2020	6	P5:			
20	17801	2/13/2020	7	P35ს9		ს8	746
21	16741	6/4/2020	7	P9454		81	2673

Queries & Connec... ▾ ✕

Queries | Connections

1 query

▦ tblSales
335 rows loaded.

Figure 3.15: Excel data imported and the Queries & Connections task pane

A Data Model is a construct inside an Excel workbook that relates two or more data sets as a relational database does. Generally, that means that two data sets have a common column that relates the data. In the following example, both the sales transactions data and the salesperson data have a SalesPerson column.

There are three ways to add a data set to the Data Model. First, when you load the data, you can choose the Load To option on the Power Query Navigator screen and check the "Add this data to the Data Model" check box on the Import Data dialog. Second, if you are importing more than one data set at the same time, Excel will automatically add them to the Data Model. Finally, if you've already imported the data, as in this example, you can choose Query ⇨ Load To on the Ribbon to show the Import Data dialog and check the box. The Query tab on the Ribbon is a context tab and is only visible when imported data is selected.

Using the third option will reload the data and replace the existing import with whatever is currently in the file. Excel warns you that you are replacing the data with the message, shown in Figure 3.16. If the source file hasn't changed, you can safely ignore the warning.

It's possible to have only one data set in the Data Model, but it has limited utility compared to having two or more data sets that relate to each other. Nevertheless, you can see your single-table Data Model in Power Pivot. You first have to enable the Power Pivot add-in. To do that, choose File ⇨ Options to show the Excel Options dialog. On the Add-ins tab, choose COM Add-ins from the Manage drop-down and click the Go button. In the COM Add-ins dialog, check the box next to Microsoft Power Pivot For Excel and click OK, as shown in Figure 3.17.

Figure 3.16: Excel's warning when adding an existing data set to the Data Model

Figure 3.17: Enable the Power Pivot add-in in Excel.

Enabling the add-in will add a Power Pivot tab to the Ribbon. On that tab, there is an Add to Data Model tool that provides a fourth option for adding an existing data set to the Data Model when you already have the Power Pivot add-in enabled. To see the Data Model, click Manage on the Power Pivot tab on the Ribbon to launch Power Pivot. Figure 3.18 shows the Power Pivot interface.

There are tabs along the bottom of Power Pivot showing all the data sets in the Data Model, similar to the worksheet tabs in a workbook. Since there is only one data set in the example so far, there is only one tab.

To add another data set, close Power Pivot and return to Excel. Follow the steps from the previous section to import the text file named Salespersons.txt. Select Load To from the Power Query Navigator screen to show the Import Data dialog and check the Add this data to the Data Model check box.

Select Manage from the Power Pivot tab on the Ribbon to re-launch Power Pivot. There are now two tabs along the bottom representing the two data sets in the Data Model. Depending on your data, Power Pivot may automatically create the relationship between the two data sets. In this case where one data set is from Excel and the other is a text file, Power Pivot won't know how the data relates so you'll have to create the relationship manually.

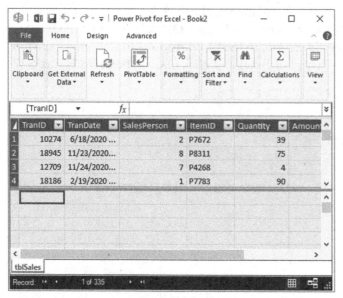

Figure 3.18: The Power Pivot interface

On the Design tab of the Power Pivot Ribbon, select Create Relationships to show the Create Relationships dialog. Select each of the data sets in the drop-downs and select the SalesPerson column in both tables, as shown in Figure 3.19.

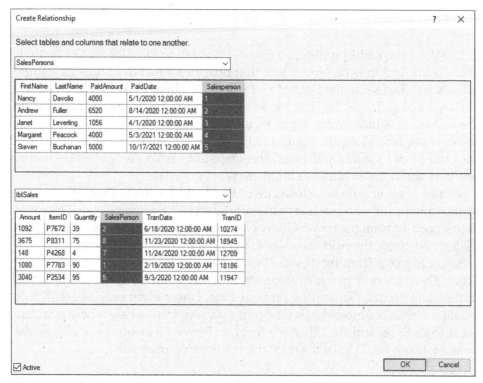

Figure 3.19: Creating a relationship in Power Pivot

Click the OK button to create the relationship. By doing this, you've told Power Pivot that those two columns are common between the two data sets. On the Home tab of the Power Pivot Ribbon, choose Diagram View. Diagram View is a different way to see your Data Model. Instead of tabs across the bottom showing you the data in each data set, the data sets are shown in boxes showing the fields. It also shows any relationships that have been created, represented by a line between the two data sets. In Figure 3.20, the mouse is shown hovering over that relationship line causing the two SalesPerson fields (the related fields) to be highlighted.

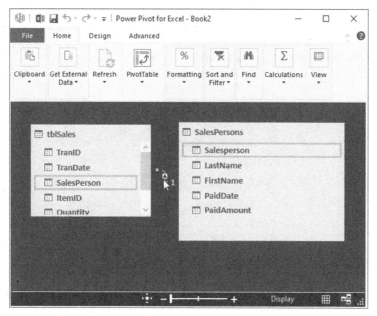

Figure 3.20: Power Pivot's Diagram View shows relationships.

The relationship shown in Figure 3.20 has an asterisk at one end nearer the tblSales data set and a 1 at the other end nearer the SalesPersons data set. Power Pivot has correctly recognized this relationship as one to many, meaning that for each record in SalesPersons there are many related records in tblSales.

Now that a relationship has been established, you can create a PivotTable based on the Data Model. Close Power Pivot and return to Excel. Select Insert ⇨ Tables ⇨ PivotTable on the Ribbon to show the Create PivotTable dialog. Choose the Use This Workbook's Data Model option as shown in Figure 3.21.

The resulting PivotTable, shown in Figure 3.22, includes both data sets in the field list. You can select fields from either table and Excel now understands the relationship between them. For example, drag the LastName field from Salespersons to the Rows area and the Amount field from tblSales to the Values area to create a PivotTable like the one shown in Figure 3.23.

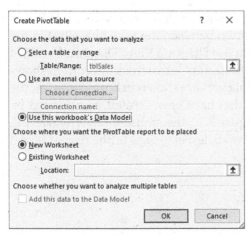

Figure 3.21: Create a PivotTable based on the Data Model.

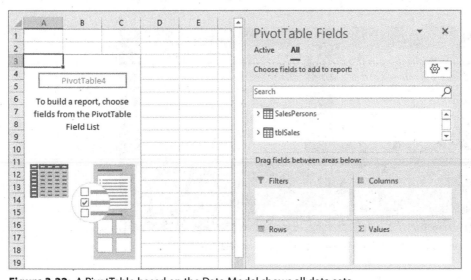

Figure 3.22: A PivotTable based on the Data Model shows all data sets.

Power Pivot is a very powerful tool in Excel and this section is only a brief introduction to its capabilities. I'll discuss some other aspects throughout the rest of this chapter, but if you want to go deeper into all that Power Pivot has to offer, a separate book devoted to it is probably in order.

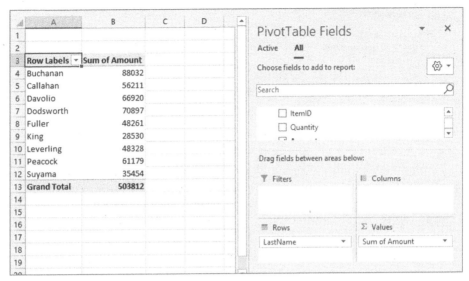

Figure 3.23: A PivotTable summing sales by salesperson's last name

Access Databases

In addition to the file-based queries, like those in the previous two sections, Power Query can also import data sets from Access databases. An Access database is still just a single file, but it contains more complex data structures than you typically find in file imports.

> **NOTE** The file for the examples in this section is named `Northwind.accdb` and can be found at `www.wiley.com/go/datavizwithexcel/`.

To import data from an Access database, open a workbook and select Data ➪ Get Data ➪ From Database ➪ From Microsoft Access Database on the Ribbon. Navigate to the Access database file and click Open. Excel displays the Power Query Navigator dialog that you're familiar with from the previous sections, as shown in Figure 3.24.

The Navigator dialog shows all the tables and queries in the database that you can import. To import a single table or query, simply select it and click the Load button. A new sheet is created with the table or query loaded into an Excel table. Figure 3.25 shows a portion of the data from loading the Orders table from the Northwind database.

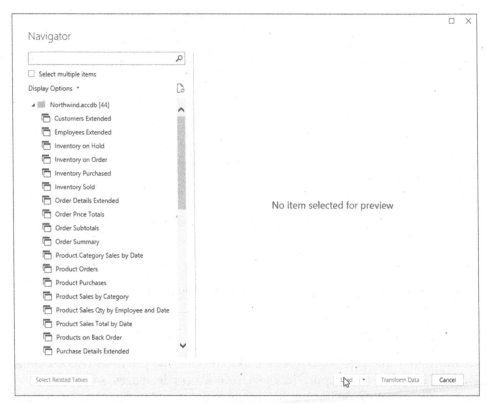

Figure 3.24: The Power Query Navigator dialog for importing data from an Access database

	A	B	C	D	E	F	G
1	Order ID	Employee ID	Customer ID	Order Date	Shipped Date	Shipper ID	Ship Name
2	30	9	27	1/15/2006 0:00	1/22/2006 0:00	2	Karen Toh
3	31	3	4	1/20/2006 0:00	1/22/2006 0:00	1	Christina Lee
4	32	4	12	1/22/2006 0:00	1/22/2006 0:00	2	John Edwards
5	33	6	8	1/30/2006 0:00	1/31/2006 0:00	3	Elizabeth Andersen
6	34	9	4	2/6/2006 0:00	2/7/2006 0:00	3	Christina Lee
7	35	3	29	2/10/2006 0:00	2/12/2006 0:00	2	Soo Jung Lee
8	36	4	3	2/23/2006 0:00	2/25/2006 0:00	2	Thomas Axen
9	37	8	6	3/6/2006 0:00	3/9/2006 0:00	2	Francisco Pérez-Olaeta
10	38	9	28	3/10/2006 0:00	3/11/2006 0:00	3	Amritansh Raghav
11	39	3	8	3/22/2006 0:00	3/24/2006 0:00	3	Elizabeth Andersen
12	40	4	10	3/24/2006 0:00	3/24/2006 0:00	2	Roland Wacker
13	41	1	7	3/24/2006 0:00			Ming-Yang Xie
14	42	1	10	3/24/2006 0:00	4/7/2006 0:00	1	Roland Wacker
15	43	1	11	3/24/2006 0:00		3	Peter Krschne
16	44	1	1	3/24/2006 0:00			Anna Bedecs
17	45	1	28	4/7/2006 0:00	4/7/2006 0:00	3	Amritansh Raghav
18	46	7	9	4/5/2006 0:00	4/5/2006 0:00	1	Sven Mortensen
19	47	6	6	4/8/2006 0:00	4/8/2006 0:00	2	Francisco Pérez-Olaeta
20	48	4	8	4/5/2006 0:00	4/5/2006 0:00	2	Elizabeth Andersen
21	50	9	25	4/5/2006 0:00	4/5/2006 0:00	1	John Rodman

Figure 3.25: The Orders table from the Northwind database

As with the other imports, any changes to the source data can be reflected in Excel by simply refreshing the imported table. The Navigator dialog also allows you to import multiple items at one time. Start with a new workbook and again choose Data ⇨ Get Data ⇨ From Database ⇨ From Microsoft Access Database from the Ribbon. At the top of the Navigator dialog, check the Select Multiple Items check box. The dialog now displays check boxes next to each item, allowing you to select more than one. Select the Orders and Order Details tables as shown in Figure 3.26 and click the Load button.

Figure 3.26: Select multiple data sets in the Navigator dialog.

When you import multiple items, Power Query doesn't load them onto worksheets as it does when you import a single item. Instead, it automatically adds them to the Data Model. From the Ribbon, choose Power Pivot ⇨ Manage to open Power Pivot and click Diagram View on the Home tab of the Power Pivot Ribbon. As shown in Figure 3.27, the Data Model recognized a relationship between the two tables already created in Access and creates the same relationship in the Data Model.

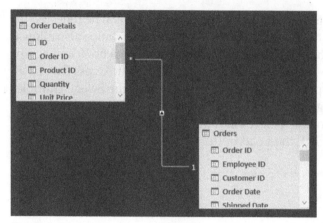

Figure 3.27: Existing Access relationships are already created in the Data Model.

With the Data Model in place, you can load a single data set to a worksheet or create a PivotTable from the data. To load a single table, first return to Excel. The Queries & Connections task pane is probably still visible from when you imported the data. If it's not, click Queries & Connections from the Data tab on the Ribbon to display it. Right-click one of the data sets and choose Load To from the context menu, as shown in Figure 3.28, to show the Import Data dialog, shown in Figure 3.29.

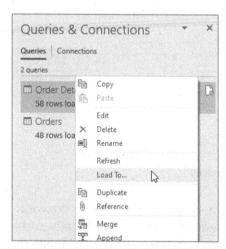

Figure 3.28: Loading a single table from the Queries & Connections task pane

The Import Data dialog remembers the settings from when that query was last imported. Because you imported more than one data set, the default of Only Create Connection and Add This Data To The Data Model are selected. Choose Table and keep Add This Data To The Data Model checked to load the single data set to a worksheet. It won't add another copy to the Data Model, but unchecking it would have removed it.

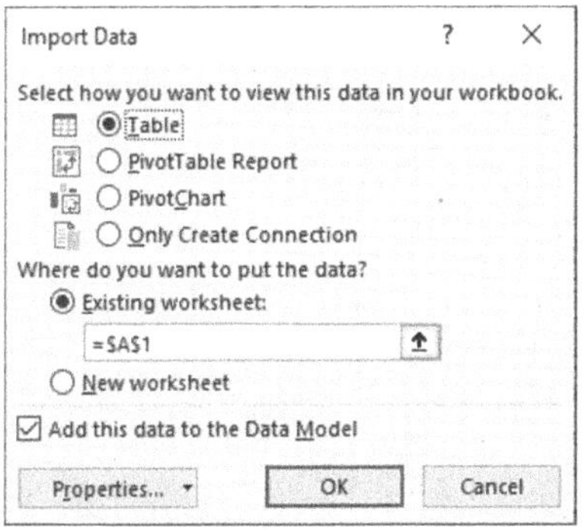

Figure 3.29: The Import Data dialog

It's more common that you would create a PivotTable from the Data Model rather than loading a single data set. To create a PivotTable, choose Insert ➪ Tables ➪ PivotTable from the Ribbon to show the Create PivotTable dialog. Choose the Use This Workbook's Data Model option, as shown in Figure 3.30, and click OK.

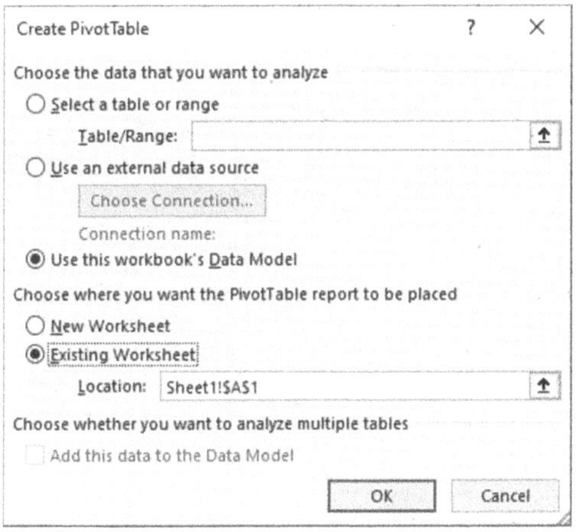

Figure 3.30: Create a PivotTable from the Data Model.

The Orders and Order Details queries are shown in the PivotTable Fields task pane as shown in Figure 3.31. The PivotTable understands the relationships in the Data Model and you can use fields from either query, such as to show the total quantity of items sold on each day.

Power Query also has the ability to determine which tables are related to each other before you import them. That way you can import all the tables related to, for example, the Orders table even if you aren't familiar with the database design.

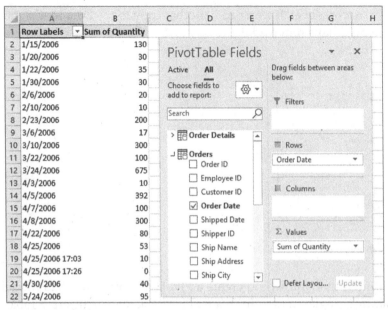

Figure 3.31: A PivotTable based on the Data Model

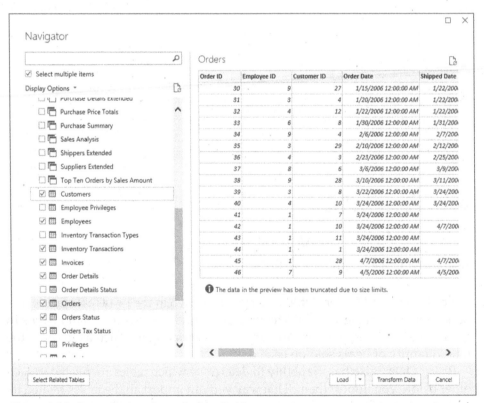

Figure 3.32: Power Query selects all related tables.

In the Power Query Navigator dialog, check the Select Multiple Items check box and check the Orders table. Click the Select Related Tables button at the bottom of the dialog. After a bit of processing, Power Query will select all the related tables as shown in Figure 3.32.

The Orders table has a foreign key named Customer ID that's related to the primary key in the Customers table, so Customers is checked. The same is true for all the other tables Power Query automatically selected. All the tables are loaded, the relationships are automatically created, and the Power Pivot Diagram View looks like the one in Figure 3.33.

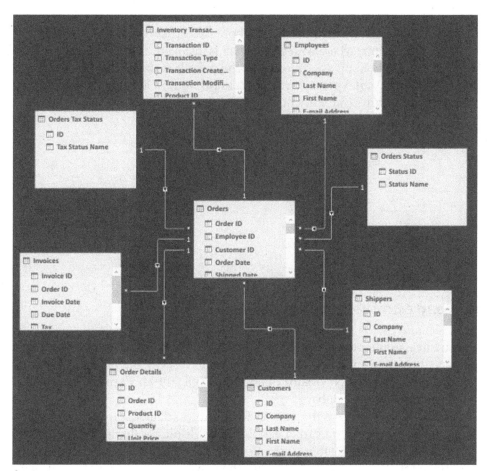

Figure 3.33: Selecting related tables creates all the relationships in the Data Model.

SQL Server Databases

Another common data store from which to import is Microsoft SQL Server. Unlike Access, SQL Server isn't a file-based program but a service running on a server or your local machine that connects to the data.

SQL Server has different versions that vary based on the needs of your organization. For this section, I'll be using SQL Server Express. The SQL Server Express version is a free version that runs on your local machine rather than its own separate server.

Microsoft provides a sample database for SQL Server called AdventureWorks. The Express version of SQL Server can be found on Microsoft's website at www .microsoft.com/en-us/sql-server/sql-server-downloads. The AdventureWorks sample database is a separate download from Microsoft's website and can be found at docs.microsoft.com/en-us/sql/samples/adventureworks-install-configure.

To load data from SQL Server, choose Data ➪ Get Data ➪ From Database ➪ From SQL Server Database from the Ribbon. Excel displays a dialog where you enter the server name where your SQL Server is installed, as shown in Figure 3.34. If you're using the Express edition with the default installation, connect using the server name **.\sqlexpress**. If you don't know your SQL Server name, contact the database administrator at your organization.

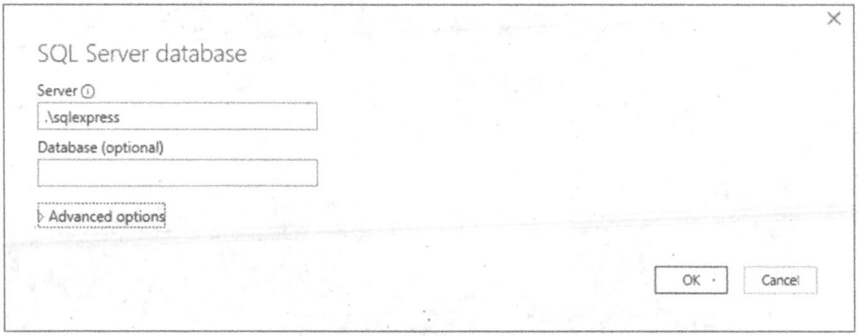

Figure 3.34: Excel's dialog for entering the SQL Server name

You can also enter the name of the database in the dialog to limit the list that's displayed on the Navigator dialog. Click OK to display the Navigator dialog. Figure 3.35 shows the Navigator dialog for a SQL Server Express server with the AdventureWorks database.

From here, the process is the same as for an Access database from the previous section. For example, you can check the Select Multiple Items check box and check the SalesOrderHeader and SalesOrderDetail tables and click Load to load them into the Data Model. Because the AdventureWorks database already contains a relationship between those two tables, Power Pivot creates the same relationship automatically. Figure 3.36 shows the Power Pivot Diagram View, which you can see by selecting Manage from the Power Pivot tab on the Ribbon and then choosing Diagram View from the Home tab on the Power Pivot Ribbon.

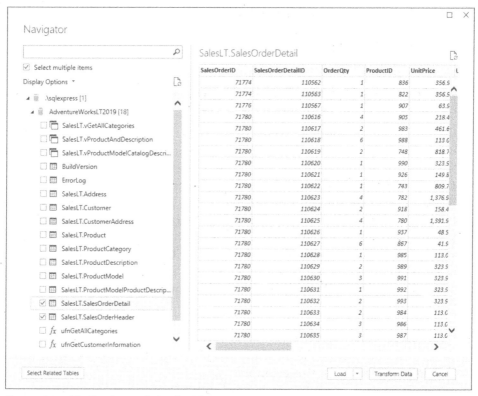

Figure 3.35: The Navigator dialog for SQL Server

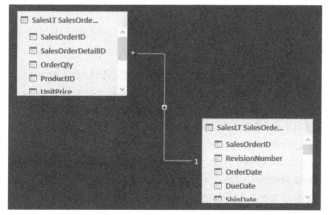

Figure 3.36: Power Pivot's Diagram View for the SalesOrderHeader and SalesOrderDetails tables

In this chapter, I've shown some common data sources for loading data via Power Query in Excel. Excel can import many more types of data sources, including Salesforce, Azure, Microsoft Exchange, and MySQL. The process for connecting to these data sources varies slightly, but once you're connected, the process for loading the data is the same.

Transforming Data in Power Query

In the previous sections I showed how to load data from various external sources using Power Query and Power Pivot. In addition to simply loading data and automatically creating relationships, Power Query allows you to manipulate, or transform, the data before it's loaded into Excel.

Power Query uses the M formula language to transform the data. To learn the M language requires a whole book of its own, but I'll show you some basics. And while you can write your own M code, Power Query writes it for you in the background as you manipulate the data using the Ribbon. For most of what you'll need to do, you won't even need to know that the M code is there.

To see how Power Query transforms data, follow these steps:

1. Choose Data ⇨ Get Data ⇨ From Database ⇨ From Microsoft Access Database from the Ribbon.

2. Choose your Access database file and click Open. I'll use the Northwind sample database for this example.

3. Check the Select Multiple Items check box at the top of the Navigator dialog.

4. Select the Orders and Order Details tables.

5. Click the Transform Data button at the bottom of the Navigator dialog as shown in Figure 3.37.

Clicking Transform Data will open the Power Query Editor, as shown in Figure 3.38. The left side of the editor lists the queries as Excel's Queries & Connections task pane does. The main area of the editor shows the data for whichever query is selected on the left. The Query Settings task pane on the right shows the steps Power Query has taken to transform the data.

The Applied Steps section of the Query Settings task pane shows that Power Query has already taken two steps to transform the data. The first step was created when you selected the Access database to use and the second step was selecting the item in the database to load.

From the View tab on the Power Query Ribbon, choose Advanced Editor. The Advanced Editor is where you can view and modify the M code that Power Query is writing in the background. Figure 3.39 shows the Advanced Editor window. The two lines in the let portion of the code are the two steps it has taken.

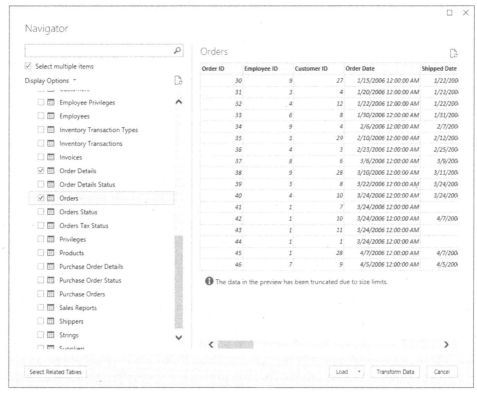

Figure 3.37: Click the Transform Data button on the Navigator dialog.

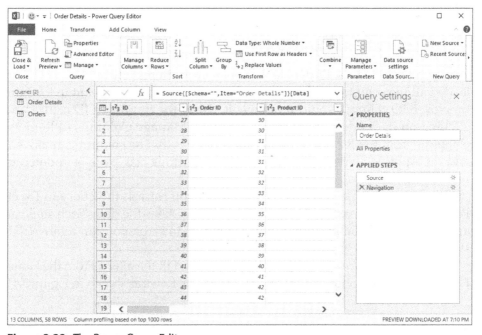

Figure 3.38: The Power Query Editor

Figure 3.39: The Advanced Editor

The syntax of the M code can appear a little daunting. But Power Query writes the code for you so it's not necessary to know how to write M code to be able to get the benefits of using Power Query. Even if you don't understand all the nuances of the code, you can see that the first line is identifying the file and the second line is identifying the table within the file.

Power Query has a Ribbon with tools you can use to transform the data. I'll describe some of those tools in the following sections.

Managing Columns and Rows

When you selected the Orders table as one of the items to load, Power Query loaded all the columns in the table. If, for example, you don't want to load the Employee ID column, you can remove it. Select the Employee ID column by clicking on its header. Then choose Home ⇨ Manage Columns ⇨ Remove Columns from the Ribbon, as shown in Figure 3.40. The column is removed, and the Applied Steps section of the Query Settings task pane is updated to record this step.

Now the query has three steps. Each time you refresh the query in Excel, Power Query will execute the three steps as it updates the data. Each step has an X next to it. If you perform a transformation in error, you can remove that step by clicking the X.

You can also reduce the number of rows you load in the query. From the Home tab on the Ribbon, choose Reduce Rows ⇨ Remove Rows as shown in Figure 3.41.

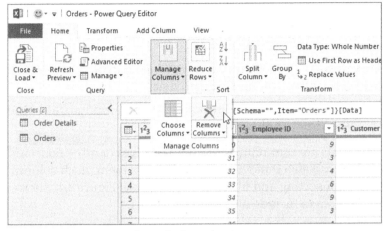

Figure 3.40: Remove a column from a query.

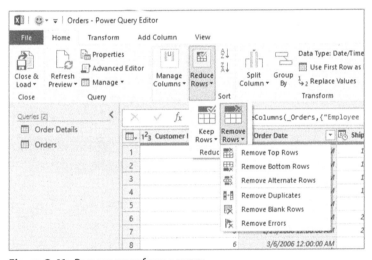

Figure 3.41: Remove rows from a query.

The Remove Rows drop-down contains the following tools:

- **Remove Top Rows:** Use this tool if your data contains header rows that you want to exclude.

- **Remove Bottom Rows:** Use this tool if your data contains footer rows that you want to exclude.

- **Remove Alternate Rows:** Use this tool if each record is on two lines and you want to keep only one of them.

■ **Remove Duplicates:** This tool removes duplicate rows based on the columns selected even if the other columns contain unique data. Select all columns to remove duplicate records.

■ **Remove Blank Rows:** This tool removes rows where the columns selected are blank even if the other columns contain data.

■ **Remove Errors:** If a previous step introduced errors into the data, you can remove those rows with this tool.

The Remove Rows tools are commonly used with text files or other nonstandard data formats. You can also remove rows by filtering them. Each column contains a drop-down for sorting and filtering. For example, Figure 3.42 shows how to filter the order data to include only January orders.

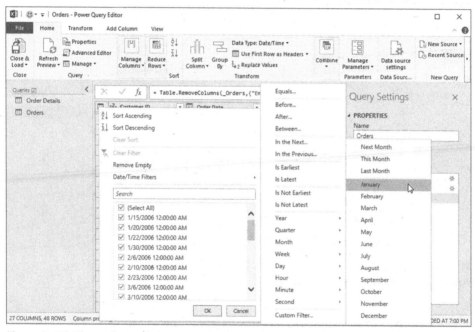

Figure 3.42: Filter orders with January order dates.

Certain steps in the Query Settings task pane display a gear icon to the right. This indicates that you can edit that step. Clicking the gear icon displays a dialog that varies depending on how that step transforms the data. Figure 3.43 shows the dialog displayed if you click on the gear icon for the step that filters the order date.

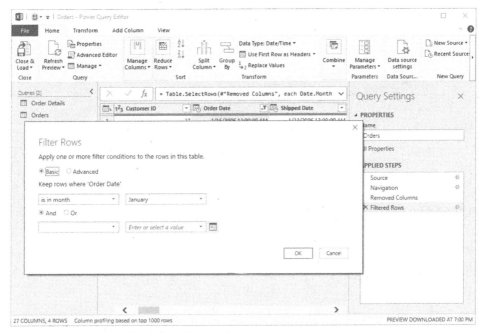

Figure 3.43: Edit a step by clicking the gear icon.

Transforming Columns

The Transform tab on the Power Query Ribbon contains tools for manipulating individual columns in your data. Some of the tools apply to columns with any kind of data and others are specific to numbers and dates. When you've completed all your transformations, click the Close & Load tool on the Home tab of the Ribbon to load your transformed data into Excel.

Transforming Data Types

The Data Type tool displays the data type Power Query has assigned to the selected column. It also allows you to change the data type. For example, if you have part numbers that are numeric but you want them to be treated as text, you can change the data type of that column to Text. Another common data type transformation changes a datetime to a date. Figure 3.44 shows the results of changing the Shipped Date column from datetime to date.

Power Query will allow you to change a data type even if it doesn't make sense. For example, the Ship Name column is a text column containing the name of the customer. Changing that column to a Whole Number data type results in errors in the data, as shown in Figure 3.45.

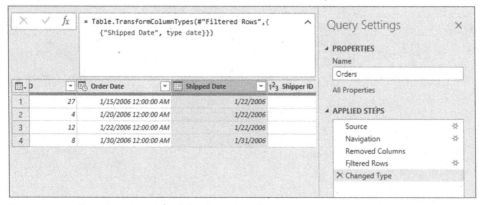

Figure 3.44: Changing the shipped date to a date data type

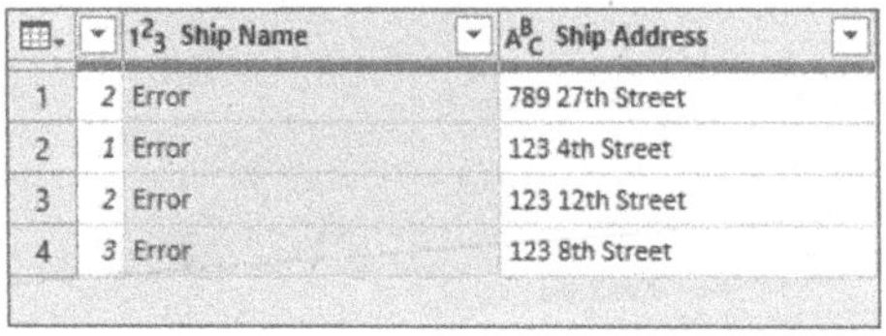

		1²₃ Ship Name		AᵇC Ship Address	
1	2	Error		789 27th Street	
2	1	Error		123 4th Street	
3	2	Error		123 12th Street	
4	3	Error		123 8th Street	

Figure 3.45: Changing to an improper data type results in errors.

If you change the data type of two or more columns without any steps in between, Power Query combines those changes into one step. If you make an error, like changing the Ship Name to Whole Number, you can delete the step, but it will delete all the changes in that step, not just the last one. If you don't want to delete and re-create the step, you can edit the code in the formula bar. Figure 3.46 shows the formula bar with the bad code selected. You can then press the Delete key and the Enter key to change that step. You have to be careful to only delete the part of the code that relates to the problem or you'll get an error. You may find it easier to delete the whole step and start over.

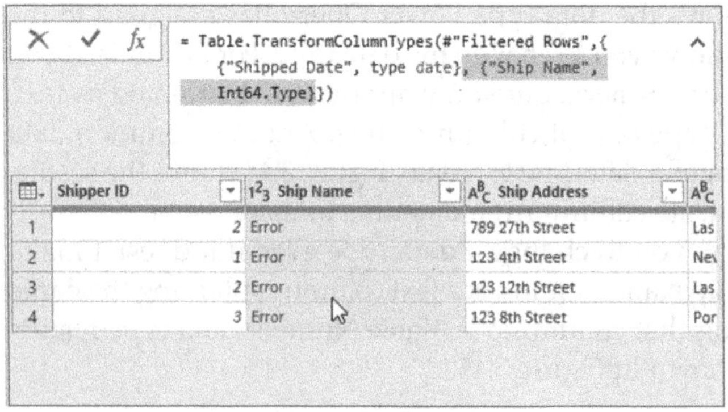

Figure 3.46: Editing a step in the formula bar

The Replace Value tool allows you to perform a find-and-replace transformation on a column. Clicking this tool shows the Replace Values dialog where you type the value to find and what text you want to replace it with. Figure 3.47 shows the Replace Values dialog used to replace the word *Street* with the abbreviation *St*.

Replace Values

Replace one value with another in the selected columns.

Value To Find

Street

Replace With

St

▷ Advanced options

OK   Cancel

Figure 3.47: Replace values in a column.

Transforming Numbers

There are several transformations that apply to only columns with a numeric data type. The simplest of these are under the Standard drop-down on the Transform tab of the Ribbon. With the options under the Standard drop-down, you can perform basic mathematical operations on a column. Figure 3.48 shows the effect of multiplying the Shipping Fee column by 10.

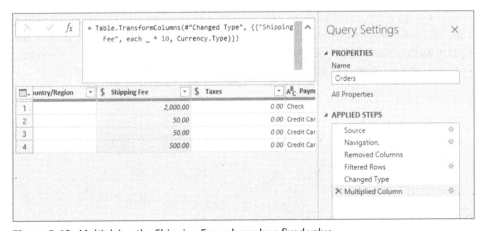

Figure 3.48: Multiplying the Shipping Fee column by a fixed value

Another common numeric transformation is rounding. The Rounding drop-down contains the following list items:

- **Round Up:** Rounds up to the nearest whole number.
- **Round Down:** Rounds down to the nearest whole number.
- **Round:** Displays a dialog box where you enter a custom number of decimal places to which you want to round. You can also round to the nearest tens, hundredths, thousandths, and so on by entering a negative number. For example, entering **-3** rounds to the nearest thousandths.

Figure 3.49 shows the Unit Price column on the Order Details query after applying the Round Up function.

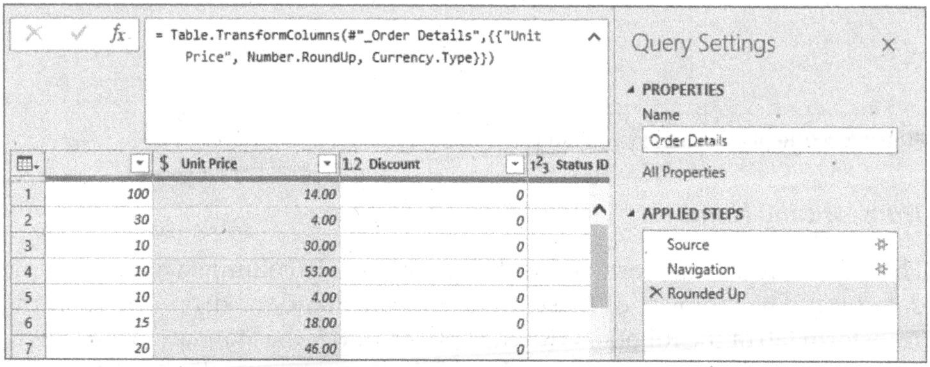

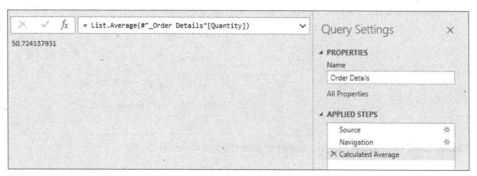

Figure 3.49: Round Up rounds to the nearest higher whole number.

The tools under the Statistics drop-down allow you to perform aggregate functions on a column like sum, minimum, and maximum. These tools reduce the data set to one number. Figure 3.50 shows the Average tool applied to the Quantity column of the Order Details query. The single number that is the result is the only data that would be returned to Excel.

Figure 3.50: Statistics functions return a single value.

Splitting Columns

The Split Columns drop-down on the Home tab provides several options for splitting a column into two or more columns. The tools under Split Columns are as follows:

- **By Delimiter:** Displays a dialog where you select or enter a character on which to split the column, shown in Figure 3.51. You can split on the first occurrence, last occurrence, or every occurrence of that character.

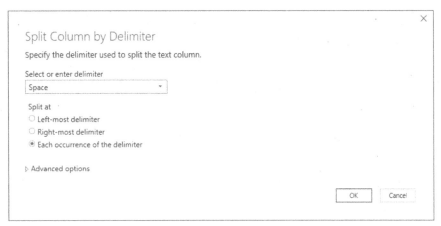

Figure 3.51: The Split Column By Delimiter dialog

- **By Number Of Characters:** Displays a dialog where you enter the number of characters after which the column is split. You can split on that number of characters once from the left or right or repeatedly. For example, if you split a 20-character value on five characters repeatedly, the result would be four columns.

- **By Positions:** Displays a dialog where you enter a comma-separated list of ascending integers indicating on which position to split the column. The first integer must be zero or all data to the left of the first integer will be ignored. For example, entering 0,4,7 results in three columns containing the first three characters, characters four through six, and characters seven through the end of the string, respectively.

- **By Lower Case to Upper Case:** Splits the value every time a lowercase character is followed by an uppercase character. Spaces are considered neither lowercase nor uppercase.

- **By Upper Case to Lower Case:** Splits the value every time an uppercase character is followed by a lowercase character.

- **By Digit to Non-Digit:** Splits the value every time a numeric character is followed by a non-numeric character. Spaces are considered non-numeric.

- **By Non-Digit to Digit:** Splits the value every time a non-numeric character is followed by a numeric character.

Figure 3.52 shows the Ship Address column of the Orders table after splitting by digit to non-digit. The resulting three columns contain the street address, the street number, and the remaining characters, respectively.

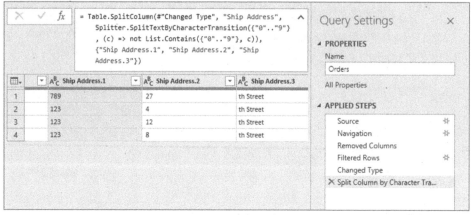

Figure 3.52: Splitting a value by digit to non-digit

You can also split columns using the Column From Examples tool on the Add Column tab of the Ribbon. This has the advantage of leaving the original column intact. For example, to add a column with just the street number of the Shipping Address column of the Orders table, select the Shipping Address column and select Column From Examples ⇨ From Selection from the Add Column tab of the Ribbon. Power Query will add a new column and allow you to type an example of how you would split the first row, as shown in Figure 3.53.

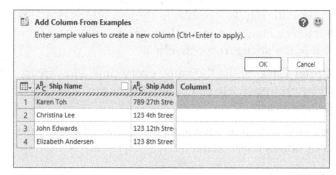

Figure 3.53: Adding columns from examples

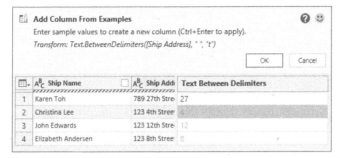

Figure 3.54: Power Query uses an example to determine how to split the remaining rows.

Type **27** into the first row under Column1 and press Ctrl+Enter. Figure 3.54 shows that Power Query guessed how to split the remaining three rows.

You may have to enter more than one example to give Power Query enough data to properly split the column. Click OK to create the new column at the end of the data set, as shown in Figure 3.55.

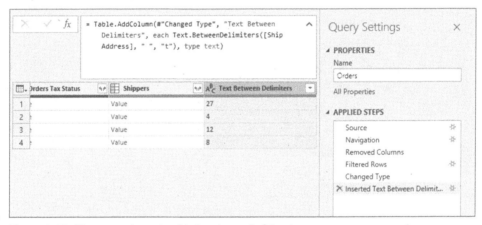

Figure 3.55: The new column is added to the end of the data set.

Power Query contains a lot more transformations than I'm able to show in this chapter. Fortunately, Microsoft's website is full of documentation and many more examples.

Visualization Primer

The Fundamentals of Effective Visualization

In This Chapter

- Creating an Effective Visualization
- Driving Meaning with Color
- Focusing Attention on Text
- Showing Insights with Charts

In this chapter, I discuss the visual elements that make up a dashboard and the components of those elements. Proper use of components like color and text can be the difference between an effective and ineffective chart.

Creating an Effective Visualization

Dashboards and the data visualization elements that make them up are meant to tell a story to the user. The following sections contain some principles that will help you make the most effective charts and help ensure the message gets through.

Keep It to a Single Screen

Your chart or dashboard should fit on one screen or one sheet of paper. If the user has to scroll when viewing the dashboard on a computer monitor, it will distract from the message. This is particularly true if there are related elements both at the top and bottom of the dashboard. The purpose of the dashboard is to tell a story quickly, and forcing users to hold some information in their memory while they scroll down to see the related data does not further that goal.

> **NOTE**   There will be times when you simply have too much data to fit on one sheet. One possible solution is to give the user the ability to drill down into dashboard elements to see more detail. Microsoft offers a stand-alone application called PowerBI that facilitates this. PowerBI is beyond the scope of this book, but as PowerBI matures, there are more and more resources available to help you learn to use it.

In other cases, the user may have to print the chart or dashboard to take it to a meeting where there is no access to a computer. A dashboard that spans multiple sheets of paper will be less attractive and harder to distribute.

To fit your dashboard to one printable page, set the Print Area so that only the dashboard is printed. Select the range around the dashboard and choose Page Layout ⇨ Print Area ⇨ Set Print Area from the Ribbon. Next, set the scaling for the page. In the Scale To Fit group of the Page Layout tab of the Ribbon, change the Width and Height drop-downs to **1 page**, as shown in Figure 4.1.

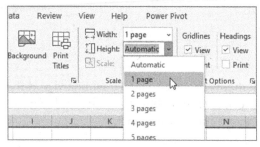

Figure 4.1: Scale a worksheet to fit on a single page.

Scaling a worksheet to fit on a single page is not a cure-all. If you have a large dashboard and scale it to one page, the individual elements, particularly text, may become too hard to read. Try not to scale below 75% of the original dashboard. The Scale tool on the Page Layout tab of the Ribbon shows the percent scaled when the Width and Height tools are set. Figure 4.2 shows an example where scaling to one page is the same as scaling to 66% of the original.

Figure 4.2: The Scale tool displays the actual scaling percentage.

What do you do when your scale percentage drops below 75%? As with good writing, the key to a good dashboard is good editing. Do you have elements on the page that don't further the story? Is there a chart type that you could use that would take up less space? Editing can be difficult, but it will almost always result in a more effective dashboard.

Make It Attractive

This may seem obvious, but it needs to be said. A visually pleasing chart will engage the user more than an ugly one. Remember that the goal of the chart is to tell a story about the data. If the user is focused on the design because it's unappealing, the story isn't getting through.

There was a time when Excel's default chart styles left something to be desired. Fortunately, newer versions of Excel produce a pretty attractive chart by default. That means less editing of the colors, styles, and text is necessary to get the final product you want.

One important aspect of a visually pleasing dashboard is balance. Balance is not concerned with the details of the data but with how the density of the data is displayed across the elements.

Your dashboard doesn't have to be symmetrical to be balanced; only the amount of ink and white space should be similar for all areas of the dashboard. If you squint and look at your dashboard from a few feet away, you can get an idea if the dashboard is balanced. Figure 4.3 shows an extreme example of a dashboard where one element is significantly denser than the others.

Tell the Story Quickly

Once you have the user's attention with an attractive chart, you have a limited amount of time to get the message across before they lose interest. The rule of thumb is that if a user doesn't understand what the chart is saying in five seconds, they will lose interest and turn their attention elsewhere.

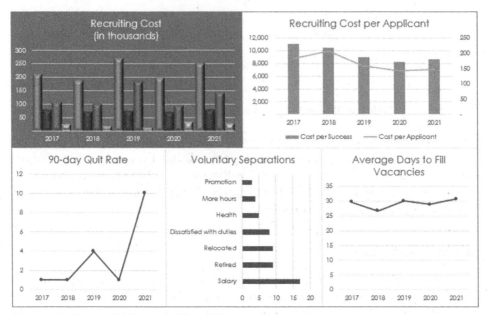

Figure 4.3: An out-of-balance dashboard due to one dense element

I don't know if there's any science behind the five-second rule. I imagine it depends on the user. There are some users who are immensely interested in what the chart says about the data and will decipher even a poorly designed chart to get at it. Conversely, there are users who don't particularly care, and if it's your job to convince them of something, you'll want to do it quickly. Nevertheless, the spirit of the five-second rule leads to at least two virtuous habits.

First, if you need to get the message out quickly, you'll be more likely to design a clean and simple chart. Eliminating clutter and making generous use of white space will help the message come through. Figure 4.4 shows a chart with a lot of clutter and the same chart with the clutter removed. The cleaner chart is easier to read, making the message understood sooner.

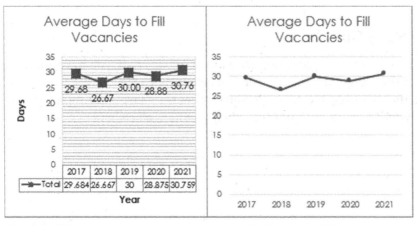

Figure 4.4: Eliminating clutter makes the chart easier to understand.

The second habit the five-second rule encourages is keeping the chart's story simple. A chart that tries to tell too many stories at once or incorporates every piece of related data you can find will be like a puzzle the user has to solve to understand the meaning. In most cases, each element on a dashboard should make one point. The chart in Figure 4.5 tries to include too much data and would be better split into multiple charts.

Figure 4.5: A chart with too much data is hard to read.

That doesn't mean that your chart can't contain a lot of detail. Some of the best charts have layers. At first glance, your chart might show a general trend. As the user is drawn into the chart, some of the individual data points have an interesting story of their own. The chart in Figure 4.6 has 51 data points that show the median income per US state plus the District of Columbia. That's a lot of data points, but the slope between the highest and the lowest is immediately interesting and can draw the user in. Next, the color-coded regions show an interesting pattern. And finally, if the user is from the US, they will no doubt find their state to see where it falls on the chart.

Make the Story Consistent with the Data

The story your chart tells must come from the data. How you get to that story will vary based on who's requesting the chart, who will be reading the chart, and what kind of data you have to support the story.

For example, you may have a lot of data that you're interested in and want to explore. You don't have a particular problem you're trying to solve, and nobody is asking you to produce a chart. So, you start creating charts, not for publication, but for exploration to see what trends or anomalies exist within the data. In these cases, the story is almost always consistent with the data because it was born from the data. There are cases, however, where a sample of the data shows a trend that you try to apply to a larger population and it just doesn't work.

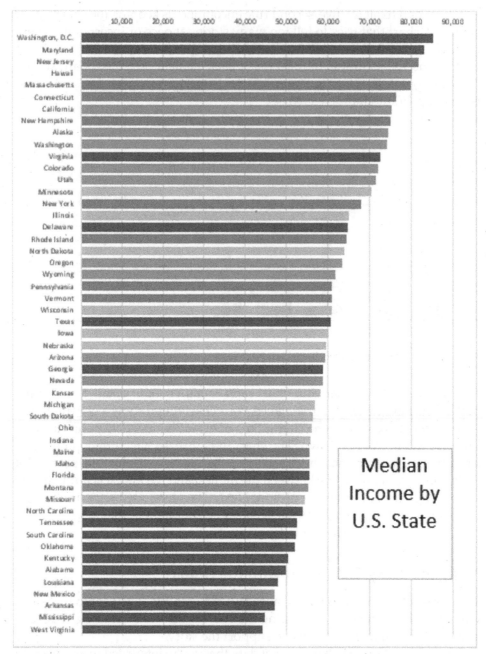

Figure 4.6: A chart with three layers of complexity

Another situation is when you have a data set and a particular problem to solve. In this case you generally start with a hypothesis, like revenues are lower on rainy days. Then you start constructing charts to see if the hypothesis is true. If it is true, you can clean up the chart for publication and include it in a dashboard. If the data shows that it's not true, you need to throw out that hypothesis and start again with a new one. You will likely have learned something from prior failed attempts that will help you form a new hypothesis.

The most dangerous situation is when someone else is supplying the hypothesis, particularly when that person has an agenda. Even if they don't have an agenda, they don't want to be proven wrong. And if they do have an agenda, they may try to force a story that the data simply can't support. In those cases, it's best to have some ideas for alternate stories so you can guide the user down a positive path rather than simply try to block them from a story that doesn't work.

Choose the Proper Chart

Some chart types are better suited to certain stories than others. Later in this chapter, I discuss specific chart types and the stories they support. In later chapters, I go into even more detail on each individual chart type.

Depending on the story the chart is telling, you'll generally have a few chart types that you can use. When you choose which acceptable chart type to use in your dashboard, consider the following:

- **Space:** Some chart types use more real estate than others. If you're short on space, choose the type that uses the least area.

- **Balance:** Earlier in this chapter I talked about balancing the density of your dashboard. If you're out of balance because you have an element whose density doesn't match the others, consider a different acceptable chart type to balance things out.

- **Expectations:** In your industry or your organization, certain charts are always of a certain type. If the five-year revenue chart has always been shown as a line chart, changing it to a column chart may make it harder to read.

Figure 4.7 shows the same five-year revenue chart as a pie chart, a line chart, and a column chart. Time based charts are not suited to pie charts, but either a line chart or the column chart is acceptable for this data.

Stock charts are an excellent example of using a chart type based on expectations. Every stock chart looks similar to the one in Figure 4.8. If you were to vary from this widely recognized standard, it would take focus away from the message.

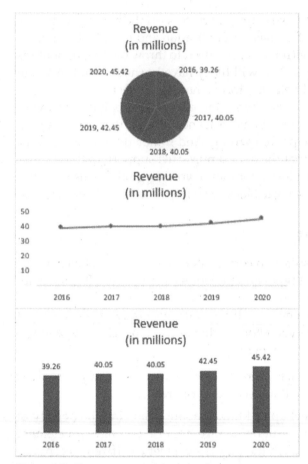

Figure 4.7: Five-year revenue in three chart types

Figure 4.8: A typical stock chart

Driving Meaning with Color

Color is an import aspect of dashboard building and chart creation. Understanding what role color is playing on your chart or in your dashboard will help you choose a color scheme that's best for your situation. Color can be misused, so I included some tips later in this chapter to help you avoid some common pitfalls.

How to Use Color

How color is applied to a chart generally falls into three categories:

- Color that represents the data's value
- Color that's meant to draw attention to one or more data points
- Color that used to group similar items to show a trend

These categories are broad, but thinking about color in these terms will help you choose a color application that improves the effectiveness of your chart.

Varying Color as Data Values Vary

The most straightforward use of color is to increase the color's intensity as the data values increase. Figure 4.9 shows a map of the United States where the color of the state represents that state's population. The higher the population, the darker the color.

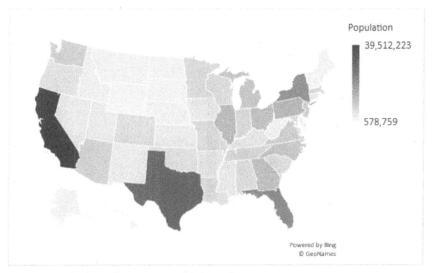

Figure 4.9: Darker colors represent higher values.

In this case, a single color is used and is made darker or lighter to match the data. Your color scale doesn't have to be monochromatic, however. If you choose to use multiple colors in your color scale, typically greens and yellows represent smaller values and reds and blues represent larger values.

This comes from the spectrum of visible light. On the extremes of the visible light spectrum are red and indigo. In the center are yellow, green, and light blue. A multi-color scale should start in the center of this spectrum and move to one extreme or the other, but not both.

Using Sharp Contrast to Highlight Data

Another common use of color is to highlight one or more data points on a chart. The color contrast draws the reader's eye to the important information and increases the speed of understanding.

The important part of using color in this way is the contrast between the important data point or points and the remainder of the chart. If you use gray-scale for most of the chart, just about any bright color will provide the necessary contrast. While a bright color against grayscale is a stark contrast, you don't have to take it to that extreme. You can use a very dark version of a color against a lighter background of the same color. Or you can use a complementary color as the highlight.

You should only use this technique to highlight one or two data points in your chart. If you try to highlight too many, it loses its effectiveness and the highlighted data points don't stand out as well. Figure 4.10 shows a column chart with one data point in contrast to draw the reader's eye to it.

Figure 4.10: Use color to highlight a data point.

Grouping Data with Color

You can also use color to group related data together. This may aid in a reader's understanding of the data or it may reveal trends that would otherwise be hidden if the data weren't grouped.

Figure 4.11 shows a chart of gross margin by subcategory for an office supply store. As is common with these types of bar charts, the values are ordered from most at the top to least at the bottom.

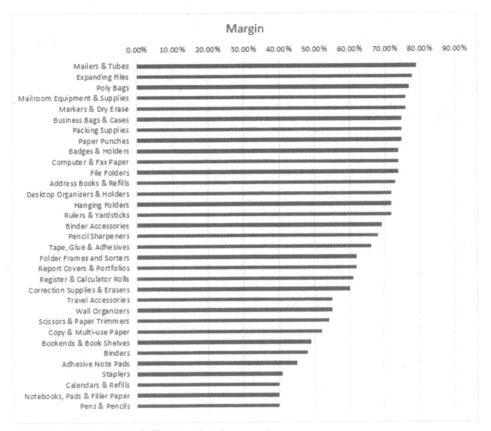

Figure 4.11: A bar chart of office supply subcategories

By adding color to group the subcategories into categories, you can add a new layer of information. The chart in Figure 4.12 shows the same data grouped using colors (shown as shades of gray in the figure). It shows the same information as Figure 4.11. It also shows that a good number of subcategories in the shipping category are closer to the top, indicating a strong category.

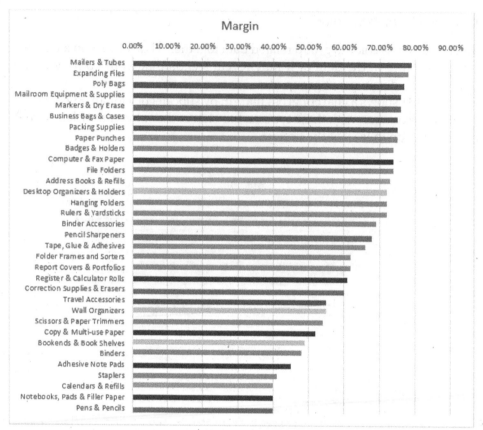

Figure 4.12: Grouping a bar chart with color

Tips on Color Use

The previous sections are about why you would use color on a chart. In the following sections, I discuss some tips for using color effectively.

Use White Space

The most important color in your chart is white. Effectively using white space can be the difference between an attractive, easy-to-read chart and a cluttered puzzle that the reader struggles to understand. When I say white, I mean any solid, very light color. It doesn't actually have to be white, and sometimes a subtle hue can be used to great effect.

White space directs the reader's eye to the data. Make the background of your chart white. Avoid dark or saturated colors as a background as they will lessen the contrast between the background and the data. A negative space chart where the data is light and the background is dark provides contrast. But it's gimmicky and it's likely your readers will be focused on its unexpected presentation rather than the message.

White space is more than just the background color on the chart. The more clutter you have on your chart, the less white space and the less focus on the data. Borders, axes, and leader lines are all elements on a chart you should consider removing. That doesn't mean you should remove them in all cases. Sometimes they add value. But don't accept them just because they are the default.

Use a Simple Color Pallet

Use the simplest color pallet you can without sacrificing meaning. Start with one color and only add more if you need them. Excel does a good job with default colors in most cases. But don't blindly accept the defaults.

If you have more than five or six colors on a chart, you should rethink the structure. Maybe you should combine some data points. Or maybe the colors aren't adding to the meaning.

One way you can end up with too many colors is if you use a legend. I discuss using text elements in charts, like legends, later in this chapter. If you use a legend, you have to have a way for the reader to match up the legend to the data point and that's usually color. If you use data labels instead of legends, you may be able to reduce the number of colors you use.

Use Colors That Are Consistent with the Data

Keep the colors consistent with the data and with social norms. For example, don't use blue shades to represent heat and red shades to represent cold. That may seem obvious, but when Excel picks colors for you, it may not understand the context of your data, so be aware of the relationship between color and data.

Another expectation is that lower numbers will be lighter and larger number will be more saturated. If your data is a measure of the same thing, like duration of time, use different shades of the same color where small to large corresponds with light to dark.

On the other hand, if your data measures different things, like categories, don't use the same color for two categories. The reader may make an association that doesn't exist. Adjacent category colors don't have to be on the opposite ends of the color wheel, but they need to contrast enough to be distinct.

Use Enough Contrast

For beginner chart makers, the problem is usually too much contrast, not too little. However, there is a more recent trend of very subtle color variations. It makes the chart look clean, simple, and modern. But it suffers from the problem of being difficult to read for many people. Light gray text on a white background is fine for marketing, like the box your phone came in, but make sure you have enough contrast in your charts so that people over 30 don't have to struggle to see it.

Use Non-data Pixels When Necessary

Charts can contain lines that aren't data. Chart borders, chart area borders, axes, and leader lines are all examples of pixels on your chart that don't represent data. It doesn't mean you should always eliminate them, but they should have to earn their way on to you chart.

Non-data pixels can help to provide context. A line chart with a lot of values almost always has to have a vertical axis. If it doesn't, the reader won't know the scale of the chart without data labels, and that can get messy. A line chart that shows only a few data labels, however, can be the best of both worlds.

If you have a panel chart, you may find that chart borders help to visually separate the charts and make them easier to read. You can also alternate backgrounds with a light color to achieve the same effect. Whenever you need non-data pixels to help with the meaning or improve the aesthetics of your chart, make sure they don't overpower the data pixels.

Focusing Attention on Text

Charts are primarily graphical elements. But without text, there would be no context for the reader to makes sense of the chart. The best charts use the right amount of text in the right places to give meaning to the graphical elements.

Fonts

The default font in Excel is currently Calibri (Body). You don't have stick with the default, but it's a suitable option. If you choose not to use the default, choose a simple, readable font that doesn't detract from the chart's message or force your readers to struggle to read it. Stay away from script-like fonts and gimmicky fonts like Comic Sans or Broadway.

You may want to change your font to match a broader presentation or because your organization has a defined style guide. Never mix fonts in the same chart unless you have a specific reason for doing so. That doesn't mean you can't use bold or italics in the same font family, however.

For font sizes, a good rule to follow is a 1.5:1 ratio for title to chart text. Chart text includes axes, data labels, legends, and notes. Excel uses approximately this ratio by default. You can mix font sizes much more freely than font families.

You don't want so many different sizes that it's distracting, but if you prefer more than just two you can safely add one or two more. However, if you're simply scaling the whole chart up or down, stick to the 1.5:1 ratio unless you have a particular preference otherwise.

The easiest way to change the font for a chart element is to select that element and use the Font group on the Home tab of the Ribbon. You can also right-click on an element and choose Font from the context menu. If you make some changes and want to go back to the default, there's a Reset To Match Style menu item on the context menu. Right-click on an element to revert only that element back to the default or right-click on the chart to revert all elements back to the default.

Legends

Legends are separate areas on a chart that explain what certain aspects of the chart mean. Most commonly they are color coded to match the colors in the chart. Sometimes legends are necessary, but if you can avoid them, especially large legends, you should. They separate the data from the explanation and cause the reader to look in two places. Smaller legends, like the one in Figure 4.13, cause less of a problem because the reader can easily hold two or three pieces of information in their memory while their focus is on the chart. But when you get to five, six, or seven labels in your legend, the reader will be shifting focus constantly.

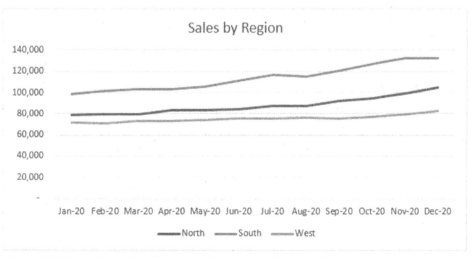

Figure 4.13: A small number of legend entries are easy to remember.

The best option in lieu of legends is data labels, which I discuss later. When data labels aren't practical, there are a few other options. You can move the legend to inside the chart area so the user doesn't have to move their focus so far away.

Not all charts will be so accommodating, and when your chart is updated, what once was a strategic placement of a legend might not work anymore.

Another option is to merge the chart title and the legend, as shown in the chart in Figure 4.14. You can change the color of individual words in your title to serve as your legend. If you have more than a few entries, this gets unwieldy. And for only a few entries, it works just a like a small legend. But if you're short on space or just want your chart to be as clean as possible, it's a good option. To change the color of individual words in a chart title, select the title, then click again to get the text insertion cursor. At this point, you can select individual words and use the Ribbon to change them.

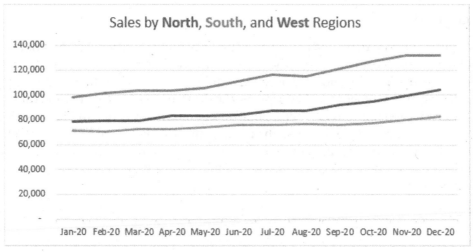

Figure 4.14: Merging the legend and chart title

Axes

Like legends, axes provide context to the data in your chart. Axes are tougher to eliminate than legends, but they are not always necessary. In Figure 4.15 the vertical axis provides no value because the data labels provide the exact value and they're in the most convenient place.

In other charts, like the one shown in Figure 4.14, both axes are necessary. The alternative of including both the date and the value for each data point would be impossible to fit on the chart.

Keep the number formatting simple on your axes. Always include commas when the numbers are large enough. If you can denote the currency in the chart title, axis title, or in a note, you can eliminate the currency symbols from the axes and it will make your chart look less cluttered. Scale the numbers on your axes to match the scale of the data. For example, don't include decimals on a chart that shows revenues in the millions of dollars. In fact, you may choose to scale numbers that large to the thousands. If you do, be sure to note it in the axis title or the chart title.

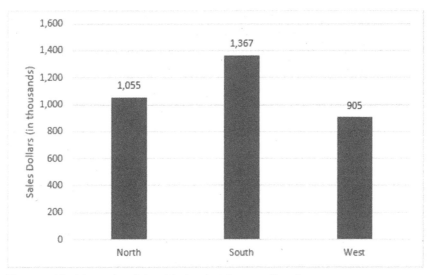

Figure 4.15: A legend and data labels serve the same function.

Data Labels

Data labels are the best way to add context to your chart because the explanation of the data is adjacent to the visual element representing that data. Data labels aren't always practical, however, particularly if there are a lot of data points.

You may not need to show every data label to get the chart's message across. The chart in Figure 4.16 only shows the first and last values for each series in a data label. Those six values provide the only context the reader needs, and there's no need to include intermediate data labels or an axis.

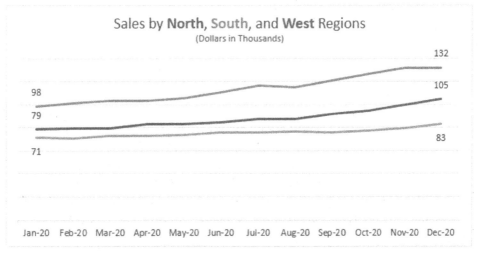

Figure 4.16: Showing first and last data labels provides context.

A great use of data labels is to highlight certain values. You can use this technique in conjunction with an axis to provide both scale and information about important data points. Figure 4.17 shows a chart with an anomalous data point labeled with an explanation.

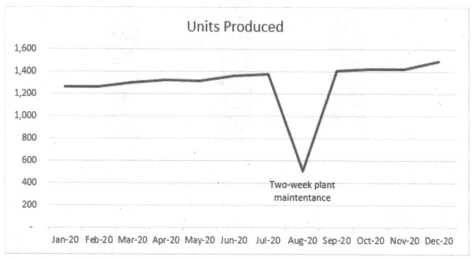

Figure 4.17: An anomalous data point labeled for clarity

Showing Insights with Charts

There are a lot of chart types to choose from. In Part III of this book I discuss the more common chart types in more details. The following sections provide a quick introduction to what chart types are appropriate for comparing data, displaying composition of data, and showing relationships.

Comparisons

For comparing data over time, line charts and column or bar charts are the most common chart types. Since time is a continuous variable, a line chart is appropriate. However, time can also be easily broken down into discrete measures of days, months, quarters, and years. When you separate the time variable in that way, a column or bar chart is also appropriate.

Line charts are great for spotting trends and anomalies. For example, if you have a list of store receipts that doesn't add up to the daily total, you could plot the receipts on a line chart, as shown in Figure 4.18. You can see that 1:00 to 3:00 p.m. is an anomaly, and you're probably missing the receipts from that time period. This is an example of using a chart to mine the data rather than tell a story.

Figure 4.18: A chart to mine data to find anomalies

If you're plotting a lot of categories over time, the bar or column chart options become a little messy. It's best to stick with a line chart if there are more than three categories to plot. Even line charts can get hard to read when you have too many data points overlapping. In those cases, a panel of line charts might be the better option.

If you're comparing data over a noncontinuous variable, such as, for example, by region or by department, the bar or column charts are excellent choices. There isn't a lot to distinguish whether to use a bar or column chart. If your category text length is long, a bar chart gives you more room. Otherwise, you may simply choose one or the other to add variety to a dashboard.

Compositions

When you want to visualize what makes up your data, you can use a pie chart, bar chart, stacked bar chart, waterfall chart, or tree map. When you only have a few variables, the pie chart is the most common. With more data points, consider switching to a bar chart. Figure 4.19 shows a pie chart with too many data points and Figure 4.20 shows the same data as a bar chart.

To show composition over multiple categories, a stacked bar chart is a great option. If only the component parts are relevant, you can use a 100% stacked bar chart where each bar is the same length, as shown in Figure 4.21. If both the component parts and the total are relevant, a stacked bar chart like the chart in Figure 4.22 is the correct choice.

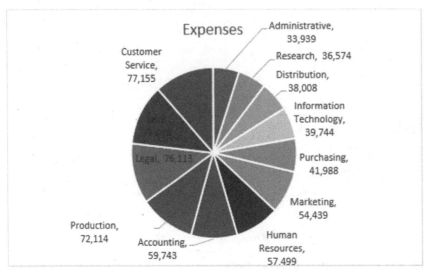

Figure 4.19: A pie chart with too many data points

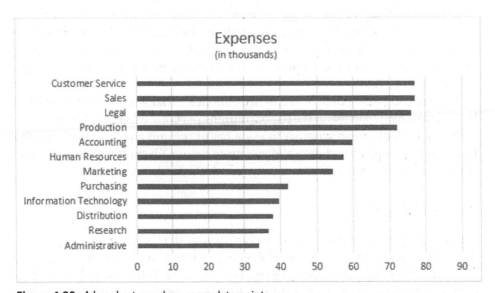

Figure 4.20: A bar chart can show more data points.

If the parts of the whole are composed of both positive and negative values, a waterfall chart is a good choice. These charts show the ups and downs that make up a total in a way that's cumbersome for other chart types, like pie charts. Waterfall charts also have subtotal data points for data sets that require them.

Tree maps are appropriate when your data is hierarchical. You can encode a lot of information in a tree map, showing not only how larger categories make up a whole but also how smaller subcategories make up the larger categories.

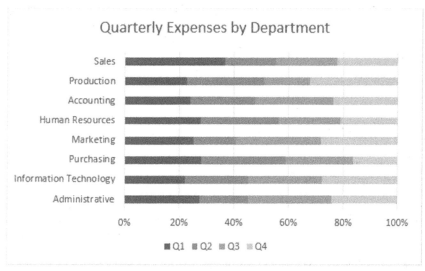

Figure 4.21: A 100% stacked bar chart focuses on the components.

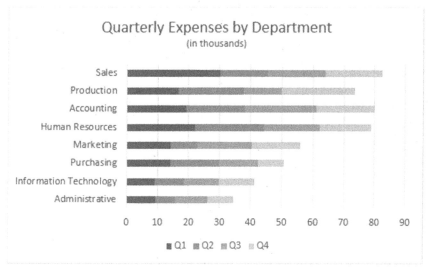

Figure 4.22: A stacked bar shows the components and the total.

Relationships

Showing the relationship between two numeric variables is what the scatter plot, also known as the XY chart, was made for. Scatter plots are excellent for visualizing whether the two variables correlate, that is, if changes to one variable indicate a predictable change in the other variable. Figure 4.23 shows a scatter plot that shows the relationship between temperature and units sold.

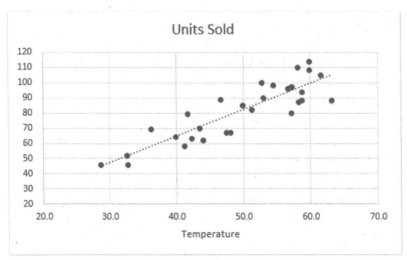

Figure 4.23: A scatter plot shows the relationship between two variables.

Often a trendline is added to XY charts, like the dotted line in Figure 4.23. The closer the points are to the trendline, the higher the correlation of the two variables. At the extremes, highly correlated and not at all correlated, you may find the trendline unnecessary. But it gives the reader an anchor by which to judge how far the data points stray.

A numeric third variable can be added and the chart type changed to a bubble chart. A bubble chart is simply a scatter plot where the size of the points indicates the value of the third variable. If the third variable is categorical, you can use color to differentiate the data.

Non-chart Visualizations

In This Chapter

- Understanding Custom Number Formats
- Using Icons
- Creating Sparklines

Not every data visualization in Excel is a chart. Whether you use a chart or a data table to tell your story, properly formatting the numbers is crucial to making the data clear and easy to read. In this chapter, I explain custom number formats and provide examples for you to use in your data table and chart. Also, Excel provides a few visualizations other than charts. I show how to use the Conditional Formatting features to create Color Scales, Icon Sets, and Data Bars and how to create and customize Sparklines.

Understanding Custom Number Formats

Excel provides a robust mechanism for controlling number formats. You are probably familiar with number formats like Currency and Accounting, but you have a lot more control over the formatting than just the built-in number formats. In the following sections, I describe how to build a custom number format, including changing the font color and adding conditions.

The Four Sections of a Format

Every number format has between one and four sections separated by semi-colons. Each section governs the format for a specific condition of the number, like whether it's positive, negative, or zero. If the format has only one section, it applies to every condition. Figure 5.1 shows how the format 0.00 applies to various numbers and has no effect on text.

	A	B
1	Values	Formatted
2	1024	1024.00
3	-1024	-1024.00
4	0	0.00
5	text	text
6		

Figure 5.1: A one-section number format applies to all numeric conditions and doesn't affect text.

> **NOTE**   The file for the figures in this section is named `Chapter5Figures.xlsx` and can be found at `www.wiley.com/go/datavizwithexcel/`.

For formats with two sections, the first section applies to positive numbers and zero and the second section applies to negative numbers. Like a format with one section, a two-section format doesn't affect text. Figure 5.2 shows how the format 0.00; 0.00- puts the negative sign on the right for negative numbers.

	A	B
1	Values	Formatted
2	1024	1024.00
3	-1024	1024.00-
4	0	0.00
5	text	text

Figure 5.2: The second section governs negative numbers.

When you add a third section to a number format, it controls how zero is formatted. In this case, the first section is only positive numbers and the second section is only negative numbers. The format 0.00;0.00-;"zero" replaces zero values with the word *zero*, as shown in Figure 5.3.

	A	B
1	Values	Formatted
2	1024	1024.00
3	-1024	1024.00-
4	0	zero
5	text	text

Figure 5.3: The third section controls zero values.

Finally, the fourth section, if included, controls how text is displayed. The @ symbol is the placeholder for the text that is actually typed in the cell, and you can add more characters to it. Figure 5.4 shows how the format `0.00;0.00-;` `"zero";@" and more text"` affects a text entry.

⊿	A	B
1	Values	Formatted
2	1024	1024.00
3	-1024	1024.00-
4	0	zero
5	text	text and more text

Figure 5.4: The fourth section affects text entries.

You can omit any of the four sections to show no value for that condition. But you still have to include the semicolon so Excel knows you're omitting it. For example, the format `;-0.00` will only show negative numbers and text. Cells with positive numbers and zeros will appear blank (but they're really not). To that end, you can hide anything a user types in a cell with the format `;;;;`. You can still see the value in the formula bar, so it's not a security measure.

Special Characters

Customer number formats are mostly made up of special characters. That is, the characters stand for something other than their literal values. Putting them all together in one format can make it difficult to read. But with a little practice, you'll be able to decipher any custom number format.

Digit Placeholders

The two most basic characters are 0 and #. The 0 character represents any digit. If there is not a digit where the 0 is, a 0 is displayed. The number 25.62 is displayed as 0025.620 with the format `0000.000`. Because there are no digits in the thousands, hundreds, and thousandths places, a zero is displayed there. The # character also represents a single digit. If there is no digit in that place, nothing is displayed. Figure 5.5 shows several numbers formatted with `#,##0.00`.

⊿	A	B
1	Values	Formatted
2	25.62	25.62
3	225.62	225.62
4	1225.62	1,225.62
5		

Figure 5.5: The # character shows only digits that exist.

In the example in Figure 5.5, I want to include a comma for numbers over a thousand. To do that, I need to have a placeholder for all the digits I want to show. If I were to use a 0 character, numbers under a thousand or a hundred would look strange. Using the # character, I can show digits where they exist and not show them where they don't.

Commas and Periods

The comma is a special character that divides numbers into thousands. In the example from the previous section, I used the # character as placeholders and a comma to separate the thousands and hundreds places. Even though I only included one comma in that number format, Excel interprets that to mean that I want a comma every three digits. The same number format, `#,##0.00`, formats a larger number as 1,225,225.62 by putting a comma everywhere you would expect.

A common use of commas in number formats is to show larger numbers in thousands or millions rather than show every digit. The number format `#,##0,` displays 1,000,000 as 1,000. Note there are no placeholders after the comma at the end. To show a number in millions, include two commas with no placeholders, like `#,##0,,`. That format displays 1,000,000 as 1. When you scale a number that way, be sure to note it so the readers aren't confused. It's typical to include a parenthetical like *(in thousands)* somewhere on the document to note the scale.

The period is another special character used to divide numbers. As you probably expect, it divides numbers between the whole and fractional parts. The first period in your number format will divide the number between whole and decimal, and any other periods will simply display as a period. It's not common to use more than one period in a number format.

If you're scaling a number with commas, the period will divide the number at that scale. The number format `0.0,,` will display the number 1,225,225.62 as 1.2. First the number is scaled to the millions because of the two commas at the end, then the period separates the whole number from the decimal.

Text

You can include any text in a number format by enclosing it in double quotes. For example, the format `0.0,," million"` will display 1,225,225.62 as 1.2 million. You can also include text at the front of a number. The format `""A surplus of "#,##0;"A deficit of "#,##0` will prepend one text string in front of a positive number and another in front of a negative number.

There are several characters that you can include without enclosing in double quotes, including +, -, $, and parentheses. These are such commonly used characters that Microsoft must have decided to allow you to use them without double quotes to make the formats more readable. You'll find there are other characters that aren't on the official list but also don't require double quotes.

The format `#,##0,k` displays 123456 as 123k. The k character didn't require any double quotes because it doesn't have any other meaning.

But other alphabetic characters do have meaning, and if you don't enclose them in quotes, they will return unwanted results. Try formatting the number 2021 as The year 2021. You can do it with the format code `"The year "0`. If you don't include the quotes, however, you will get an error that Excel doesn't understand the format. If you just use the format `The year`, the result will be T01905 051905ar. That strange output includes the characters T, a, r, and space that have no other meaning and are simply displayed. But the characters h, e, and y mean hour, four-digit year, and two-digit year, respectively.

Underscore

The underscore character creates white space so that you can line up values from different sections of the number format. The most common use is when the negative section of the number format includes parentheses to signify the value is below zero. Figure 5.6 shows the effects of the format `#,##0;(#,##0)` that uses parentheses for negative values and no underscores. The commas don't line up as you'd expect them to.

	A	B
1	Values	Formatted
2	1024	1,024
3	-1024	(1,024)
4		

Figure 5.6: Characters in a number format can cause numbers to not line up.

By changing the format to `#,##0_);(#,##0)`, you tell Excel to include the same amount of white space to the right of a positive number that a closing parenthesis would use. That way, when you have both positive and negative numbers, the commas and periods line up, as shown in Figure 5.7.

	A	B
1	Values	Formatted
2	1024	1,024
3	-1024	(1,024)
4		

Figure 5.7: The underscore character helps align values.

You can add as much white space as you need by repeating the underscore character. If you wanted, for example, to show your negative numbers with the abbreviation neg at the end, like 1,024 neg, then you could use the format `#,##0_ _n_e_g;#,##0" neg"` to keep positive and negative numbers aligned. There are four underscores followed by the characters space, n, e, and g.

Asterisk

Whatever character follows an asterisk is repeated in the cell to fill up the available space. The format `*-` will fill a cell with dashes regardless of what number is entered. If you change the column width, the number of dashes increases or decreases to fill the new width.

The most common use of the asterisk is to align a currency symbol, like a dollar sign, for different lengths of values. Figure 5.8 shows how three different numbers are affected by the format `$* #,##0`. The space following the asterisk is repeated to fill the available room between the dollar sign and the start of the digits, aligning the dollars signs on the left.

	A	B
1	Values	Formatted
2	1024	$ 1,024.00
3	-1024.1	$ (1,024.10)
4	0	$ -

Figure 5.8: Use an asterisk to align a currency symbol.

Escaping Special Characters

There are two ways to use a special character to represent its own value rather than its special value. You can enclose the character in double quotes as I explained in a previous section with the format `"The year "0`. The other way is to precede the character with a backslash. The \ character tells Excel to display the next character literally and don't try to interpret it as special.

The format `T\h\e \y\e\a\r 0` produces the same results as `"The year "0`. Instead of putting the whole string in quotes, the special characters h, e, and y are escaped with a backslash. The characters a and r are not special characters, but Excel inexplicably escapes them with a backslash whether you enter it or not. Generally, if you have one or two characters to escape, use the backslash, otherwise quotes are easier to read.

The Accounting Number Format

Now that you know the basics of custom number formats, you can start to read Excel's built-in formats and understand how they work. The Accounting format uses several of the special characters from this section. Select a cell and press Ctrl+1 to open the Format Cells dialog. On the Number tab, select Accounting, then select Custom. The first category you select will change the format, and selecting Custom after that will show you that the built-in format is constructed. Figure 5.9 shows the Custom category after Accounting was first selected.

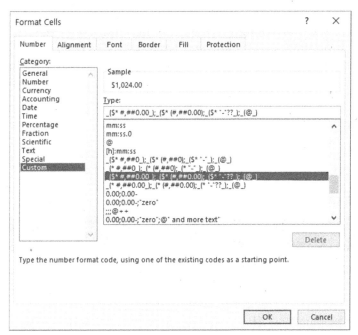

Figure 5.9: Select the Custom category to see how a built-in category is constructed.

The format _($* #,##0.00_);_($* (#,##0.00);_($* "-"??_);_(@_) contains all four sections for positive, negative, zero, and text values. Each section starts with _(to create white space equal to the width of an opening parenthesis. Normally this is done to allow for an actual opening parenthesis for a negative number. But the left-most character in the negative section is a dollar sign, so this extra white space is probably just for aesthetics.

The next character is a dollar sign, which displays as itself with no escaping necessary. The asterisk-space combination comes next to push the dollar sign to the left of the cell so they are aligned regardless of the length of the number. Following the repeating spaces are the # and 0 placeholder characters with a comma and period included. The final character sequence in the positive section is _) and creates white space on the right side equal to the width of a closing parenthesis.

The negative section looks very similar to the positive section. One difference is the opening parenthesis between the dollar sign and the left-most digit in the number. The opening parenthesis is another special character that doesn't require escaping. The other difference is that instead of white space being created on the right, an actual closing parenthesis is displayed.

The zero section displays a dash under the decimal point. By now, you probably can already see that some white space and a dollar sign are left aligned, there is white space on the right, and the dash is enclosed in quotes. This section could also have been written as _($* -??_) or _($* \-??_) as the dash doesn't require escaping. The question mark is another digit placeholder character. While the # character doesn't show anything if there is no digit and the 0 character shows a zero if there is no digit, the ? character displays a space when there is no character. This pushes the dash to the left by two digits. It's the same as the format _($* -_0_0_).

Date and Time Formats

Excel uses the characters m, d, and y to represent months, days, and years in various ways. Table 5.1 shows the codes for displaying parts of a date.

Table 5.1: Format codes for displaying parts of a date

FORMAT CODE	DESCRIPTION	EXAMPLE FOR JAN 9, 2021
m	Displays the month number as one or two digits	1
mm	Displays the month number as two digits including the leading zero where necessary	01
mmm	Displays a three-letter abbreviation of the month's name	Jan
mmmm	Displays the full month's name	January
mmmmm	Displays a one-letter abbreviation of the month's name	J
d	Displays the day number as one or two digits	9
dd	Displays the day number as two digits including the leading zero where necessary	09
ddd	Displays a three-letter abbreviation of the day's name	Sat
dddd	Displays the day's full name	Saturday
yy	Displays the year as two digits	21
yyyy	Displays the year as four digits	2021

You can include slashes or dashes to separate the date parts. For example, mm/dd/yyyy returns 01/09/2021 and m-d-yyyy returns 1-9-2021 for January 9, 2021. Of course, you can use any character you like to separate them, but slashes and dashes are the most typical.

In charts, it's helpful to be able to make the dates as short as possible, so they all fit when you have many of them on an axis. Another common custom number format for dates is to define a period. For instance, the number format "For the Year Ended "m/d/yyyy returns For the Year Ended 12/31/2021 for December 31, 2021 and can be used in a chart's title or in a note.

For times, Excel uses the characters h, m, and s for hours, minutes, and seconds, respectively. For the m character, Excel uses its position in the number format to determine if it's a month or a minute. By default, it stands for month, but if it appears after an h character or before a colon, Excel interprets it as a minute. Minutes can only be two characters at most, so Excel will interpret more than two m characters as a month regardless of its context.

As with dates, a single h, m, or s character will display that part with one or two digits. Two characters, such hh, mm, or ss, displays two digits and includes a leading zero where necessary. If you put the single-character format code in brackets, Excel displays the elapsed time rather than the time of day. For example, the format code [h] returns 1060920 for January 15, 2021 because that's how many hours have elapsed since January 1, 1900, the date from which Excel starts counting. This is useful when you're working with payroll data or other time-based data that isn't the time of day.

Include the code AM/PM, am/pm, A/P, or a/p after your time codes to display the time using a 12-hour clock. For example, the format code m/d/yyyy h:mm AM/PM displays 1/15/2021 1:35 PM if you apply it to 1/15/2021 13:35 entered in a cell.

Conditional Custom Number Formats

By default, the four sections of a number format are positive numbers, negative numbers, zero, and text. However, you can redefine two of those sections to use different conditions. The other two sections define text and the default format for any number that doesn't meet the conditions. To define a condition, enclose a comparison operator and a number in square brackets before the number format.

For example, the format condition [>=1000000]0.0,,"M";[<1000000]##0 ,"K" will display numbers greater than or equal to one million as a number scaled to millions with a single decimal place followed by an M and numbers less than one million as a number scaled to thousands followed by a K. With that format, the number 1,010,576 is displayed as 1.0M and the number 795,422 is displayed as 795K.

A common use of conditional number formats is to control color. Custom number formats support eight named colors and 56 total colors. The eight named colors are black, green, white, blue, magenta, yellow, cyan, and red. To change the color of a number, include the named color in square brackets at the start of the number format. The format [Blue]0 will format numbers with no decimal places and color them blue.

To make negative numbers red, include the named color at the start of the negative section. The format #,##0.00;[Red] #,##0.00 will color positive numbers and zero; however, the cell's formatting is set (black, by default), and negative numbers will be red.

If you want to use a color other than one of the eight named colors, you append the color's index number to the word Color and put it in square brackets. The eight named colors are Color1 through Color8. Color9 through Color56 can be used in a number format as, for example, [Color9]. The 56 colors correspond to Excel's original color palette that was removed from the user interface after Excel 2003 but lives on in number formats. You can't see this palette in Excel, so you have to experiment with the numbers to see what colors they represent.

Now you can combine conditionals and colors in a format. The color comes first, then the conditional, then the number format. For example, the format [Blue] [>=20] 0; [Magenta] [>=10] 0; [Green] 0 will color any number greater than or equal to 20 as blue, numbers greater than 10 as yellow, and any other number as green. Text will be colored according to the cell's color because no fourth section was included.

When working in cells on a worksheet, Excel's Conditional Formatting feature (Home ⇨ Conditional Formatting on the Ribbon) is an easier way to control font color. But if you want to conditionally control font color in a chart, you have to build the correct custom number format.

Using Icons

Excel's Conditional Formatting feature contains three options for non-chart visualizations. These graphics are rendered inside the cell and don't have to be placed. As the cell changes size, the graphics will adjust to fill the cell. Each option is customizable to match your theme in color and style.

Color Scales

Excel's Conditional Formatting feature has a Color Scales option that applies colors based on the relative values in the cells. To use this feature, select a range of cells with values, choose Conditional Formatting ⇨ Color Scales from the Ribbon, and choose one of the built-in color scale options. Figure 5.10 shows the expanded Color Scales Ribbon item and Figure 5.11 shows a range of 11 numbers with the Green - Yellow - Red Color Scale applied to it.

NOTE The file for the figures in this section is named Chapter5Figures.xlsx and can be found at www.wiley.com/go/datavizwithexcel/.

The lowest number in the range is colored red, the highest number is green, and all the numbers in between are colored on a gradient scale between those two colors. Numbers close to the minimum number are shades of orange, numbers in the middle of the range are yellows, and numbers nearer to the maximum number are lighter greens.

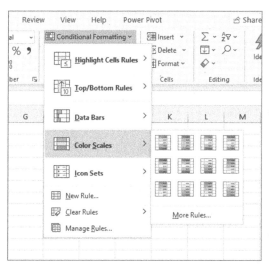

Figure 5.10: The Color Scales gallery on the Ribbon

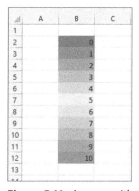

Figure 5.11: A range with the Green - Yellow - Red Color Scale applied

You can choose from six three-color scales like the one in the previous example and six two-color scales. The two-color scales set the color for the minimum and maximum numbers and the numbers in between gradually transition from one color to the other.

In addition to the built-in color scales, you can create your own custom scales. To see how this works, apply the Green - Yellow - Red Color Scale to a range. Then choose Home ➪ Conditional Formatting ➪ Manage Rules from the Ribbon to display the Conditional Formatting Rules Manager, shown in Figure 5.12.

The Rules Manager shows all the conditional formatting rules you've applied to the currently selected cells. You can change it to show all the conditional formatting rules for the whole worksheet by changing the Show formatting rules for: drop-down. Select the Graded Color Scale rule and click the Edit Rule button to display the Edit Formatting Rule dialog, shown in Figure 5.13.

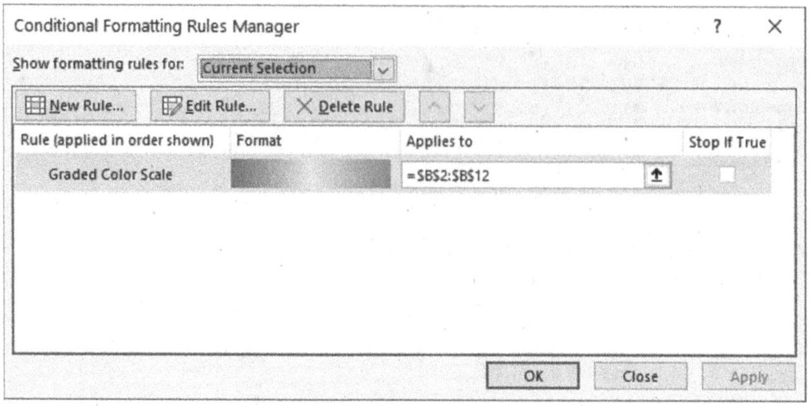

Figure 5.12: The Conditional Formatting Rules Manager

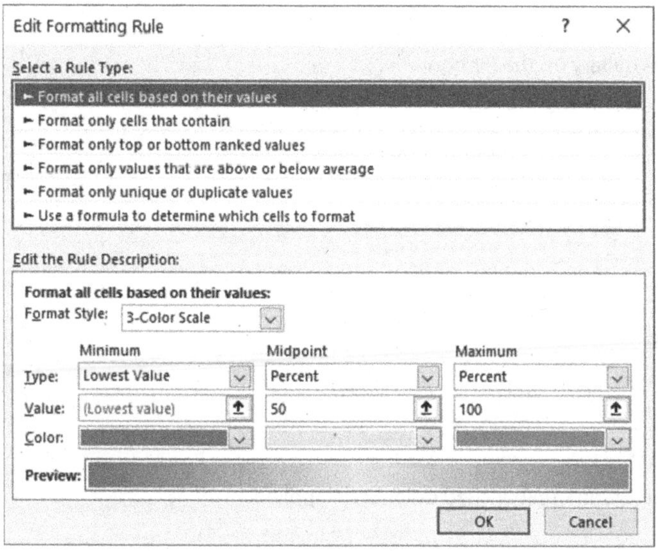

Figure 5.13: The Edit Formatting Rule dialog

You can create any type of conditional format from this dialog. By applying a built-in rule and editing it, you can see how it was constructed. The top section of the Edit Formatting Rule dialog shows all the rule types. The rule type for a color scale is "Format all cells based on their values." The bottom section contains the options specific to the selected rule type.

The rule shown in Figure 5.13 has a Format Style of 3-Color Scale, the lowest value set to red, the highest value set to green, and the value at the 50th percentile set to yellow. A preview bar is shown at the bottom so you can see how the colors will change as the values change. A Format Style setting of 2-Color Scale looks similar except that the midpoint section is hidden. Figure 5.14 shows the rule when a 2-Color Scale is selected.

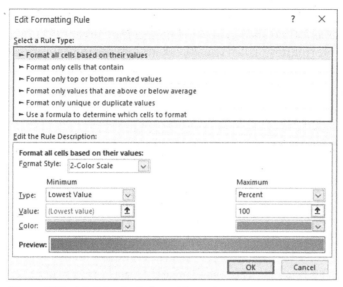

Figure 5.14: A 2-Color Scale formatting rule

When customizing a color scale formatting rule, choose one of these types:

- **Lowest/Highest Value:** Excel calculates the lowest or highest value in the range. Lowest Value and Highest Value are not options for the Midpoint.

- **Number:** You can enter a number for Minimum, Midpoint, or Maximum. Numbers less than the Minimum will be colored the same as the Minimum and numbers greater than the Maximum will be colored the same as the Maximum. If you enter a number for Midpoint, Excel will adjust the gradient of the colors. For example, a Midpoint closer to the Minimum in a Green - Yellow - Red scale will skew the overall gradient to red. The value for Number can also point to a worksheet cell.

- **Percent:** Excel calculates the value by subtracting the lowest value from the highest value, multiplying by the percent entered, and adding the result to the lowest value. You enter a whole number to represent the percent and don't include the percent sign (%). Percent ensures the color gradient is proportional to the numbers in the range. The value for Percent can point to a worksheet cell.

- **Formula:** You can enter any valid worksheet formula that returns a number, date, or time. An invalid formula prevents any formatting from being applied.

- **Percentile:** This type uses the number's position in the list rather than a proportional percent. In a range of 10 cells, the eighth number will represent the 80th percentile even if it is close to the Minimum. Use the Percentile type when you want a consistent color gradient regardless of how evenly spread the value are. Figure 5.15 shows ranges with uneven value with the Percent type shown on the left and the Percentile shown on the right. Both formatting rules use 20, 50, and 80 for the Minimum, Midpoint, and Maximum values, respectively. The value for Percentile can point to a worksheet cell.

◢	A	B	C	D	E
1					
2		0		0	
3		1		1	
4		2		2	
5		3		3	
6		4		4	
7		5		5	
8		80		80	
9		81		81	
10		82		82	
11					

Figure 5.15: Two ranges with the Percent and Percentile format styles applied in a 3-color rule

In Figure 5.15, the Percent rule colors all the low numbers the same as the Minimum because they are all less than 20% of the difference between the highest and lowest values. The Percentile rule, on the other hand, shows the value 4 as yellow because it's the 50th percentile even though it's a small percentage of the range.

The Edit Formatting Rule dialog also allows you to select custom colors. You can select colors that match your overall color scheme rather than accepting the default. You can even select the same color for two values. For example, you can select the same color for Minimum and Maximum and a different color for Midpoint when you want to highlight extremes regardless if they're high or low. Figure 5.16 shows a range and a rule using this technique.

◢	A	B	C
1			
2		8	
3		15	
4		18	
5		28	
6		30	
7		39	
8		50	
9		80	
10		82	
11		85	
12		96	
13			

Figure 5.16: Use the same color for Minimum and Maximum to highlight extreme values.

Data Bars

Another non-chart visualization option in the Conditional Formatting feature is Data Bars. When you apply Data Bars to a range, Excel fills a portion of the cell with a colored bar based on the cell's value. If you change the width of the column, the Data Bars grow or shrink proportionally. Figure 5.17 shows a range of random numbers with Data Bars applied.

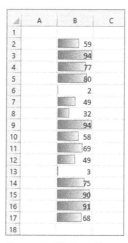

Figure 5.17: Data Bars applied to a range

To apply a Data Bars Conditional Format to a range, select the range, choose Home ⇨ Conditional Formatting ⇨ Data Bars from the Ribbon, and select one of the built-in Data Bars. You can select either a gradient fill or a solid fill Data Bar. Gradient-fill Data Bars are darkest on the right side of the bar and gradually become lighter as you move left.

If you don't like any of the built-in Data Bars, you can create a custom format. Choose More Rules on the Data Bar gallery to show the New Formatting Rule dialog, shown in Figure 5.18.

As with Color Scales from the previous section, the top portion of the dialog shows that the "Format all cells based on their values" rule type is selected. When Data Bar is selected as the format style, the options in the lower section change. The Show Bar Only check box will hide the underlying values in the range when checked.

The Minimum and Maximum values have the same options as Color Scales in the previous section and they work the same. The exception is that the Data Bar style also has an Automatic type for these values. If you choose Lowest Value, the cell with the lowest value will not show any formatting. It is showing a Data Bar of zero length, and that may be confusing. The Automatic type calculates a Minimum that is less than the lowest value so that all cells show

Figure 5.18: The New Formatting Rule dialog

something. For the Maximum, the Automatic and Highest Value types don't seem to be different from one another.

In the Bar Appearance section, you can choose Solid Fill or Gradient Fill, the color of the bar, Solid Border or No Border, and the color of the border. The Negative Value and Axis button shows the Negative Value and Axis Settings dialog shown in Figure 5.19.

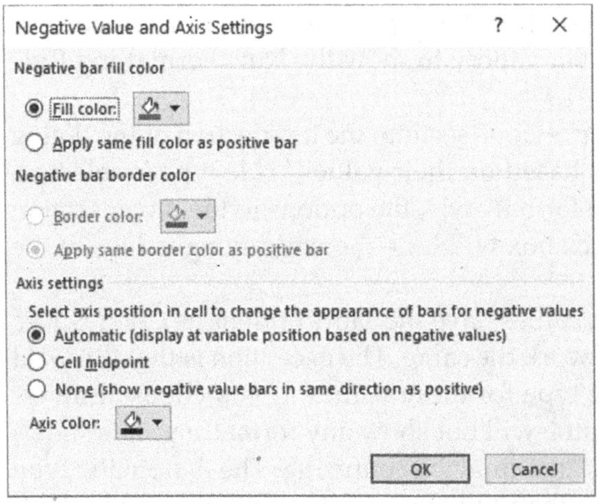

Figure 5.19: The Negative Value and Axis Settings dialog

For negative values, you can choose to show a different color bar and border or use the same colors as for positive values. There are three options for determining where the bar starts when you have positive and negative values. The default is that Excel determines a variable position based on the relative values in the cells. For proportionally smaller negative values, the axis will be closer to the left edge of the cell. You can force the bars to start in the middle of the cell regardless of relative values by choosing the Cell Midpoint option button. Or you can choose to show negative bars in the same direction as positive bars and use color to differentiate them. Figure 5.20 shows a range with positive and negative values where negative values have a different color and extend to the left.

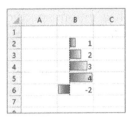

Figure 5.20: Negative Data Bars extending to the left and differently colored

The Bar Direction drop-down defaults to Context. If your worksheet is set up as left to right—that is, column A is the left-most column—then the bars will display left to right. You can change the Bar Direction setting to force the bars one way or the other. Generally, accepting the default is the best choice.

Icon Sets

The final non-chart visualization option in the Conditional Formatting feature is Icon Sets. Icon Sets are a set of small graphical elements that are placed in the cell and vary with the value in the cell. Figure 5.21 shows a list of values from this year and last year. An Icon Set format is applied to the difference column to indicate whether the value increased and by relatively how much.

⊿	A	B	C	D	E
1					
2		Last Year	This Year	Difference	
3		14,388	24,593 ⬆	10,205	
4		19,898	10,497 ⬇	(9,401)	
5		13,681	22,538 ⬆	8,857	
6		17,189	22,359 ⬀	5,170	
7		13,980	28,393 ⬆	14,413	
8		21,861	19,793 ⬂	(2,068)	
9		10,599	23,449 ⬆	12,850	
10					

Figure 5.21: A directional Icon Set applied to a range

To apply an Icon Set to a range, select the range and choose Home ⇨ Conditional Formatting ⇨ Icon Sets to display the Icon Set gallery. Select one of the built-in Icon Sets or choose More Rules to create a custom Icon Set.

The Icon Sets in the gallery are divided into four groups. The Directional group contains four colored graphics and three gray-scale graphics and are meant to show the direction of the numbers relative to the other numbers in the range. The Shapes group contains simple shapes where either the shape or color (or both) varies based on the cell's value. The graphics in the Indicators group are more complex shapes that also vary by color or shape. Finally, the Ratings group contains stars and small icons meant to look like charts. The icons in this group are filled in more or less based on the value of the cell.

The New Formatting Rule dialog, shown in Figure 5.22, has options specific to Icon Sets. Like Data Bars, there is a checkbox to show only the formatting and hide the underlying values.

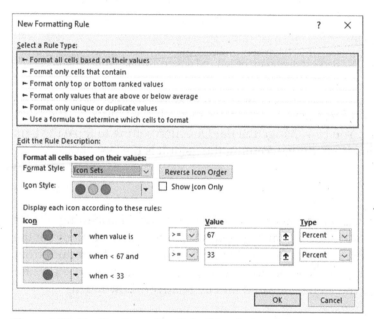

Figure 5.22: The New Formatting Rule dialog for Icon Sets

The Reverse Icon Order button will switch the colors so that, for example, green represents the lower numbers and red represents the higher numbers. Click the button a second time to return to the original color order. The colors in Icon Sets are not customizable. The Icon Style drop-down lets you choose which icons to use and is the same as the built-in Icon Set gallery.

Depending on how many icons are in the Icon Style option you choose, a matching number of rules appears at the bottom of the dialog. For each rule, select the icon you want to use, a condition operator, a value, and a value type.

The built-in sets all contain icons that are similar to each other, but you can mix and match icons to create a custom set.

The Icon drop-down, shown in Figure 5.23, shows all the icons available. It also includes a No Cell Icon option. You can use that if you only want to show icons for big movers and not clutter the range for smaller changes.

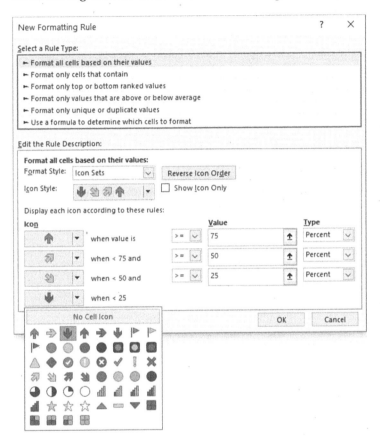

Figure 5.23: The Icon drop-down allows you to create custom Icon Sets.

The Type drop-down determines how you want to split the range of values. You can choose between Percent, Number, Percentile, and Formula. These options work just like with Color Scales and Data Bars. The final icon will always represent whatever is not caught in one of the other rules. The Conditional Operator drop-down lets you choose between greater-than-or-equal-to or greater-than. There is no option for less-than. If you want to reverse the order, click the Reverse Icon Order button and choose the appropriate greater-than option.

Creating Sparklines

A Sparkline is a simple visualization rendered entirely within a cell. You can use a Sparkline in place of a chart when you want to a quick, simple way to show a trend in the data. With Sparklines, you give up some formatting options that you have with full-blown charts and you're limited to one series.

NOTE   The file for the examples and figures in the followings sections is named `Sparklines.xlsx` and can be found at `www.wiley.com/go/datavizwithexcel/`.

Types of Sparklines

There are three types of Sparklines in Excel: Line, Column, and Win/Loss. Figure 5.24 shows each type applied to simple income statement data.

	A	B	C	D	E	F	G
1							
2		**2016**	**2017**	**2018**	**2019**	**2020**	**Trend**
3	Sales	100,245	102,249	106,339	110,593	105,441	
4	Cost of Sales	59,145	63,395	62,741	68,568	65,373	
5	Gross Margin	41,100	38,854	43,598	42,025	40,068	
6	Operating Expenses	12,029	10,225	9,571	13,271	9,953	
7	Net Income	29,071	28,629	34,027	28,754	30,115	
8							
9		**2016**	**2017**	**2018**	**2019**	**2020**	**Trend**
10	Sales	100,245	102,249	106,339	110,593	105,441	
11	Cost of Sales	59,145	63,395	62,741	68,568	65,373	
12	Gross Margin	41,100	38,854	43,598	42,025	40,068	
13	Operating Expenses	12,029	10,225	9,571	13,271	9,953	
14	Net Income	29,071	28,629	34,027	28,754	30,115	
15							
16		**2016**	**2017**	**2018**	**2019**	**2020**	**Trend**
17	Sales	#N/A	2,004	4,090	4,254	(5,152)	
18	Cost of Sales	#N/A	4,250	(654)	5,827	(3,195)	
19	Gross Margin	#N/A	(2,246)	4,744	(1,573)	(1,957)	
20	Operating Expenses	#N/A	(1,804)	(654)	3,700	(3,318)	
21	Net Income	#N/A	(442)	5,398	(5,273)	1,361	
22							

Figure 5.24: Three types of Sparklines

The Line and Column types are similar to the charts with the same names. They show how the data is trending. The slope of the line chart and the relative heights of the columns indicate if the trend is up or down and the severity of the changes in the data. That is, a steeper upward slope or a greater difference in the column heights means the changes in the values are larger.

The Win/Loss type displays a bar above a horizontal axis for increases and one below for decreases. Unlike the other two, three is no indication of the size of the change, just whether it went up or down. Generally, the data that drives a Win/Loss Sparkline is the change in some other data, while the data for the Line or Column Sparkline is the original data.

For Line and Column Sparklines, each row is scaled independently of the other rows in the same group. That is, the lowest point in a line or the smallest column represents the smallest number in that row, not the smallest number of the whole range. This is most evident in 2018 Net Income number in Figure 5.24. Its line and column heights are almost to the top of the cell because its value is the highest in its row. But those line and column heights are similar to the highest value in the Sales row even though the Net Income value is much smaller than the Sales value. Later in this chapter, I'll show how you can adjust the scaling of a Sparkline group.

Creating a Sparkline

To create the Sparklines in Figure 5.24, enter the data shown or open the sample workbook. Select the range B3:F7 and choose Insert ⇨ Sparklines ⇨ Line from the Ribbon to display the Create Sparklines dialog shown in Figure 5.25.

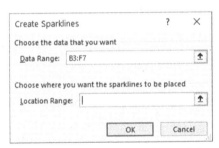

Figure 5.25: The Create Sparklines dialog

The selected range is automatically populated in the Data Range box. In the Location Range box, enter or select the range G3:G7 and click OK. The Sparkline group is inserted into the range and there is a border around the entire group indicating it is currently selected, as shown in Figure 5.26. A Sparkline tab also shows on the Ribbon whenever you have a Sparkline group selected.

⯅	A	B	C	D	E	F	G	H
1								
2		2016	2017	2018	2019	2020	Trend	
3	Sales	100,245	102,249	106,339	110,593	105,441		
4	Cost of Sales	59,145	63,395	62,741	68,568	65,373		
5	Gross Margin	41,100	38,854	43,598	42,025	40,068		
6	Operating Expenses	12,029	10,225	9,571	13,271	9,953		
7	Net Income	29,071	28,629	34,027	28,754	30,115		
8								

Figure 5.26: A newly inserted Sparkline group is selected

Repeat that procedure for the other two ranges on the worksheet. Select Column for the second range and Win/Loss for the third range from the Sparkline gallery. If you make a mistake and need to start over, use the Clear tool on the Sparkline tab of the Ribbon to delete the whole Sparkline group.

Sparkline Groups

When you create a Sparkline in Excel, you're actually creating a Sparkline group. The idea is that when you make a formatting change, you want that change to affect every Sparkline in the group, not just the one you have selected. Sparklines were designed to be small visualizations over multiple data sets, so the group model fits them well.

You can change the source data for an individual Sparkline in a group and the Sparkline will remain a part of the group. That means that any other changes you make to the group will still apply to the individual Sparkline. To change the source data for one Sparkline, select it and choose Sparkline ➪ Edit Data ➪ Edit Single Sparkline's Data from the Ribbon. The Edit Sparkline Data dialog, shown in Figure 5.27, allows you to enter a new range for the single Sparkline.

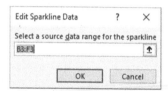

Figure 5.27: The Edit Sparkline Data dialog allows you to change the source data for a single Sparkline.

You can also split a Sparkline group into two. Simply select the cells with the Sparklines you want to be in their own group and choose Sparkline ➪ Ungroup from the Ribbon. You can select only one cell to make a group of one Sparkline. To combine groups, select all the cells you want in the same group and choose Sparkline ➪ Group from the Ribbon.

There's one more operation you can perform on a Sparkline that won't affect others in the group. You can delete individual Sparklines, leaving the others intact. Figure 5.28 shows the Clear tool on the Sparkline tab of the Ribbon. From that tool, you can delete one or more individual Sparklines or you can delete the whole group to which the individuals belong.

Customize a Sparkline

There aren't as many formatting options for Sparklines as for regular charts. That's to be expected since Sparklines are meant to be simple visualizations. But there are few customizations you can make.

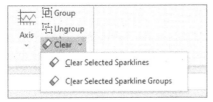

Figure 5.28: Use the Clear tool to delete individual Sparklines or the whole group.

Changing the Source Data

In the previous section, I showed how to change the source data for a single Sparkline. There is also the option of changing the source data of the whole group. Choosing Sparkline ⇨ Edit Data ⇨ Edit Group Location and Data from the Ribbon displays the Edit Sparklines dialog as shown in Figure 5.29. It looks exactly like the Create Sparklines dialog except for the title.

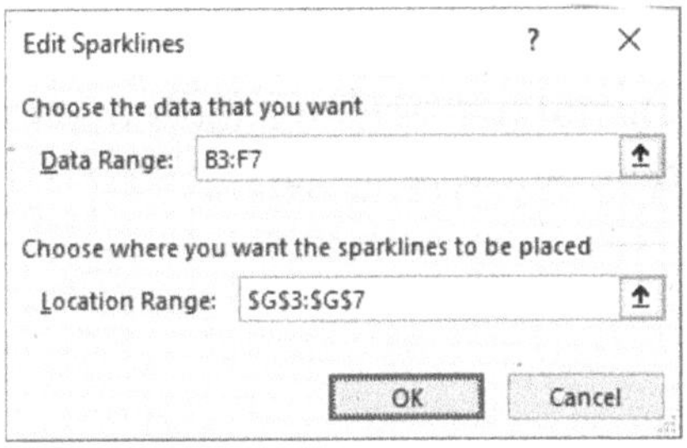

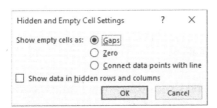

Figure 5.29: Change the group's source data in the Edit Sparklines dialog.

Another tool under the Edit Data drop-down is Hidden & Empty Cells. This tool displays the Hidden and Empty Cell Settings dialog shown in Figure 5.30. From here, you can choose to show empty cells as gaps in the Sparkline, as zero values, or you can connect the data points on either side of the empty cell. The Show data in hidden rows and columns check box determines whether hidden rows and columns are rendered in the Sparkline.

Figure 5.30: The Hidden and Empty Cell Settings dialog

Changing the Color and Thickness

The Show group on the Sparkline tab of the Ribbon contains six check boxes for showing markers—dots for the individual data points—on the Sparkline. The check boxes are as follows:

- **Markers:** Show a marker for every data point.
- **High Point:** Show a marker for only the highest point. If there are multiple highest data points, a marker is shown for all of them.
- **Low Point:** Show a marker for the lowest point or lowest points if there are more than one.
- **Negative Points:** Show markers for only points below zero.
- **First Point:** Show a marker for only the first data point.
- **Last Point:** Show a marker for only the last data point.

If you check the Markers check box, the others become redundant as every data point already has a marker.

The Style group on the Sparkline tab of the Ribbon contains tools that let you change the color and weight of the Sparklines. The Style gallery, shown in Figure 5.31, contains several color options.

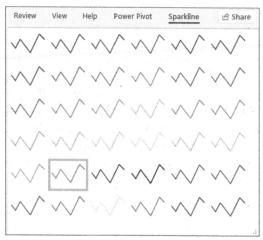

Figure 5.31: Change a Sparkline's color using the Style Gallery.

In addition to the Style Gallery, the Sparkline Color drop-down allows you to apply any available color to a Sparkline. The drop-down also has a Weight tool, shown in Figure 5.32, to change the thickness of the Sparkline from the default of 3/4 points.

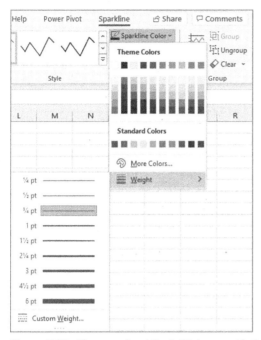

Figure 5.32: Change a Sparkline's thickness with the Weight tool.

The Marker Color tools allows you to set the color for markers if they are shown. In has the same options, such as High Point and Last Point, that the Show group has for displaying them. The single marker options will override the color for all markers. For example, if you set the color for all markers to red and the last point marker to green, the last point will show as green.

Adjusting the Axis

Excel provides a few options for controlling the axis of a Sparkline. The Ribbon item Sparkline ⇨ Axis contains the following options:

- **General Axis Type:** With this type, each data point is equally spaced across the cell.
- **Date Axis Type:** With this type, the horizontal axis values are assumed to be dates, and they are spaced according to the number of days between values rather than equally. Figure 5.33 shows the two Sparklines from the same data. One is set to General Axis Type and the data points are equally spaced, and the other is set to Date Axis Type and the data points are spaced according to the values.

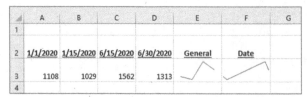

Figure 5.33: Comparing the General and Date Axis Types

- **Show Axis:** If your data has both positive and negative numbers, a line representing zero is rendered in the Sparkline. If all the numbers are either positive or negative, no line is shown. Figure 5.34 shows three Sparklines in a group with Show Axis set. Only the middle Sparkline renders an axis because it contains both positive and negative values.

⊿	A	B	C	D	E
1					
2	1	2	3	4	
3	14	17	12	11	
4	10	14	-2	11	
5	-13	-10	-11	-14	
6					

Figure 5.34: Sparklines with positive and negative values will show an axis

- **Plot Data Right-to-Left:** This reverses the order of the values.
- **Vertical Axis Minimum:** If you choose the automatic option, each Sparkline is scaled on its own and the data points of other Sparklines in the group are not considered. If you choose the Same For All Sparklines option, the Sparkline is rendered using the lowest data point for the entire group as the minimum for all Sparklines. Finally, you can hard code a value for the minimum.
- **Vertical Axis Maximum:** These options are the same as the Vertical Axis Minimum. If you choose the Same For All Sparklines option for both the minimum and maximum, all the Sparklines in the group will be rendered on the same scale. The left Sparkline in Figure 5.35 has the minimum and

⊿	A	B	C	D	E	F	G	H
1								
2		2016	2017	2018	2019	2020	Automatic	Group Scaling
3	Salaries	68,451	69,136	69,827	72,620	76,251		
4	Rent	25,432	25,432	25,432	27,975	30,773		
5	Advertising	41,888	41,888	41,050	41,871	42,290		
6	Depreciation	16,449	16,613	16,779	16,611	16,445		
7	Admin Expenses	32,227	32,549	32,874	32,217	31,573		
8								

Figure 5.35: Comparing the scaling options for Sparklines

maximum set as Automatic for Each Sparkline and the right Sparkline is set to Same For All Sparklines.

With automatic scaling, you can see the trends for each expense classification independently. There appears to be wild swings for each row. But with scaling across the whole group, you see that the expenses are much more stable.

Using Shapes to Create Infographics

In This Chapter

- Working with Shapes
- Framing Data with Shapes
- Creating Custom Infographics
- Adding Other Illustrations

In addition to charts, Excel has other drawing objects, called shapes, that you can use to enhance your charts or that you can combine to create your own infographics in lieu of charts. In more recent versions, Microsoft has added even more drawing options known as icons. In this chapter, I'll show you how to get started working with shapes, including some examples of how to combine shapes to add interesting effects to your charts. I'll also provide an introduction to the various types of icons included in Excel.

Working with Shapes

Excel provides a rich ecosystem of drawing objects called shapes. There are dozens of built-in shapes to choose from, and Excel allows you to manipulate them in so many ways that the number of shapes is limitless. In this chapter,

I'll show you how to work with shapes, including adding them, customizing them, and using them in connection with charts to make interesting frames around your data.

Inserting Shapes

When you insert a shape on a worksheet, you are adding the shape to the drawing layer. The drawing layer sits over the top of the cells, which is why you can move shapes around irrespective of the grid. To insert a shape, choose Insert ➪ Illustrations ➪ Shapes to show the shapes gallery, a portion of which is shown in Figure 6.1.

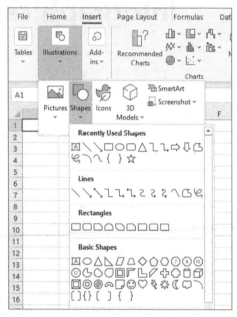

Figure 6.1: Insert a shape from the Shapes Gallery.

The shapes in the gallery are organized into sections of similar shapes to help you find what you're looking for more easily. Once you've found the shape you want, click it and click in the worksheet where you want to place the shape. The point on the worksheet you click becomes the top-left corner of the shape and the shape is inserted at its default size.

Instead of clicking where the top-left corner of the shape will be, you can click and drag to draw a shape at something other than the default size. Figure 6.2 shows a rectangle inserted at the default size (on the left) and another rectangle in the process of being inserted using the click and drag method. You can see that the cursor becomes a large cross, and you can vary not only the size of the shape but also the proportions. The default is a square, and the shape being created in Figure 6.2 is wider than it is tall.

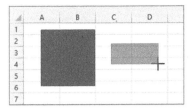

Figure 6.2: Insert a shape by clicking and dragging.

TIP   If you hold down the Shift key while inserting a shape using the click and drag method or by resizing from a corner sizing handle, Excel will maintain the default proportions of the shape while still allowing you to control the size.

Don't worry if you don't get the shape exactly in the right location or the right size. It's easy to move and resize shapes. Single-click a shape to select it. Your cursor will turn to a four-sided arrow and the sizing handles on the shape will become visible, as shown in Figure 6.3.

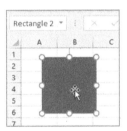

Figure 6.3: Selecting a shape displays its sizing handles.

To move a shape, simply drag it with your mouse and release at the desired location. To resize a shape, click and drag one of the sizing handles. The corner sizing handles will change the height and width at the same time. The other sizing handles only increase one dimension.

If you want to keep the center of the shape in place while you resize it, hold down the Ctrl key while you drag one of the sizing handles. For example, dragging the bottom, center sizing handle down will increase the height and maintain the top-left position. But holding down the Ctrl key will increase the height both up and down, as shown in Figure 6.4. The darker area is the original shape, and the lighter areas show you the size of the shape if you release the mouse button.

Excel names each shape with the shape's generic name and a number. When you select a shape, you can see its name in the Name box to the left of the formula bar. Figure 6.5 shows that an oval shape was named Oval 4, indicating it was the fourth time an oval was inserted on the worksheet, including those that were deleted. You don't need to change the names of the shapes unless you plan to manipulate them in a macro or you just like to keep things organized.

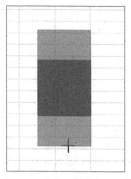

Figure 6.4: Hold down the Ctrl key when resizing to maintain the center position.

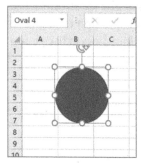

Figure 6.5: Excel names each shape inserted.

Customizing Shapes

Shapes have properties beyond just size and position that you can change. Recall that to select a shape, you single-click it. If you double-click a shape, you enter Edit mode. In Edit mode, you can enter or edit text inside the shape. If you single-click a shape and start typing, Excel will automatically put you in Edit mode. Another method for entering Edit mode is to right-click the shape and choose Edit Text from the context menu.

When you select a shape, the Shape Format tab on the Ribbon becomes visible. The first group on the Shape Format tab has the same gallery from the Insert menu that allows you to insert a new shape. It also contains a tool for inserting a text box that is identical to inserting a text box from the gallery. The Edit Shape tool allows you to change the selected shape to a different type of shape or to show the edit points to manipulate the shape. I discuss edit points later in this chapter.

The next group on the Shape Format tab allows you change the overall style of the shape. The default style when you insert a shape will depend on the theme of your workbook. But you can easily change the shape's style using the Shape Styles Theme Style gallery, which changes the shape's theme independent of the workbook's theme. Click the up or down arrow to scroll through the gallery's rows or click the drop-down arrow to see the whole gallery, as shown in Figure 6.6.

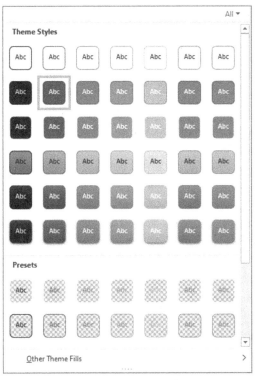

Figure 6.6: Change a shape's style from the Shape Styles Theme Style gallery.

If you don't want any of the predefined styles, you can create a custom style using the other drop-downs in the Shape Styles group of the Shape Format tab. With the Shape Fill tab, you can change the interior color of the shape, change the interior to a picture, or add a gradient to the fill color. Figure 6.7 shows the preset gradient options. If you choose More Gradients, Excel will show the Format Shape task pane, where you can create any gradient you want.

The Shape Outline tool lets you change the color of the shape's border. You can also increase the thickness of the border or change it to dashes or styles that are supposed to look more like freehand drawings. The Shape Effects tool contains all the standard effects tools like shadows, beveled edges, and 3D effects.

The WordArt Styles group allows you to apply WordArt styles to the text in your shape. If you are in Edit mode, only the selected text will get the style. If the shape is selected and you're not in Edit mode, all the text in the shape will be styled. Be very conservative if you apply a WordArt style. Most of them make the text very difficult to read.

To make your dashboard accessible to the visually impaired, click Shape Format ⇨ Alt Text to show the Alt Text task pane. You can enter a description of the shape to be read by a screen reader or you can mark the shape as decorative to tell the screen reader to ignore it entirely. If you have text in your shape, you may not need alternative text.

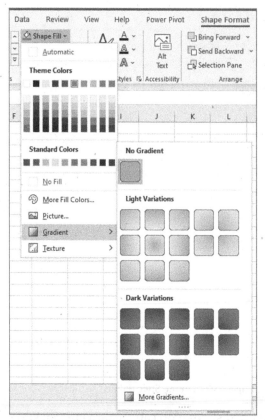

Figure 6.7: Change the gradient with a preset gradient from the gallery.

The Arrange tab contains tools to determine which shape is on top if you have overlapping shapes and a tool to show the Selection task pane. The Selection task pane is useful if you have a lot of shapes or your shapes are small or otherwise hard to select directly with your mouse.

If you have more than one shape selected, you can use the Align Objects tool to help you align the shapes. For example, if you have an arrow shape that's pointing at a rectangle shape, you could use the Align Middle tool to make sure those two shapes are aligned properly. Figure 6.8 shows the Align Middle tool being used on two selected shapes.

Excel doesn't provide visual alignment guides as a dedicated graphics software application would, so the alignment tools are invaluable when placing shapes. The Snap To Grid and Snap To Shape tools apply to all the shapes in the workbook. When Snap To Grid is enabled, the edge of the shape will align with the cell gridlines when you get it close enough. When Snap To Shape is enabled, the edge of the shape will be aligned with the edge of a nearby shape, again, when you are within a certain distance of that edge.

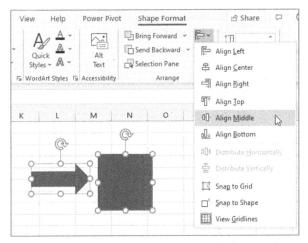

Figure 6.8: Use the alignment tools to help aligning shapes.

The last group on the Shape Format tab is the Size group. Rather than resizing a shape with your mouse, you can enter the exact dimensions for height and width. The Size group has an icon in the lower-right corner that will show the Format Shape task pane. Other groups also have this icon, and they take you to the part of the Format Shape task pane that's relevant to that group. Most, if not all, of what you need to do can be done from the Shape Format tab on the Ribbon. But if something seems lacking, the Format Shape task pane may have more options.

Framing Data with Shapes

Presenting a single number or a simple data set can be impactful, but they also sometimes appear too plain amid fancier charts on a dashboard. Figure 6.9 shows a simple gauge chart that's part of a dashboard containing financial information.

Figure 6.9: A simple gauge chart from a financial dashboard

NOTE   The examples in this section can be found in the workbook named `FramingDatawithShapes.xlsx` on this book's companion website at www.wiley.com/go/datavizwithexcel.

Creating a Banner

Instead of using a chart title, you can combine shapes to create a banner across the top of the chart. This will give the chart some depth and visual appeal without distracting from the data. To create a banner, follow these steps:

1. Delete the chart title by selecting it and pressing the Delete key.

2. Choose Insert ⇨ Illustrations ⇨ Shapes and select Rectangle from the gallery. Then click on the worksheet to insert a default rectangle.

3. Resize the rectangle so that it's slightly wider than the chart, as shown in Figure 6.10. To get the same amount of rectangle on either side of the chart, start by making the rectangle the exact width of the chart. Then widen the rectangle while holding down the Ctrl key. This keeps the middle of the shape in the same place and extends each end.

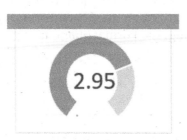

Figure 6.10: Position a rectangle across the top of the chart.

4. Change the shape fill and shape outline to match the colors in the chart.

5. Choose Insert ⇨ Illustrations ⇨ Shapes and select Isosceles Triangle, and insert it onto the worksheet.

6. Change the shape fill to one shade darker than the rectangle and set the shape outline to No Outline.

7. Right-click the triangle and click Format Shape to show the Format Shape task pane.

8. Change the rotation to 270° to make the triangle point left.

9. Change the height and width properties and position the triangle just below the rectangle and outside the borders of the chart, as shown in Figure 6.11.

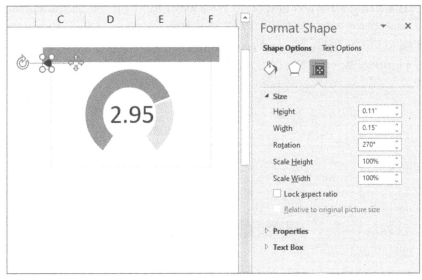

Figure 6.11: Position a triangle below the rectangle.

TIP   You may find it easier to zoom in on your worksheet when working with small shapes. Choose the Zoom tool on the View tab of the Ribbon and select one of the magnifications or choose Custom and enter your own. You can also hold down the Ctrl key and use the scroll wheel on your mouse to change the zoom.

10. Select the triangle and press Ctrl+C and Ctrl+V to make a copy of it. Excel will place the new triangle right on top of the old one, and the new triangle will be selected.

11. Move the new triangle to the other side of the chart and change its Rotation to 90°. Figure 6.12 shows the status of the shapes through this step.

Figure 6.12: Position another triangle on the other side of the chart.

12. Select the rectangle and click Shape Format ➪ Arrange ➪ Bring Forward twice so the rectangle is on top of the triangles. Excel maintains an order for all the shapes on a worksheet called the z-order. When shapes overlap, the shape with higher z-order covers up the shape with the lower one.

The Bring Forward and Send Backward tools on the Shape Format tab change the z-order of the selected shape.

13. Select the rectangle and enter **=$B$1** in the formula bar, as shown in Figure 6.13.

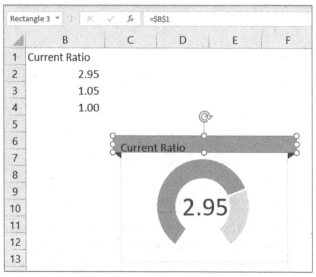

Figure 6.13: Use a formula to show text in a shape.

14. With the rectangle still selected, click Home ⇨ Alignment ⇨ Middle Align and Home ⇨ Alignment ⇨ Center to center the text both vertically and horizontally.

15. Change the font color of the text to match the chart colors. Figure 6.14 shows the finished product.

Figure 6.14: Combined shapes to frame a chart title

Creating a Binder Tab

Similarly to using banners, using a binder tab is a way to add a label that is visually appealing to a chart. Figure 6.15 shows a column chart from a financial dashboard above the same chart with the chart title and legend replaced with shapes.

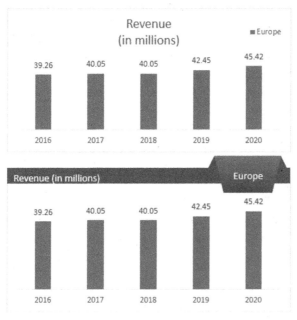

Figure 6.15: Replacing the chart title and legend with shapes

This uses the same technique as the banner from the previous section. Shapes are combined and layered to give the illusion of depth. Figure 6.16 shows an exploded view of the shapes involved.

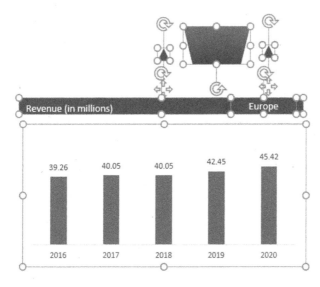

Figure 6.16: An exploded view of the binder tab chart

To create this effect, start with a rectangle that spans the top of the chart. Next, insert a trapezoid and two isosceles triangles. Flip the trapezoid vertically so that the narrower end is at the bottom. Fill the rectangle and triangles one shade darker than the chart color. Fill the trapezoid the same color as the chart and apply a gradient that's darker on the top and lighter on the bottom. Because you flipped the trapezoid vertically, this will make the bottom darker.

Remove the legend from the chart. Replace the chart title with a single space. If you remove the chart title entirely, the columns will fill the space and get too close to the other shapes. Figure 6.17 shows the chart title selected.

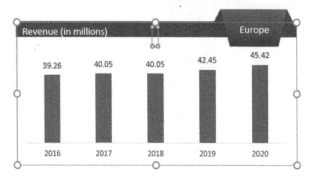

Figure 6.17: An invisible chart title keeps the other elements from filling the vertical space.

Resize and arrange the shapes across the top of the chart. Insert a text box for the caption in the trapezoid. If you entered text directly in the trapezoid, it would be upside down because we flipped the shape vertically. You can flip the text back to right side up using 3-D rotation, but that tends to distort the text. To ensure the text is properly aligned, resize the text box to be the same height as the rectangle and the same width as the widest part of the trapezoid. Then center the text vertically and horizontally. Figure 6.18 shows the size of the text box in relation to the other shapes.

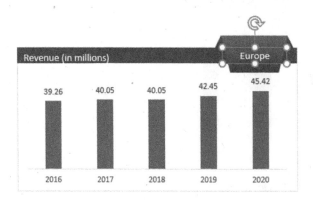

Figure 6.18: Make the text box larger than necessary to ensure the text aligns with neighboring shapes.

Working with Multiple Shapes

There are a few things you can do to make working with a lot of shapes easier. In this example, there are only five shapes outside of the chart, so they're pretty easy to keep track of. But if you have five charts and wanted to use the same shape-framing technique on all of them, it would be harder to manage.

You can change the name of your shapes from the default to something meaningful to you. Select the shape and type a new name in the name box to the left of the formula bar. Figure 6.19 shows that the trapezoid was renamed trp Binder Tab.

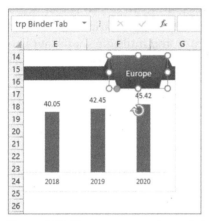

Figure 6.19: You can rename shapes to better manage them.

If you want to move or copy shapes, particularly if you've painstakingly arranged them, you'll want to move them all together. Selecting shapes that are small and overlap with the mouse is not always easy. Excel provides a Selection task pane to make the job easier. First select a shape so the Shape Format tab is shown on the Ribbon. Then click the Selection Pane tool in the Arrange tab to show the task pane. Figure 6.20 shows the Selection task pane.

Figure 6.20: Use the Selection task pane to make selecting shapes easier.

The Selection task pane shows all the shapes on the worksheet with the selected shape highlighted. The original chart and the revised charts are also shapes, so they are listed too. All the shapes have been renamed with an abbreviation for what kind of shape they are and some description to help identify them. For example, the binder tab is made up of a trapezoid and two triangles, and it's easy to see which shapes those are.

The eye icon next to each sheet is used to show or hide individual shapes. You can also show or hide all shapes using the buttons on the top of the task pane. You might want to temporarily hide a shape while working on another shape that's partially obstructed.

You can hold down the Ctrl key while clicking on shapes to select more than one shape. That's true in the Select task pane too. Hold down the Ctrl key while clicking on the shape names in the task pane and multiple shapes will be selected. Figure 6.21 shows all the shapes associated with the binder tab chart title selected. It would be difficult to select all those shapes without the task pane.

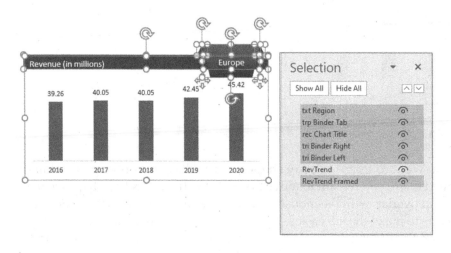

Figure 6.21: Hold down the Ctrl key to select multiple shapes in the Selection task pane.

The last tip for dealing with multiple shapes is groups. You can group shapes together so that you can manipulate them as one. Start by selecting the shapes you want to group. Then click Shape Format ⇨ Arrange ⇨ Group Objects ⇨ Group. Figure 6.22 shows the five shapes that make up the binder tab grouped together. Excel named the group Group 8, but you can change that in the name box.

You can now select the group, copy it, change the text box text, and position the entire group over another chart. This ensures consistency across your dashboard and is a huge time saver.

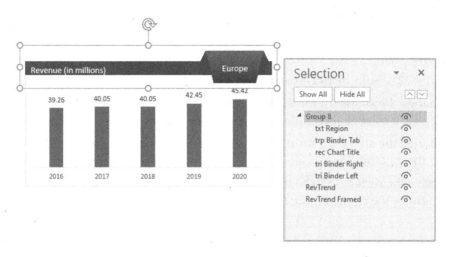

Figure 6.22: Group shapes to work with them as a single unit.

Creating Simple Charts with Shapes

As I mentioned earlier in this chapter, charts are shapes. They also live on the drawing layer in Excel. You can combine shapes with charts to draw attention to a particular piece of data or to add more data in the same amount of space.

In the previous section, I added shapes to a column chart in lieu of chart titles and legends. In this section, I'll add a shape to the chart to provide additional information. Figure 6.23 shows a chart of house sales for a real estate office. The office has a goal of selling houses in 15 days or fewer, and the percentage of houses that met that goal has been added to the chart.

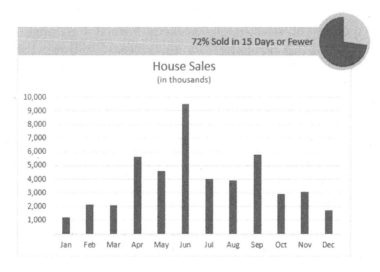

Figure 6.23: House sales for a real estate office

To create this effect, follow these steps:

1. Add an oval, a partial circle, a rectangle, and a text box anywhere on the worksheet.

2. Enter **72% Sold in 15 Days or Fewer** in the text box.

3. Change the shape fill for the rectangle and the oval to be the same color. Choose a color that complements the chart but does not match it.

4. Change the shape fill for the partial circle to a darker shade than the fill for the rectangle and oval.

5. Resize the rectangle to be the same width as the chart and about half the height of the circle. Figure 6.24 shows the shapes through this step.

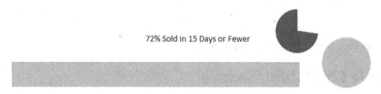

Figure 6.24: Format the shapes to complement the chart.

6. Next, get the shapes close to their position relative to each other. They don't need to be near their final destination near the chart.

7. Show the Selection task pane by clicking Shape Format ⇨ Arrange ⇨ Selection Pane. Hold down the Ctrl key and select the text box, partial circle, oval, and rectangle.

8. From the Ribbon, choose Shape Format ⇨ Arrange ⇨ Align Objects ⇨ Align Middle. This will make sure shapes are perfectly aligned.

9. While the shapes are still selected, choose Shape Format ⇨ Arrange ⇨ Group Object ⇨ Group from the Ribbon to create a group that will be easier to move around. Figure 6.25 shows the shapes and the Selection task pane.

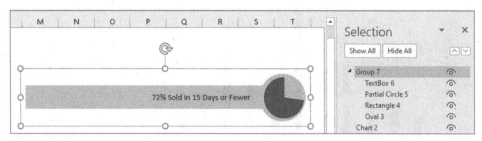

Figure 6.25: Group shapes to make them easier to move.

If you don't like the position of the pie chart when you move the group to the top of the column chart, ungroup the shapes, reposition to the desired location, repeat the steps to align the middles, and regroup the shapes.

Creating Custom Infographics

You can customize shapes beyond just size and rotation. Some shapes have additional sizing points, called adjustment points, that allow you to change a characteristic of the shape other than its height or width. Figure 6.26 shows the Callout: Up Arrow shape with the standard eight sizing points plus four adjustment points.

Figure 6.26: Some shapes have additional sizing points.

In the case of the Callout: Up Arrow shape, the top-most adjustment point changes the width of the arrow. The left-most adjustment point changes the height of the callout box without changing the overall height of the shape. The right-most adjustment point changes the height of the arrow. Finally, the remaining adjustment point changes the width of the connector between the arrow and the callout box.

By manipulating these adjustment points, you can create a shape that's quite a bit different than the original. Figure 6.27 shows the Callout: Up Arrow shape changed to custom infographics that could be used in place of a simple column chart.

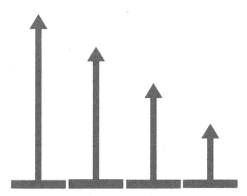

Figure 6.27: Use additional sizing points to create custom shapes.

Shapes also have edit points. To see them, right-click on the shape and choose Edit Points from the context menu. The shape in Figure 6.28 has 11 edit points. The two edit points at the outside base of the arrows have been pulled down to make a pointier arrow head.

Figure 6.28: Use edit points to further customize a shape.

The lines between the edit points are called segments, and they are also editable. Figure 6.29 shows the context menu when you right-click on a segment.

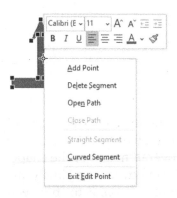

Figure 6.29: Right-click on a segment to modify it.

Using this context menu, you can add edit points beyond the default points or change other characteristics of the segment. Right-clicking on an edit point as opposed to a segment shows a slightly different context menu, as shown in Figure 6.30.

You can change the edit point from one type to another, such as changing from a corner point to straight point. The different types of points determine how you can manipulate them. Changing shapes using edit points can be tricky. You need a steady hand and a creative streak. Once you get a shape you like, be sure to copy it into another workbook for future use.

Adding Other Illustrations

Excel provides thousands of royalty-free and copyright-free icons and images that you can add to your worksheets. The icons are Scalable Vector Graphics

Figure 6.30: Right-click on an edit point to modify it.

(SVG), which means you can resize them without any loss of quality. SVG images contain instructions on how to render the image rather than pixels. This allows them to render the image at any size.

Click Insert ➪ Illustrations ➪ Icons from the Ribbon to show the dialog used to insert illustrations, shown in Figure 6.31. This same dialog box is used to insert stock images, icons, and other illustrations. Select the item from the list across the top to choose what you want to insert.

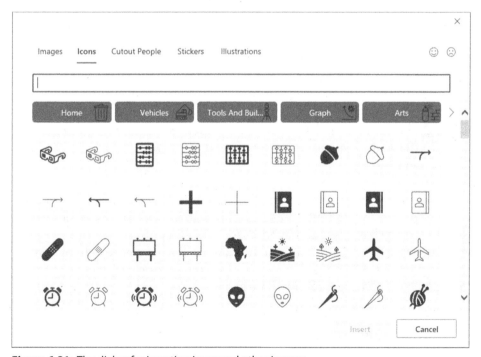

Figure 6.31: The dialog for inserting icons and other images

In the Icons section, there is a search box and a list of predefined search terms. You can click one of the buttons to type the search term into the search box and limit the icons you can see. Scroll right using the arrow next to the buttons to see more suggested search terms. You can also type your own search terms in the search box. Figure 6.32 shows the icons Excel finds when you search for the term *finance*.

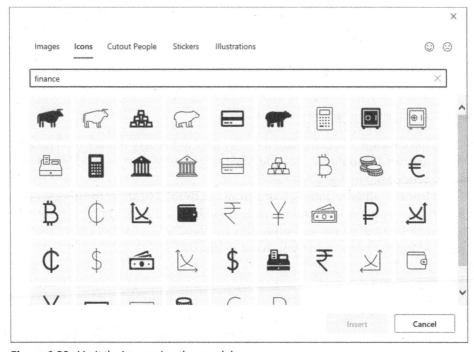

Figure 6.32: Limit the icons using the search box

NOTE   This example can be found in the workbook named `CutoutPeopleSign` `.xlsx` on this book's companion website at `www.wiley.com/go/` `datavizwithexcel.`

The Cutout People section of the illustration dialog contains thousands of images of people in different poses. You can search by name using the button below the search bar to see all the poses for a certain person. You can use your own search terms here, as you can in the Icons section. If you search for *sign*, as shown in Figure 6.33, you get images of a person holding a sign.

To add text to that sign, follow these steps:

1. Choose Insert ➪ Illustrations ➪ Icons from the Ribbon.

2. Select the Cutout People section.

3. Enter **sign** in the search box.

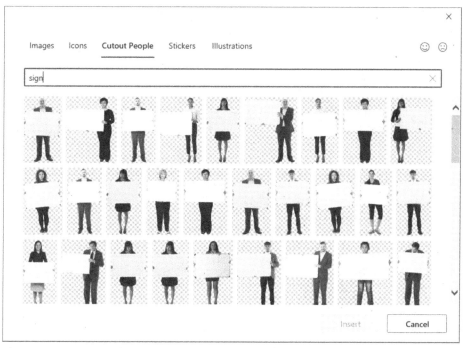

Figure 6.33: Search in the Cutout People section.

4. Select one of the images and click Insert.

5. Resize the image if necessary.

6. Choose Insert ⇨ Illustrations ⇨ Shapes ⇨ Text Box and click near the sign to place the text box, as shown in Figure 6.34.

Figure 6.34: Add a text box to the sign.

7. Resize and rotate the text box to the approximate position and dimensions of the sign, as shown in Figure 6.35.

Figure 6.35: Resize and rotate the text box to better fit the sign.

8. Enter text into the text box and format it, such as by changing the font, size, and color.

9. Center the text both vertically and horizontally using the tools in the Alignment group of the Home tab of the Ribbon.

10. Right-click on the text box and choose Format Shape to show the Format Shape task pane.

11. On the Text Options tab, check the Wrap Text In Shape check box, as shown in Figure 6.36.

12. On the Shape Options tab, change the fill to No fill and the line to No line if necessary. This makes the text box transparent and it appears that the text is part of the other image. Figure 6.37 shows the final product.

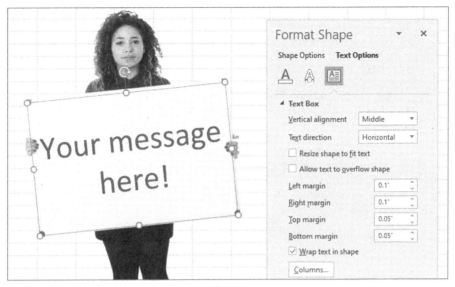

Figure 6.36: Wrap the text within the text box.

Figure 6.37: Make the text box transparent.

Tell a Story with Visualization

Visualizing Performance Comparisons

In This Chapter

- Single Measurements
- Column Charts
- Bullet Charts
- Clustered Column Charts
- Funnel Charts
- XY Charts
- Bubble Charts
- Dot Plot Charts

Excel supports many common chart types for visualizing performance measurements. Which chart type you choose depends on the nature of your data and the story you want to tell. In this chapter, I discuss some of the more common chart types for visualizing performance and provide guidance for when to use each type.

Single Measurements

Not all dashboard elements are charts. Simple tables and pictures can be part of a dashboard to great effect. The simplest element you can display is a single number. By scaling up the size of the text, adding some color, and adding icons, you can display an important number in an effective way.

Percentages are a classic example of a single measurement. A percentage can be used to show how close you are to a goal. Everyone knows that 100% is meeting the goal, and showing progress as, for example, 87% is easily under-standable by your readers. Figure 7.1 shows an example of using a percentage as part of a larger dashboard.

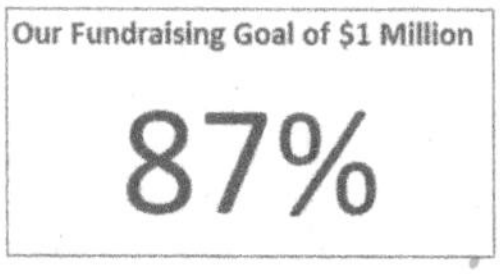

Our Fundraising Goal of $1 Million

87%

Figure 7.1: A single percentage in a dashboard

> **NOTE**   The charts in the figures for this chapter can be found on this book's companion website at www.wiley.com/go/datavizwithexcel. Each case study has its own file containing all its charts. You can find the names of those files in the sections containing the case studies.

This example is simply a percentage typed in a cell. Its font size is set to 72 points, and its color was changed to match the style of the dashboard. The cell above it has a title, and both cells are surrounded by a border to set it off from the other elements.

You can also use a percentage to show how something changed over time. You can use a conditional formatting icon to show an up arrow for an increase. Figure 7.2 uses the some of the same techniques as Figure 7.1 (i.e., larger font, color) and applies a conditional formatting rule to show an arrow icon in the cell.

Sales Increase over Last Year

⬆ 145%

Figure 7.2: A single percentage showing change

To apply the conditional formatting rule, select the cell with the percentage and choose Conditional Formatting ➪ Icon Sets ➪ Directional - 3 Arrows (Colored) from the Home tab.

Other single numbers that are not percentages can be displayed in this way. Total sales dollars, units shipped, and days without an accident are examples of single numbers that can be an impactful element in a dashboard. Make sure your single numbers are appropriately labeled and rounded to a meaningful precision. Figure 7.3 shows total sales dollars displayed in two different ways: as a raw number and as a rounded number. The rounded number conveys the same information, is more visually pleasing, and is easier to read.

Figure 7.3: Total sales dollars shown as raw and rounded

The rounded number is the same number as the raw number but is formatted with a custom number format. To format a number in millions, open the Format Cells dialog box, choose the Number tab, choose the Custom category, and type **$ #.#,," million"** in the Type box.

The dollar sign is a special character that's understood by Excel and simply displays a dollar sign—no quotes are needed around it. The next part, **#.#,,** instructs Excel to only show a number with one decimal place and to only show digits to the left of the second comma (millions). Because the word *million* isn't understood by Excel, it's enclosed in quotes so that it displays exactly as typed.

Both previous examples can also be displayed using a chart. You can easily imagine a bullet chart showing that you're 87% of the way to a goal or a column chart showing last year's and this year's sales to convey the increase. But a single number is a simple and clean dashboard element that can break up what otherwise might be similar looking charts.

Column Charts

Column charts are among the most used chart types. They are best used for comparing categories of data. Simple column charts have the category axis on the bottom, the values axis on the side, and for each category, a single value represented by the height of a column extending up from the category name.

Bar charts are column charts turned on their side. That is, the category axis is on the side and the values axis on the bottom. All the same principles and best practices apply to both column and bar charts. You might choose a bar chart if your category labels are particularly long, because they provide more horizontal space for labels. Or you might simply choose them to break up the monotony of too many column charts on your dashboard. Figure 7.4 shows the structures of a column chart and a bar chart.

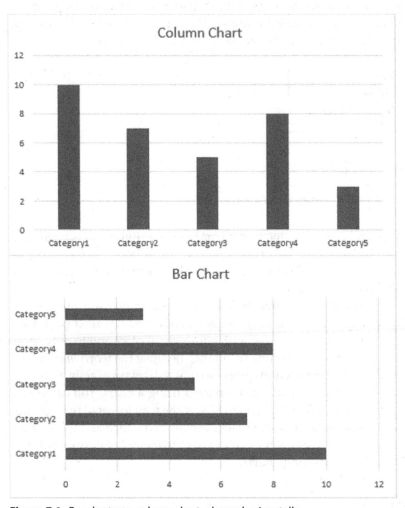

Figure 7.4: Bar charts are column charts shown horizontally.

As with virtually every other chart type, start your values axis at zero. Starting at a value other than zero distorts the reader's perception of the column heights and might be misleading. Figure 7.5 shows a column chart whose values axis doesn't start at zero.

A casual glance at the chart in Figure 7.5 will lead the reader to believe that the first category is double the second when it's only 50% larger.

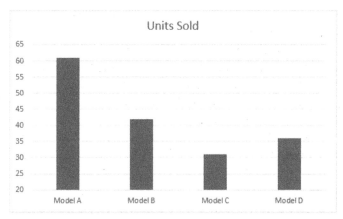

Figure 7.5: Start the values axis at zero.

Limit the number of categories in column charts to about ten. Too many categories in a single chart makes it difficult to compare. If you have more than ten categories, consider grouping them differently. How you group them depends on the story that you're trying to tell. For example, if your story is that the top three products dominate sales, you could group all products outside of the top three into one category. In Figure 7.6, the chart on the left shows too many categories. There's so much noise in the chart that the story of the top three products might get lost. The chart on the right groups all other products into a single category. It tells the same story but is easier to read.

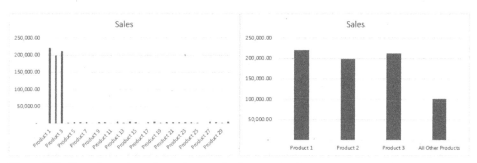

Figure 7.6: Grouping categories reduces noise in your chart.

The order of your categories can be an important factor in how the reader interprets the chart. Generally, if your categories have a natural order, you should stick with that. For example, if your categories are time based, like the quarters of a year, order them from earliest to latest. However, if your categories don't have a natural order, like products or departments, put the largest value on the left.

There is a theory that people like charts that increase from left to right, like a stock chart that's increasing. However, I believe this is an over-manipulation of the data to elicit a specific response (if the theory is indeed true). You must tell a story, but it's important to stay true to the data when you tell it. If the story you want to tell isn't supported by the data, tell a different story.

Finally, consider your reader. Your company may have a predetermined idea of the order of your categories. Or if you publish a chart on a schedule, keep the categories in the same order from one period to the next. There may be a case to change the order, such as if a new product becomes a big seller, but those changes should be rare. Don't change the order because one product had an unusually large quarter and will fall back down to a normal level next quarter.

Case Study: Sales by Quarter

Your retail apparel store groups its products into five categories: Men's Activewear, Men's Outerwear, Women's Activewear, Women's Outerwear, and Children's. Your task is to simply report the first quarter sales by product category.

NOTE The workbook for this case study is `ColumnSalesbyQuarter.xlsx` and can be found at www.wiley.com/go/datavizwithexcel.

The first step is to stage the data. Follow these steps to create the data staging area that will drive your chart:

1. On a new worksheet, type the header for a new table as shown in Figure 7.7.

	A	B	C
1	Product Category	Q1 Sales	
2			
3			
4			
5			

Figure 7.7: Table headings for Q1 sales

2. Choose Insert ⇨ Tables ⇨ Table from the Ribbon and check the My Table Has Headers check box to create the table.

3. Type the product categories in the first column of the table as shown in Figure 7.8.

	A	B	C
1	Product Category	Q1 Sales	
2	Men's Activewear		
3	Men's Outerwear		
4	Women's Activewear		
5	Women's Outerwear		
6	Children's		
7			

Figure 7.8: Product categories for Q1 sales

4. Enter the following formula in the Q1 Sales column.

```
=SUMIF(tblSalesData[Category],[@[Product Category]],tblSal
esData[Sales])
```

Check that your table resembles the table in Figure 7.9.

A	B	C
Product Category	Q1 Sales	
Men's Activewear	$61,363.86	
Men's Outerwear	$49,451.74	
Women's Activewear	$105,039.47	
Women's Outerwear	$91,291.86	
Children's	$50,141.07	

Figure 7.9: A completed Q1 sales table

5. Select the table and choose Insert - Recommended Charts. Choose the Clustered Column option. Click OK to insert the chart onto the active worksheet. Figure 7.10 shows the completed chart.

6. Optionally, you can sort the table by Q1 sales largest-to-smallest. The chart will update to reflect the new order.

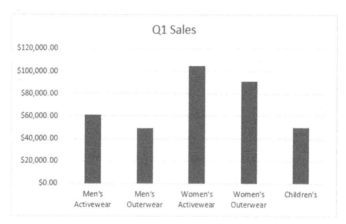

Figure 7.10: A column chart for Q1 sales

NOTE   Clustered column charts and column charts are really the same chart type. The only difference is that clustered column charts show multiple, grouped values. If you only have one value per category, choosing the clustered column chart type results in a simple column chart.

Bullet Charts

Bullet charts are used to show a featured measurement compared to a comparison measurement. Actual results vs. budgeted results and progress toward a goal are the two classic examples for this chart type. Visualization expert Stephen Few created bullet charts as a replacement for gauge charts.

The linear nature of a bullet chart makes it more flexible than the round gauge chart because it's more compact and can be displayed horizontally or vertically. When you're creating a dashboard with several charts, you'll appreciate this flexibility.

In general, linear charts, like column charts or bullet charts, make it easier to compare multiple data points than angular charts, like pie charts or gauge charts. It's a common opinion among charting experts that readers are better at comparing lengths than angles and it seems to make sense.

Bullet charts are constructed with a wider bar representing the comparison measurement and a narrower bar, representing the featured measurement, placed within the wider bar's borders. Figure 7.11 shows a typical bullet chart. You don't need to use a color gradient on a bullet chart, but if you do, going from dark to light seems to be the most common.

Figure 7.11: A typical bullet chart

Case Study: Expenses vs. Budget

You need to show actual expenses vs. budgeted expense for each of four departments. The departments are Production, Sales and Marketing, Administration, and Research and Development.

> **NOTE**   The workbook for this case study is `BulletExpenses.xlsx` and can be found at www.wiley.com/go/datavizwithexcel.

Organize your data as shown in Figure 7.12 with actual in one row and budget in another. Follow these steps to create a bullet chart.

◢	A	B	C	D	E
1	Department ▾	Produc ▾	Sales and ▾	Admini ▾	Resear ▾
2	Actual	225,000	113,000	87,000	79,000
3	Budget	250,000	120,000	80,000	90,000
4					

Figure 7.12: Bullet chart data

1. From the Insert tab, select Recommended Charts and choose the Clustered Bar chart type. Figure 7.13 shows the resulting chart.

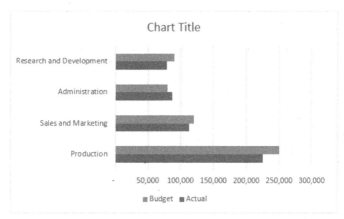

Figure 7.13: A clustered bar chart

2. Right-click the Actual series and choose Change Series Chart Type. Put the Actual series on the secondary axis. Figure 7.14 shows the Change Chart Type dialog box.

TIP   You can use the Clustered Column chart type instead of Clustered Bar. When the category axis labels are long, a Clustered Bar chart type allows more room.

3. From the Chart Elements drop-down on the Format tab, select Series "Budget" to select that series. You can also select it directly in the chart, but sometimes there is only a small area sticking out and it's hard to select. Click the Format Selection button to show the Format Data Series task pane if it's not already visible. On the Series Options tab of the task pane, change Gap Width to 90%. Figure 7.15 shows the Format Data Series task pane.

4. In the same way, select the Series "Actual" series and change its Gap Width setting to 400%. You can experiment with the Gap Width percentages to get the look you want.

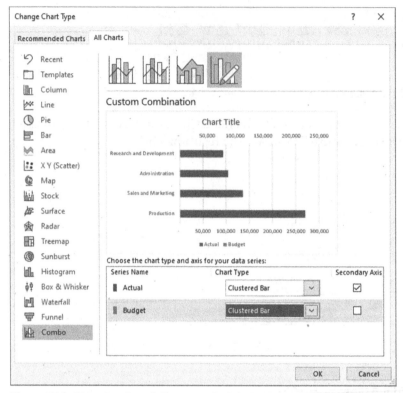

Figure 7.14: Changing the axis for one series

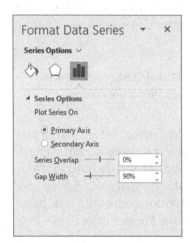

Figure 7.15: The Gap Width setting on the Format Data Series task pane

5. For each series, change fill and border colors on the Fill & Line tab of the Format Data Series task pane. Typically, the wider budget bar is a lighter color than the narrower actual bar. Figure 7.16 shows the state of the chart after this step.

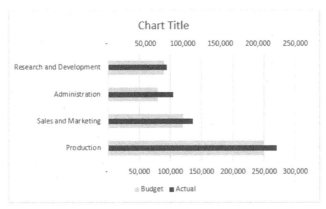

Figure 7.16: Bullet chart after gap width and color adjustments

6. Select the secondary axis and, on the Format Axis task pane, change the Minimum and Maximum values to match the primary axis. Then with the axis still selected, press the Delete key to hide the secondary axis. You can also use the on-object chart customization buttons to unselect the secondary axis as shown in Figure 7.17.

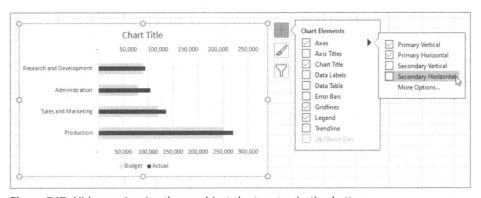

Figure 7.17: Hide an axis using the on-object chart customization buttons.

7. Finally, change the chart title to a meaningful name. Figure 7.18 shows the completed chart.

The chart shows that all departments stayed within budget except the Administration department.

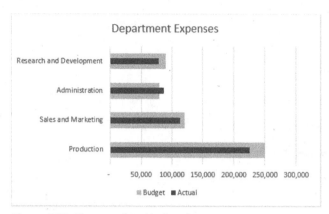

Figure 7.18: The completed bullet chart

Clustered Column Charts

In Excel, all column charts are clustered column charts. If you only have one dimension, a clustered column chart looks just like a simple column chart. When you have multiple dimensions, however, a clustered column chart allows you to compare the parts of each dimension individually. It's not suitable when you want to compare the total of each category because the parts are separated into clusters.

A stacked column chart seems to solve the problem of comparing the parts and the whole all at once. The problem with stacked charts is that after the first part, the part that starts at zero, each part starts at a different place, making it harder to see the differences. Figure 7.19 shows a stacked column chart and a clustered column chart side by side.

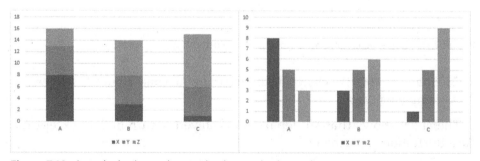

Figure 7.19: A stacked column chart and a clustered column chart

In the stacked column chart (on the left), it's difficult to see that the Y dimension is the same value for every category because each Y dimension starts in a different place. The clustered column chart (on the right) makes it easy to compare each dimension, but you sacrifice the ability to compare the total of each category. The story you want the chart to tell will guide you in which chart type is best for your situation.

Case Study: Production Defects

You measured defects at each of your four production facilities for the year. You want to compare, by quarter, the defects at each facility. Figure 7.20 shows the data that you will use for the chart.

	A	B	C	D	E	F
1	Facility	Q1	Q2	Q3	Q4	
2	Nashville	8	6	9	7	
3	Knoxville	12	15	10	11	
4	Murfreesboro	13	8	7	10	
5	Chattanooga	10	8	11	6	
6						

Figure 7.20: Defects per facility per quarter

NOTE The workbook for this case study is `ClusteredColumnDefects.xlsx` and can be found at www.wiley.com/go/datavizwithexcel.

Because clustered column charts are a native Excel chart type, creating them is easy. From the Insert tab, choose Recommended Charts and select Clustered Column. Excel does a good job of creating the chart on the first try. Change the chart title and you have a clustered column chart like the one shown in Figure 7.21.

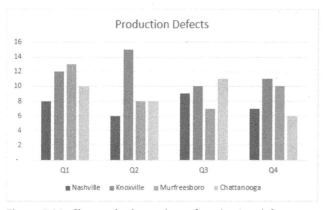

Figure 7.21: Clustered column chart of production defects

Instead of relying on the value axis for values, you can use data labels. To show data labels, right-click on each series in the chart and choose Add Data Labels. Then select the value axis and press the Delete key to hide it. Finally, select the horizontal gridlines and hide them with the Delete key. Figure 7.22 shows the chart with data labels instead of a value axis.

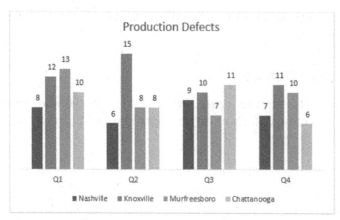

Figure 7.22: Clustered column chart with data labels

Funnel Charts

Funnel charts show progress through a series of stages, where each stage is dependent on the previous one. The first stage, a bar at the top of the chart, is the widest one. The second stage just below it is narrower to the degree that items in the first stage made it to the second stage. Each stage gets narrower and more items are weeded out. An example of a funnel chart is shown in Figure 7.23.

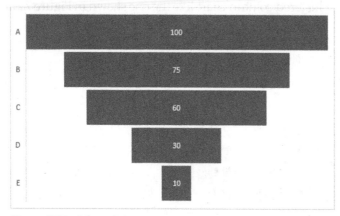

Figure 7.23: A funnel chart

The classic funnel chart shows the sales process. The top stage is generally Leads. It then flows down through stages like Qualified Leads, Quoted, Negotiated, and Won. The Leads level is at the top and is the widest. Not every lead will be qualified, and a smaller number of those leads end up in the second level, Qualified Leads. The next stage, Quoted, is smaller yet because not every qualified lead will respond when you try to contact them. Some quotes get rejected right away and never enter the Negotiated stage. And finally, not all negotiations end in a sale.

Another process well suited to a funnel chart is the hiring process, with stages like Applied, Phone Interview, First Interview, Second Interview, and Hired.

Avoid using funnel charts for showing values by category, like expense by department or sales by product. Column or bar charts are better choices for these types of data. With a funnel chart, the reader will have an expectation that the levels are dependent on each other and you should respect that.

Case Study: Sales Conversion

Steve is your lowest performing salesperson, and you want to know why. You create a funnel chart to visualize Steve's results throughout the sales process. Excel has a built-in funnel chart type that makes creating them very easy. Steve's sales process data is shown in Figure 7.24.

Figure 7.24: Sales process data

NOTE The workbook for this case study is `FunnelSalesConversion.xlsx` and can be found at `www.wiley.com/go/datavizwithexcel`.

To create a funnel chart, select the sales process data and choose Recommended Charts from the Insert tab. Then choose Funnel and click OK. Select the chart title and give your chart a meaningful title. Your chart should look like Figure 7.25.

Unlike a bar chart, a funnel chart is one series and, therefore, one color. To add some color to the chart, select the top bar to select the whole series. Then select the top bar again to select that data point. Figure 7.26 shows that the other data points' colors become very light and the task pane becomes a Format Data Point task pane. On the task pane, you can change the color for the selected data point. Select each data point and change its color, the result of which is shown in Figure 7.27.

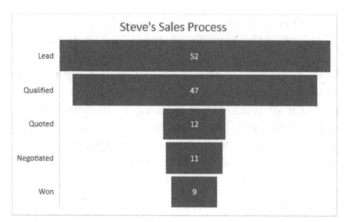

Figure 7.25: Steve's initial funnel chart

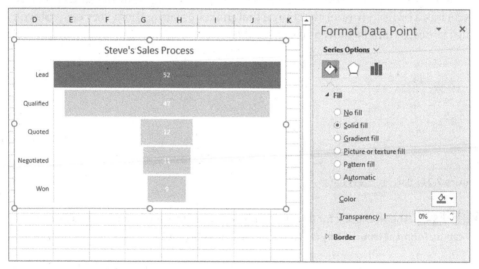

Figure 7.26: Nonselected data points are lighter.

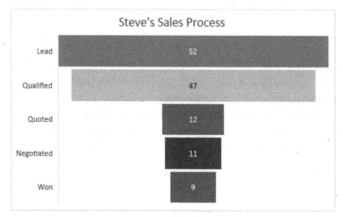

Figure 7.27: Adding color to a funnel chart

TIP   If the task pane is not visible, right-click the data series and choose Format Data Series. Once visible, the task pane will remain visible until you close it. When you select different chart elements, the task pane changes to show options for that element.

You conclude that Steve doesn't seem to have a problem closing sales, but you notice the large drop off between the Qualified and Quoted stages. Perhaps Steve needs some coaching on getting his foot in the door to provide a quote. To verify this, you create a second funnel chart for all salespeople over the same time period. Figure 7.28 shows both funnel charts side by side.

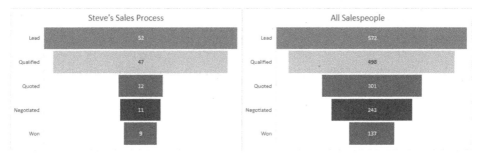

Figure 7.28: A funnel chart for Steve and one for all salespeople

Your instincts are confirmed. Company-wide, the drop off from Qualified to Quoted is more in line with your expectation.

XY Charts

XY charts are also called scatter charts or scatter plots. An XY chart is used to plot two sets of data to determine if the two sets are related. You plot one data set along the x-axis (the horizontal axis) and one along the y-axis (the vertical axis). When the sets group around a trend line, you can say they are correlated. Figure 7.29 shows an XY chart of random values with a trendline. Because the values are random, they don't follow the trendline.

XY charts look a lot like line charts. For both chart types, you can show lines, markers, or both lines and markers. The key difference between the XY chart type and the line chart type is the category axis. The category axis of an XY chart is numeric, and the distance between the plots along the x-axis are proportional to the difference in the values. In a line chart, however, the category axis is not a number. If you have numeric categories, they will be spaced out evenly along the axis regardless of their value. Figure 7.30 shows an XY chart and a line chart made from the same data. Both charts show lines and markers.

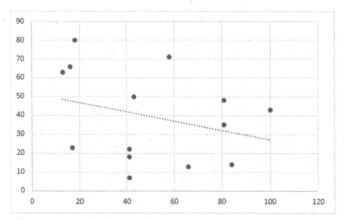

Figure 7.29: An XY chart with random values

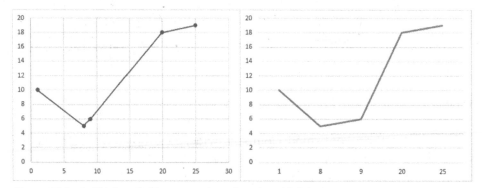

Figure 7.30: An XY chart (left) compared to a line chart (right)

The XY chart shows the second and third data points right next to each other. The line chart equally spaces the numbers along the x-axis. To the line chart, the category axis data are just labels. The fact that the data points are numbers doesn't matter in a line chart. The XY chart also defaults to major gridlines both horizontally and vertically, while the line chart defaults to only horizontal grid lines.

Case Study: Temperature vs. Sales

Your smoothie store sells a variety of juice-based and dessert smoothies. You suspect that smoothie sales drop when it's cold outside and you plot unit sales against the outside temperature. You record the average temperature for every day in April along with the total units you sold that day. A portion of the data is shown in Figure 7.31.

◢	A	B	C
1	Date ▾	Temperature ▾	Units Sold ▾
2	4/1/2020	41.3	58
3	4/2/2020	41.7	79
4	4/3/2020	43.6	70
5	4/4/2020	49.9	85
6	4/5/2020	54.4	98
7	4/6/2020	57.3	97
8	4/7/2020	56.6	96
9	4/8/2020	58.3	87
10	4/9/2020	59.8	108
11	4/10/2020	42.3	63
12	4/11/2020	28.6	46
13	4/12/2020	32.6	52
14	4/13/2020	32.7	46
15	4/14/2020	44.0	62
16	4/15/2020	59.9	114

Figure 7.31: Daily temperature and sales data

NOTE   The workbook for this case study is `XYTemperatureSales.xlsx` and can be found at www.wiley.com/go/datavizwithexcel.

To create the XY chart, follow these steps:

1. Select the range B1:C31 and choose Recommended Charts from the Insert tab.

2. Choose the Scatter chart type.

3. Select the x-axis, and in the Format Axis task pane, set the Minimum field to **20**.

4. Select the y-axis and set its Minimum field to **20** also. This removes the unnecessary white space.

5. Right-click one of the data points and choose Add Trendline.

6. From the Ribbon, select Chart Design ➪ Add Chart Element ➪ Axis Titles ➪ Primary Horizontal to add an axis title. Change the title to **Temperature**.

TIP   XY charts are one of the few charts where you don't need your axes to start at zero.

Figure 7.32 shows the completed XY chart.

Compare the chart in Figure 7.32 to the one in Figure 7.29 that contained random values. The values in the chart in Figure 7.32 don't stray too far from the trendline. This means that temperature and sales are correlated. It does not mean, however, that lower temperatures cause lower sales.

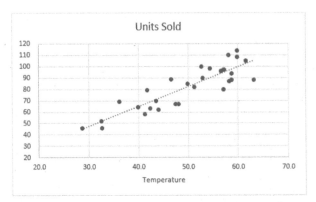

Figure 7.32: An XY chart comparing temperature to sales

To gain a little more insight into the data, you decide to see how juice-based smoothies and dessert smoothies correlate to temperature separately. You split your units sold between the two categories, as shown in Figure 7.33.

	A	B	C	D
1	Date	Temperature	Juice	Dessert
2	4/1/2020	41.3	31	27
3	4/2/2020	41.7	32	47
4	4/3/2020	43.6	31	39
5	4/4/2020	49.9	39	46
6	4/5/2020	54.4	32	66
7	4/6/2020	57.3	34	63
8	4/7/2020	56.6	36	60
9	4/8/2020	58.3	34	53
10	4/9/2020	59.8	35	73
11	4/10/2020	42.3	30	33
12	4/11/2020	28.6	36	10
13	4/12/2020	32.6	38	14
14	4/13/2020	32.7	36	10
15	4/14/2020	44.0	30	32
16	4/15/2020	59.9	39	75
17	4/16/2020	57.2	31	66
18	4/17/2020	51.3	34	48

Figure 7.33: Separated units sold data

Follow these steps to insert an XY chart from this new data:

1. Select the range B1:D31 and choose Recommended Charts from the Insert tab.

2. Choose the Scatter chart type.

3. Change the Minimum value for the x-axis to **20** on the Format Axis task pane. Leave the y-axis Minimum at zero.

4. Right-click on a data point for the Juice series and choose Add Trendline. Repeat for the Dessert series.

5. From the Ribbon, select Chart Design ⇨ Add Chart Element ⇨ Axis Titles ⇨ Primary Horizontal to add an axis title.

6. Change the chart title by selecting it and typing a new title. Figure 7.34 shows the final chart.

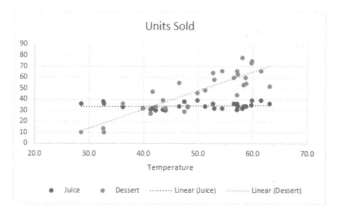

Figure 7.34: Smoothie type vs. temperature

The trendlines of the series tell you that juice-based smoothie sales are largely unaffected by temperature and it's the dessert smoothie sales that account for the drop when the temperature falls. You consider a marketing campaign that discounts dessert smoothies in colder weather.

Bubble Charts

A bubble chart is an XY chart that includes a third dimension. The size of each point of the XY chart changes to reflect this added dimension making the point look like a bubble. Figure 7.35 shows a bubble chart. The first two dimensions, X and Y, are plotted along the horizontal and vertical axes just like in an XY chart. The Z dimension is shown as larger or smaller points (bubbles) proportional to the data point's value.

The best way to size the bubbles is by making the area of the bubble proportional to the value rather than the width. Your readers will perceive a bubble that's double the area of another bubble to represent double the value. A circle's area is proportional to the square of its radius. Bubbles that are based on width will appear four times larger for values that are merely double.

For negative values in the third dimension, Excel shows a bubble whose area is proportional to the positive value of that number, but with a different fill color, usually white. Or you can elect not to show negative values at all.

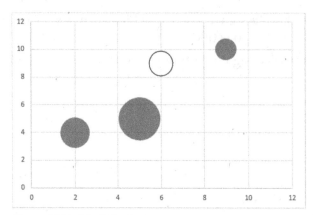

Figure 7.35: A bubble chart

Case Study: Home Mortgages

Your bank makes home mortgages. In the past, you've created XY charts plotting the number of mortgages written and the average mortgage size for each branch. Now, management wants to see how those mortgages are performing. You add a third dimension that is the number of mortgages that are in good standing. You use the data shown in Figure 7.36 to create a bubble chart displaying all three dimensions.

	A	B	C	D	E	F
1	Branch	Mortgages Written	Average Size	In Good Standing	% Good Standing	
2	Northeast	22	225,632	21	95%	
3	Southeast	36	181,443	28	78%	
4	Central	15	77,350	13	87%	
5	Midtown	8	92,161	8	100%	

Figure 7.36: Home mortgage data

NOTE   The workbook for this case study is `BubbleHomeMortgages.xlsx` and can be found at www.wiley.com/go/datavizwithexcel.

To create the bubble chart, follow these steps:

1. Select the data for the chart. Start by selecting cells B2:C5, then hold down the Ctrl key and select E2:E5.

2. Select Insert ⇨ Charts ⇨ Recommended Charts from the Ribbon. From the All Charts tab, choose XY (Scatter) and the Bubble option. Choose the example chart with only four bubbles on it. Click OK to insert the chart.

3. Right-click on one of the bubbles and choose Add Data Labels. Excel guesses that you want to show the Y value.

4. Right-click one of the data labels and choose Format Data Labels to show the Format Data Labels task pane.

5. Under Label Options, choose the Label Options section and check the Value From Cells check box. Figure 7.37 shows the Data Label Range dialog that's displayed. Select the range containing the branch names and click OK.

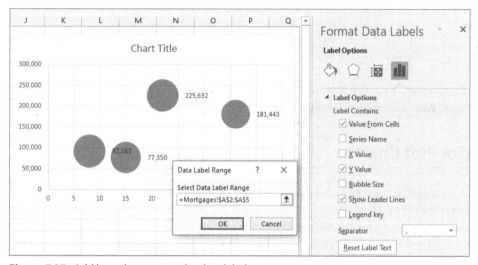

Figure 7.37: Add branch names to the data labels.

6. Uncheck the Y Value check box in the Format Data Labels task pane.

7. Change Label Position to Center.

8. From the Text Options section of the Format Data Labels task pane, choose a darker text color so that it stands out against the bubbles.

9. Click on the chart title and change the text to a more meaningful chart title.

10. From the Chart Design tab on the Ribbon, choose Add Chart Element and add axis titles for both the horizontal and vertical axes.

11. Select each axis title and change the text.

Figure 7.38 shows the final chart. While the Southeast branch is writing the most mortgages, their relatively smaller circle may indicate a problem in their process for identifying quality loans.

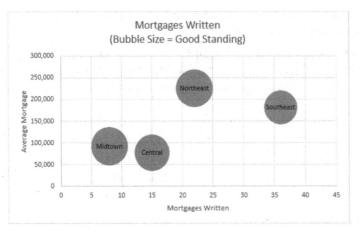

Figure 7.38: Mortgages by branch

Dot Plot Charts

Dot plots are used to show counts of items or occurrences by category. In their simplest form, they show one dot for each counted item. Figure 7.39 shows an example of dot plot recording the observation of different types of birds. Each time a bird is observed, a dot is added to that bird's column.

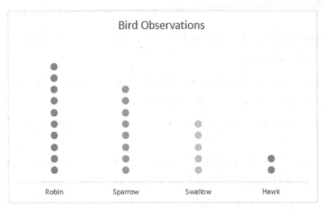

Figure 7.39: A dot plot chart of bird observations

It's important to keep the number of dots on your dot plot small so that the chart isn't cluttered or so the dots aren't stacked on top of each other. If you have too many dots, you can group the data so that each dot represents more than one item.

Simple dot plots don't offer much more than a column chart. You can combine multiple dot plots to show how an observation changes over one variable, like time, and compare that change to other categories. This allows you to see how the data spreads out over that variable.

Case Study: Production Output

You group the production employees at your manufacturing plant by tenure. The groups are less than one year, one to three years, three to five years, and greater than five years. You want to see how many products each group produces per hour.

NOTE The workbook for this case study is `DotPlotProductionOutput.xlsx` and can be found at www.wiley.com/go/datavizwithexcel.

Excel does not have a native dot plot chart type. Creating this type of chart is a little tedious. In addition to your raw data, you will need three data staging areas to get the data into a form to populate your charts. For this case study, you will be creating four different charts.

A portion of the raw data is shows in Figure 7.40. It consists of a tenure column, a units produced column, and a count column for how many times someone with that tenure produced that many units.

	A	B	C	D
1	Tenure	Units	Count	
2	<1 yr	1	0	
3	<1 yr	2	2	
4	<1 yr	3	10	
5	<1 yr	4	7	
6	<1 yr	5	4	
7	<1 yr	6	1	
8	<1 yr	7	0	
9	<1 yr	8	0	
10	1 -3 yrs	1	0	
11	1 -3 yrs	2	0	
12	1 -3 yrs	3	2	
13	1 -3 yrs	4	8	
14	1 -3 yrs	5	9	
15	1 -3 yrs	6	5	
16	1 -3 yrs	7	0	
17	1 -3 yrs	8	0	
18	3 - 5 yrs	1	0	
19	3 - 5 yrs	2	0	
20	3 - 5 yrs	3	0	
21	3 - 5 yrs	4	2	
22	3 - 5 yrs	5	10	

Figure 7.40: Raw data for units produced

The first step in creating a dot plot chart is to create a dummy series for your category axis. Since no one produces more than eight units per hour, create a range with the numbers one through eight and a row of zeros underneath it, as shown in Figure 7.41.

G	H	I	J	K	L	M	N
1	2	3	4	5	6	7	8
0	0	0	0	0	0	0	0

Figure 7.41: Dummy series for the category axis

For each of the four charts, you'll create an X values staging area and a Y values staging area. Below your dummy series, create a range with the same number of columns as the dummy series and as many rows as you'll need, plus a few extra. For this data, the most observations you made was ten, so make the range at least twelve rows to allow for future expansion. In the top left cell of your range, enter the formula =G$1, fill the formula down twelve rows, then fill all twelve rows to the right eight columns. Figure 7.42 shows the dummy series and the X values staging area just below it.

=G$1

G	H	I	J	K	L	M	N
1	2	3	4	5	6	7	8
0	0	0	0	0	0	0	0
1	2	3	4	5	6	7	8
1	2	3	4	5	6	7	8
1	2	3	4	5	6	7	8
1	2	3	4	5	6	7	8
1	2	3	4	5	6	7	8
1	2	3	4	5	6	7	8
1	2	3	4	5	6	7	8
1	2	3	4	5	6	7	8
1	2	3	4	5	6	7	8
1	2	3	4	5	6	7	8
1	2	3	4	5	6	7	8
1	2	3	4	5	6	7	8

Figure 7.42: Staging area for X values

You'll use the X values staging areas for all four charts. The Y values staging areas will be different for each chart. Create the Y values staging area for the first chart below your X values staging area, leaving at least one blank row between them. Enter the formula =G17+MIN(OFFSET($C$2,COLUMN()-7,0)-G17,1) in the top left cell of the Y values staging area range and fill the formula down twelve rows and across eight columns. The formula starts with the cell just above and adds one until it reaches the total count for that column. Once it reaches the total count, it simply repeats that number. Excel will still plot those repeating numbers, but the dots will be placed on top of each other and will appear as a single dot. Figure 7.43 shows the Y values staging area for the first chart.

=G17+MIN(OFFSET($C$2,COLUMN()-7,0)-G17,1)

E	F	G	H	I	J	K	L	M	N
		1	2	3	4	5	6	7	8
		0	0	0	0	0	0	0	0
		1	2	3	4	5	6	7	8
		1	2	3	4	5	6	7	8
		1	2	3	4	5	6	7	8
		1	2	3	4	5	6	7	8
		1	2	3	4	5	6	7	8
		1	2	3	4	5	6	7	8
		1	2	3	4	5	6	7	8
		1	2	3	4	5	6	7	8
		1	2	3	4	5	6	7	8
		1	2	3	4	5	6	7	8
		1	2	3	4	5	6	7	8
		0	1	1	1	1	1	0	0
		0	2	2	2	2	1	0	0
		0	2	3	3	3	1	0	0
		0	2	4	4	4	1	0	0
		0	2	5	5	4	1	0	0
		0	2	6	6	4	1	0	0
		0	2	7	7	4	1	0	0
		0	2	8	7	4	1	0	0
		0	2	9	7	4	1	0	0
		0	2	10	7	4	1	0	0
		0	2	10	7	4	1	0	0
		0	2	10	7	4	1	0	0

Figure 7.43: Staging area for Y values

Before you create the Y value staging areas for the other charts, create the first chart to make sure it will look like you want. When you create multiple charts, get the formatting for the first one right so you can copy it and have minimal changes to the remaining charts.

To create the first chart, select the dummy series range (G1:N2), choose Insert ⇨ Charts ⇨ Recommended Charts, and choose the Clustered Column chart type. You'll get a chart similar to the one shown in Figure 7.44.

Figure 7.44: A column chart with the dummy series

Next, add a new series to your chart. Right-click anywhere in the chart and choose Select Data. The chart contains one series, the dummy series, and you'll add eight more. Click the Add button to display the Edit Series dialog box. Set the series name to the top-left cell of your dummy series, cell G1 in this example, and leave the series value as ={1}. Click OK to dismiss the Edit Series dialog and click OK again to dismiss the Select Data Source dialog. Your chart should look similar to Figure 7.45.

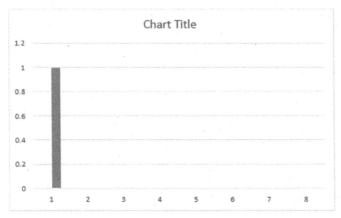

Figure 7.45: Adding a new series

The new series you added is a column type series and you need to change it to an XY Scatter type series. Right-click on the column in the chart and choose Change Series Chart Type. In the drop-down for the series labeled 1, choose Scatter with no lines as shown in Figure 7.46.

Now that the series is XY Scatter, you'll have more options in the Edit Series dialog. Right-click in the chart and choose Select Data. Select the series labeled 1 and click Edit. Complete the Edit Series dialog box as shown in Figure 7.47. The X values will come from your X values staging area and the Y values from your Y values staging area.

Dismiss the dialog boxes by clicking OK. Your chart shows the new series with a single dot at zero. It's actually 12 dots at zero all on top of each other. To add the next series, right-click on the chart and choose Select Data. Excel guesses correctly that you want to add another XY Scatter series, so you don't have to repeat the steps where you added a column series and changed it to XY Scatter. Complete the Edit Series dialog for the second series as shown in Figure 7.48.

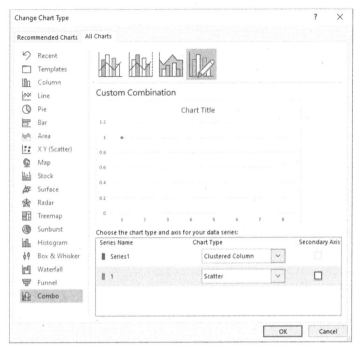

Figure 7.46: Changing the series chart type

Figure 7.47: Setting the X and Y series values

Follow those same steps to add the remaining six series, each pointing to the next column of values in the respective staging areas. You don't have to dismiss the Select Data dialog box each time. Simply continue clicking the Add button to add the next series. When you've added all eight XY Scatter series, your chart should look like the one in Figure 7.49.

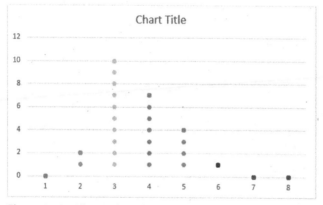

1	2	3	4	5	6	7	8
1	2	3	4	5	6	7	8
1	2	3	4	5	6	7	8
1	2	3	4	5	6	7	8
1	2	3	4	5	6	7	8
1	2						8
1	2						8

Edit Series   ? ×

Series name:
=SecondSeries!$H$1   ↥ = 2

Series X values:
=SecondSeries!$H$5:$H$16   ↥ = 2, 2, 2, 2, 2,...

Series Y values:
=SecondSeries!$H$18:$H$29   ↥ = 1, 2, 2, 2, 2,...

OK   Cancel

0	1						0
0	2						0
0	2						0
0	2						0
0	2						0
0	2						0
0	2						0
0	2	8	7	4	1	0	0
0	2	9	7	4	1	0	0
0	2	10	7	4	1	0	0
0	2	10	7	4	1	0	0
0	2	10	7	4	1	0	0

Figure 7.48: Setting the X and Y value for the next series

Chart Title

Figure 7.49: All series have been added to the chart.

Complete the following steps to format the chart. Once the formatting is complete, you'll make copies of this chart, so all the formatting should be just the way you want it.

1. Select the chart title and press the Delete key to remove it.

2. Right-click on the first series and choose Format Data Series. Choose Fill and Line and Marker in the Format Data Series task pane. Change the fill color to black and the border color to black.

3. Repeat changing the fill and border colors to black for the other series.

4. Select the vertical axis and change the Minimum value to **1.0** under Axis Options to hide the zero values.

5. In the Chart Elements dialog, choose Axes Titles and add a title for the vertical axis, as shown in Figure 7.50.

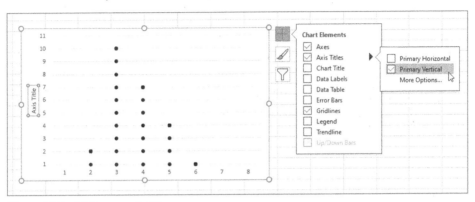

Figure 7.50: Adding an axis title

6. Select the axis title you just created, click in Excel's formula bar, type an equal sign, and select a cell from the raw data range that contains <1 yr, such as cell A2.

7. Using the top, middle fill handle, reduce the height of the chart to a desired height.

Once the formatting is complete, your chart will look similar to Figure 7.51.

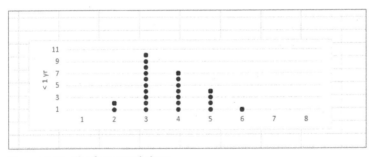

Figure 7.51: The formatted chart

When the first chart's formatting is complete, make three copies of it. Select the chart and press Ctrl+C to copy it. Select any cell in the worksheet and press Ctrl+V to paste a copy of the chart. Do that two more times so that you have four identical charts. Figure 7.52 shows all four charts.

TIP   When copying a chart, don't press Ctrl+V while the chart is still selected or Excel will add more series to the existing chart rather than making a copy of it.

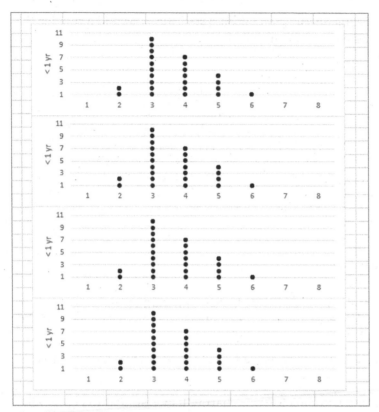

Figure 7.52: Four charts aligned vertically

Create three more staging areas for your newly created copies. Below the Y values staging area for the first chart, enter the formula `=G30+MIN(OFFSET ($C$10,COLUMN()-7,0)-G30,1)` and fill down twelve rows and across eight columns. Continue creating Y values staging areas until you have four. Each formula is slightly different because the values start at a different place in the raw data. A zoomed-out view of the spreadsheet is shown in Figure 7.53. It shows the dummy staging area in G1:N2, the X values staging area for all four charts below that, and each Y values staging area lower on the spreadsheet.

Change the data series in the new charts you just created. Start by right-clicking the second chart and choosing Select Data. For each series except the dummy series, click the Edit button and change the Y values range to point to that chart's Y values staging area.

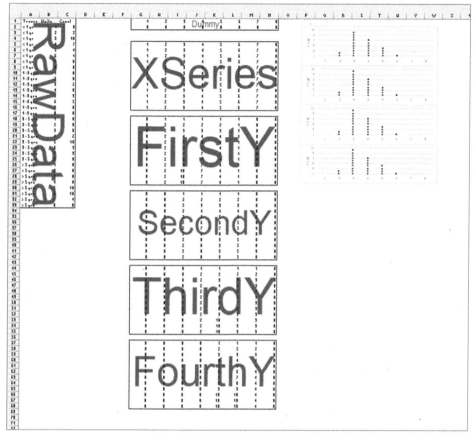

Figure 7.53: A zoomed-out view of the staging areas

Dismiss the Select Data dialog by clicking OK after you've changed each series. Select the axis title for the vertical axis and change the formula in Excel's formula bar to point to the appropriate cell in the raw data.

Finally, add a chart title to the top chart only. From the Chart Elements menu, choose Chart Title. Resize the top chart so that the plot area is the same size as the other charts. The final four charts are shown in Figure 7.54.

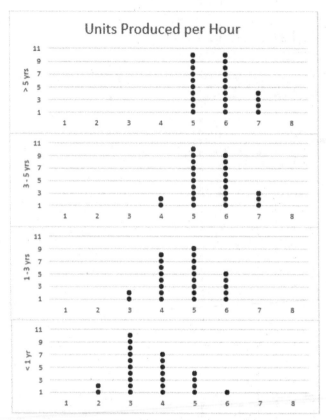

Figure 7.54: The final four dot plot charts

The final four-chart panel demonstrates that units produced per hour increase until a production employee has three years of experience and that there isn't much difference between the longest-tenure categories.

CHAPTER 8

Visualizing Parts of a Whole

In This Chapter

- Pie Charts
- Doughnut Charts
- Waffle Charts
- Sunburst Charts
- Histograms
- Treemaps
- Waterfall Charts

The chart types described in this chapter are used to demonstrate how component parts make up a whole, the relationship between components of a whole, and the cumulative effect of parts on a total. The chart type that is right for you depends on your data, the point you're trying to make, and the amount of space you have.

Pie Charts

The classic parts-of-a-whole chart is the pie chart. Pie charts have a reputation for being abused by, for example, including too many data points or making the charts 3D. If used properly, however, pie charts can be an effective visualization element. Figure 8.1 shows an example of a pie chart.

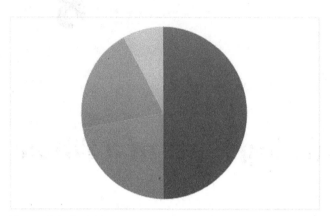

Figure 8.1: A pie chart

NOTE   The charts in the figures for this chapter can be found on this book's companion website at www.wiley.com/go/datavizwithexcel. Each case study has its own file containing all its charts. You can find the names of those files in the sections containing the case studies.

If you want to tell the story that blue is half of the total, the chart in Figure 8.1 will do fine. For an effective pie chart, you must have a limited number of data points. Six data points is the maximum number I will put on a pie chart. It's also helpful if the most prominent data points are near where 3, 6, or 9 would be if the pie chart were a clock face. If you're accustomed to reading analog clocks, you will probably find that angles near 25% and 50% are easier to interpret.

A legitimate complaint about pie charts is that they can be hard to label. If you have a lot of data points or if any of the data points are small, it's difficult to fit labels near the chart. You might resort to leader lines or a legend, causing the reader to do more work to associate the label with its related pie slice.

If you have a lot of data points, a pie chart might still be a viable option. You can group smaller data points into an "other" category to reduce the slices of the pie. Figure 8.2 shows two pie charts. The chart on the right groups the smaller data points.

The rest of the charts in this chapter can be used to visualize parts of a whole while addressing some of the complaints about pie charts.

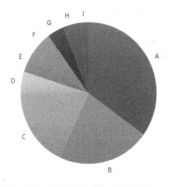
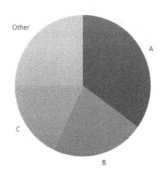

Figure 8.2: Grouping smaller data points

Doughnut Charts

Doughnut charts are pie charts with a hole in the middle. If you believe that interpreting areas or angles makes a pie chart hard to read, a doughnut chart fixes it by removing that part of the pie chart. For me, there is no real advantage to a doughnut chart over a pie chart, and I apply all the same constraints to both chart types, such as limiting the number points and avoiding small data points.

The extra white space in a doughnut chart can have an advantage. You can put the chart title in the middle of the chart to save space or you can put some data labels on the inside and some on the outside. Figure 8.3 shows a doughnut chart with the title and some of the data labels inside the doughnut.

Figure 8.3: Placing text inside a doughnut chart

When choosing a chart type, keep in mind the story you intend to tell with the data. If you want to demonstrate how each data point relates to the others, a column or bar chart is the proper choice. On the other hand, to highlight how one product relates to the total, a doughnut chart works better.

Case Study: Sales by Region

Your company sells products in four regions of the United States. You want to show how each region's sales contribute to the sales of the entire US division. The sales data by region is shown in Figure 8.4.

	A	B	C
1	Region	Sales	
2	Northeast	$ 2,942,714	
3	South and Texas	$ 1,389,021	
4	Midwest	$ 1,297,839	
5	Great Plains	$ 823,275	
6			

Figure 8.4: Sales dollars by region

NOTE   The workbook for this case study is `DoughnutSalesbyRegion.xlsx` and can be found at www.wiley.com/go/datavizwithexcel.

To create the doughnut chart, follow these steps:

1. Select your data and choose Recommended Charts from the Insert tab on the Ribbon.

2. Select the All Charts tab on the Insert Chart dialog.

3. Select the Pie gallery on the left.

4. Select the Doughnut chart type and click OK. Figure 8.5 shows the Insert Chart dialog box.

5. From the on-chart Chart Styles button, choose a chart style. Style 5 is used in this example and is shown in Figure 8.6.

6. Change the chart title to **Sales by Region**.

7. Right-click on the doughnut and choose Add Data Labels.

8. Right-click on any of the data labels and choose Format Data Labels to show the Format Data Labels task pane.

9. On the Format Data Labels task pane in the Label Options section, check Category Name and Percentage and uncheck Value.

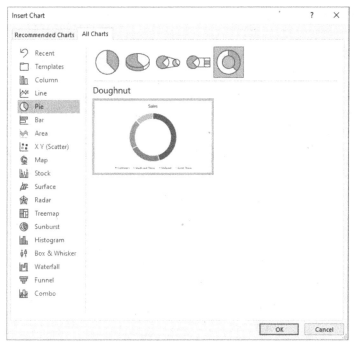

Figure 8.5: The Insert Chart dialog box

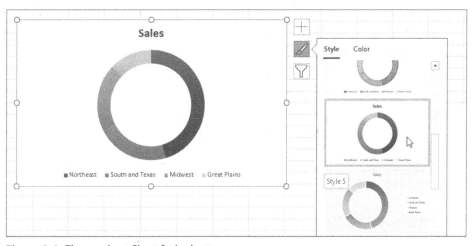

Figure 8.6: The on-chart Chart Styles button

10. On the Text Options tab, change the color of the data label text to something lighter so it stands out against the chart colors.

11. With the data labels still selected, click the Bold tool on the Ribbon's Home tab.

12. Select the legend showing the categories and press the Delete key to hide it.

13. Right-click the doughnut, choose Format Data Series, and change the Doughnut Hole Size value to a smaller percentage. Make the doughnut width large enough that the labels fit comfortably inside.

Figure 8.7 shows the final doughnut chart. It's easy to see how each region contributes to the sales of the whole division.

Figure 8.7: Sales by Region doughnut chart

Waffle Charts

Waffle charts are made up of boxes arranged in a grid. The data points are represented by coloring the number of boxes representing a data point, either as a percentage or the actual value. Some readers prefer waffle charts to circular-style charts because the rectangular areas are easier to compare. An example of a waffle chart is shown in Figure 8.8.

A typical use for waffle charts is to show one data point in relation to the whole. These waffle charts, like the one in Figure 8.8, are drawn as 100 equally sized boxes. The data point is converted to a percentage and that percentage of boxes is filled in. Other waffle charts don't use 100 boxes but use a number representing the actual total. Figure 8.9 shows a waffle chart where a box represents each of 632 retail outlets of a convenience store chain. The data points show which stores sell gas, diesel, or no fuel.

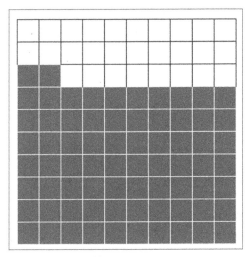

Figure 8.8: A waffle chart

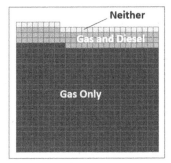

Figure 8.9: Retail outlets by fuel type

Waffle charts have one of the same disadvantages as a stacked column chart. It's difficult to compare one data point to another because they don't start at the same place. But for comparing one data point to the whole, it is an effective and visually appealing chart type.

Case Study: Employee Participation by Benefit

The Human Resources department would like to determine which employee benefits are being used. They provide you with the data in Figure 8.10 showing the number of employees enrolled in each benefit and the total number of employees. You decide to create a waffle chart for each benefit and display them side by side.

NOTE   The workbook for this case study is `WaffleEmployeeBenefits.xlsx` and can be found at www.wiley.com/go/datavizwithexcel.

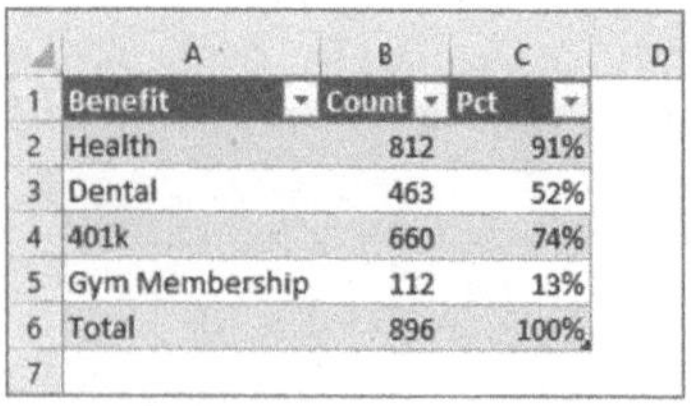

Benefit	Count	Pct
Health	812	91%
Dental	463	52%
401k	660	74%
Gym Membership	112	13%
Total	896	100%

Figure 8.10: Employee benefit use data

To create the waffle charts, follow these steps:

1. Add a new column to the table to calculate the percentage with the formula `=ROUNDUP([@Count]/$B$6,2)`.
2. Select columns E:AU and change the column width to 20 pixels by dragging the column heading border to the left.
3. In cell E10, enter the formula `=ROUND(N11+0.01,2)`.
4. In cell F10, enter the formula `=ROUND(E10+0.01,2)` and fill to the right for nine columns (to column N).
5. Fill E10:N10 down to create a 10x10 grid of formulas as shown in Figure 8.11.

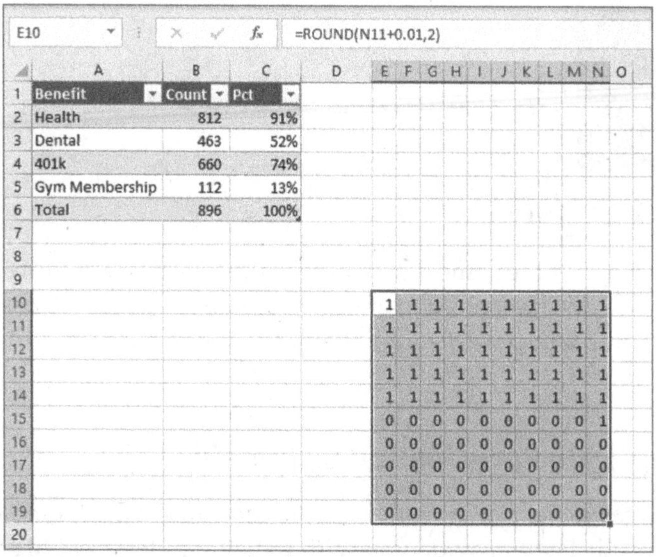

Figure 8.11: The 10x10 grid of formulas

6. Change the font color in E10:N10 to white using Home ➪ Font ➪ Font Color on the Ribbon.

7. Change the border color to dark blue. With the range still selected, choose More Borders from Home ➪ Font ➪ Borders. Choose dark blue from the Color drop-down and click the Outline and Inside buttons. Figure 8.12 shows the Border tab of the Format Cells dialog.

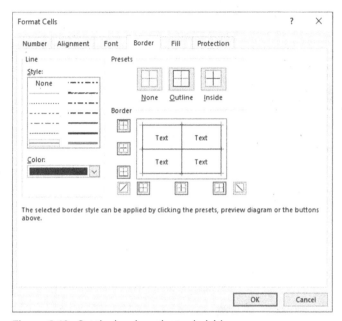

Figure 8.12: Set the border color to dark blue.

8. Choose New Rule from Home ➪ Conditional Formatting to show the New Formatting Rule dialog box.

9. Choose Format Only Cells That Contain from the Select A Rule Type list.

10. Choose Cell Value and Less Than Or Equal To from the Edit The Rule Description section of the dialog and enter =$C$2.

11. Click the Format button and set the fill to dark blue, the font color to dark blue, and the left and bottom border color to white. Click OK. The New Formatting Rule dialog is shown in Figure 8.13 and the resulting chart is shown in Figure 8.14.

12. Copy the 10x10 grid to cell P10 to create the next waffle chart.

13. With the range P10:Y10 still selected, select Manage Rules from Home ➪ Conditional Formatting from the Ribbon. Change the rule to point to =$C$3. Figure 8.15 shows the resulting two charts.

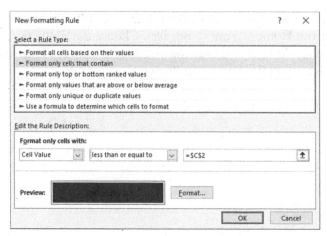

Figure 8.13: Create the conditional formatting rule.

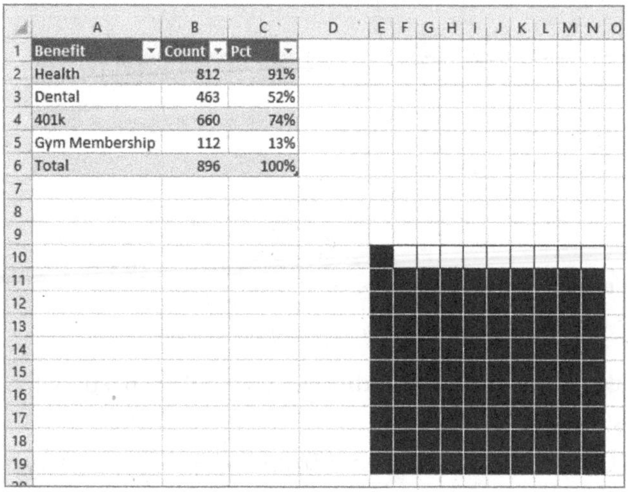

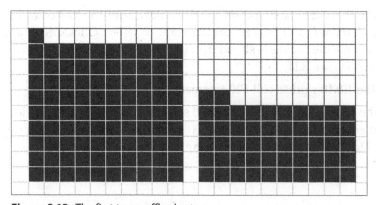

Figure 8.14: The conditionally formatted range

Figure 8.15: The first two waffle charts

14. Repeat the process by copying one of the 10x10 grids to cells AA10 and AM10 and changing the Conditional Formatting rule to point to the correct cell in the table.

15. Hide the gridlines by unchecking Gridlines on the View tab of the Ribbon.

16. Label the charts. In cell E21, enter the formula =A2. Select cells E21:N21 and show the Format Cells dialog by pressing Ctrl+1. Change Font Style to Bold, Size to 16, Color to dark blue, and Horizontal Alignment to Center Across Selection.

17. Repeat the process to label the other three charts. Figure 8.16 shows the final four waffle charts.

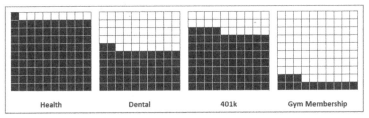

Figure 8.16: Employee benefits waffle charts

The visualization shows that the gym membership benefit is the least used benefit. Human Resources may choose to cancel the benefit, raise awareness to increase enrollment, or increase the value of the benefit.

Sunburst Charts

Sunburst charts consist of two or more concentric doughnut charts. The innermost layer is a standard doughnut chart. Each outer layer is a subset of the layer just inside it. Use a sunburst chart when you have hierarchical data and you want to show how each data point relates to the data point above it in the hierarchy. Figure 8.17 shows a typical sunburst chart.

Because the innermost layer is a doughnut chart, it is subject to the same constraints as a doughnut chart, namely limiting the number of data points and avoiding very small data points. With sunburst charts, not all inner layers have to have an outer layer. Figure 8.18 shows a sunburst chart where only one of the inner layers is extended outward. This is useful when you want to draw attention to one aspect of the hierarchy.

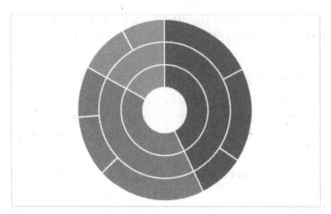

Figure 8.17: A sunburst chart

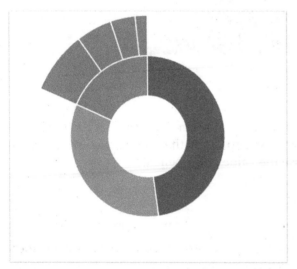

Figure 8.18: A sunburst chart with an incomplete hierarchy

Figure 8.19 shows the data that drives the chart in Figure 8.18. The data contains only one column of values (column C in this example). The "a" portion on the right is assigned the value 283. The "b" portion on the top left is the sum of all the values for "bba" through "bbd." You can repeat the "b" label in column A or leave them blank as in Figure 8.19. Whether you fill them or leave them blank, they must be all together. That is, you can't have another "b" below the "c" label or Excel will assume it's another data point.

Case Study: Manufacturing Process Time Study

The Production department completed a time-motion study for its production process. You've been assigned to create a dashboard element that shows how each process contributes to its parent process. The results of the study are shown in Figure 8.20.

⬠	A	B	C	D
2	a		283	
3	b	bba	20	
4		bbb	50	
5		bbc	30	
6		bbd	10	
7	c		199	
8				

Figure 8.19: Data layout for a sunburst chart

⬠	A	B	C	D
1	**Process**	**SubProcess**	**Detail**	**Time**
2	Preproduction	Procurement	Quoting	1:00:00
3			Purchasing	0:40:00
4		Staging		0:24:00
5	Production	Cutting		0:16:00
6		Milling		0:22:00
7		Deburring		0:08:00
8		Assembly		3:14:00
9	Post-Production	Sanding		1:12:00
10		Painting		4:33:00
11		Packaging		0:27:00
12				

Figure 8.20: Time-motion study results

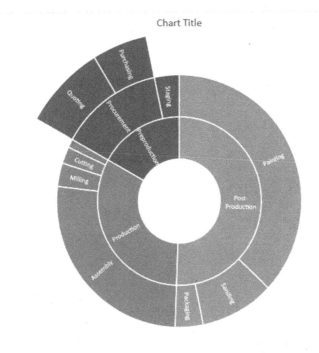

Figure 8.21: Excel's initial sunburst chart

NOTE   The workbook for this case study is `SunburstProcessTimeStudy.xlsx` and can be found at www.wiley.com/go/datavizwithexcel.

Sunburst is a built-in chart type, so creating one is easy. To create a sunburst chart, select the data and click Recommended Charts on the Insert tab of the Ribbon. On the Insert Chart dialog's All Charts tab, select Sunburst.

If your data labels are more than a few characters, Excel's initial chart is difficult to read. Excel shortens the data labels for some data points and leaves them off entirely for others. You can increase the size of the chart, as shown in Figure 8.21, until most of the labels are shown and fit.

Unfortunately, Excel doesn't give you many options when it comes to data labels on a sunburst chart. You can change what text the labels contain or how the text is formatted, but you can't move the data labels or add leader lines. If you determine that the sunburst chart is too large for your dashboard, the best option is to choose another chart type.

Histograms

Histograms are visually similar to column charts. Where column charts plot two variables, a category axis and a value axis, a histogram plots one continuous variable. Figure 8.22 shows an example of a histogram.

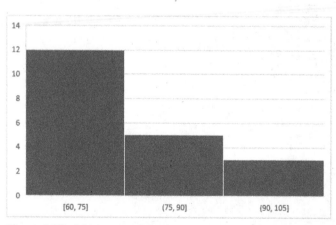

Figure 8.22: A histogram chart

A histogram takes one continuous-variable data set and divides it into bins. The chart shows the count of data points that fall into each bin. In the chart in Figure 8.22, Excel has automatically divided the data into three bins. Of the 20 data points, 12 fall into the bin of data points between 60 and 75, 5 fall between 75 and 90, and 3 fall between 90 and 105.

The value axis is always a count of data points in each bin. You can configure the category axis to control the bins. Figure 8.23 shows the Axis Options on the Format Axis task pane.

Figure 8.23: The Format Axis task pane for a histogram

What follows is an explanation of the options in the Format Axis task pane:

- **By Category:** By default, Excel groups the numerical data into bins and displays the range for each bin. If your data is already in bins, you can choose this option and include a column of bin names. Rather than count the number of data points, Excel sums the values. Figure 8.24 shows an example of a histogram formatted by category.

- **Automatic:** Excel automatically bins the data according to a formula known as *Scott's normal reference rule*. The formula is 3.5 times the standard deviation divided by the cube root of the population. Fortunately for people who struggle with those mathematical principles, the formula is automated. Its goal is to minimize the integral of the error of each bin to the mean.

- **Bin width:** Allows you to manually set the range of data points in each bin. The number of bins will be calculated based on the data and the bin width.

- **Number of bins:** Allows you to manually set the number of bins. The bin width will be calculated based on the data and the number of bins.

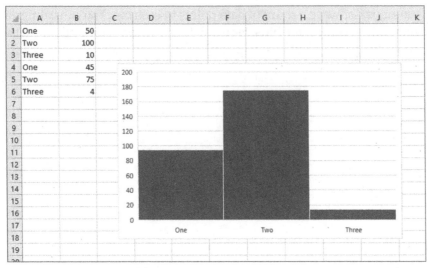

Figure 8.24: A histogram formatted by category

- **Overflow bin:** Allows you to set the right-most bin to be all data points over the number you specify. The default overflow number is three standard deviations.

- **Underflow bin:** Allows you to set the left-most bin to be all data points under the number you specify. The default underflow number is three standard deviations.

Case Study: Restaurant Ticket Totals

Your restaurant manager wants to know how much diners are spending when they visit the restaurant. She provides you with all the tickets for a month, a partial list of which is shown in Figure 8.25. You decide to create a histogram to visualize the data.

> **NOTE** The workbook for this case study is `HistogramRestaurant.xlsx` and can be found at www.wiley.com/go/datavizwithexcel.

To create a histogram, select the data and choose Insert ⇨ Recommended Charts from the Ribbon. On the All Charts tab, choose the Histogram chart type. Only select the data in column B. You're only plotting the continuous variable, ticket total, so you don't need the data in column A. Figure 8.26 shows Excel's initial histogram with a chart title added.

The data shows that tickets between 28.85 and 47.45 are the most common. Those bins aren't very intuitive for the restaurant manager, so you decide to customize them. Right-click on the category axis and choose Format Axis to display the Format Axis task pane.

◢	A	B
1	Date	Total
2	9/1/2020	30.02
3	9/1/2020	33.24
4	9/1/2020	39.43
5	9/1/2020	30.57
6	9/1/2020	36.76
7	9/1/2020	37.61
8	9/1/2020	42.60
9	9/1/2020	30.35
10	9/1/2020	35.82
11	9/1/2020	36.83
12	9/1/2020	30.86
13	9/1/2020	41.89
14	9/1/2020	34.72
15	9/1/2020	37.37
16	9/1/2020	42.64
17	9/1/2020	52.42
18	9/1/2020	54.67
19	9/1/2020	74.43
20	9/1/2020	71.61
21	9/1/2020	74.78

Figure 8.25: A partial list of tickets for a month

Figure 8.26: Histogram of restaurant tickets

On the Format Axis task pane, set the bin width to **10** to show ticket bins in $10 increments. Check the Overflow Bin and Underflow Bin check boxes and group all tickets over **$85** and **$30**, respectively. In the Number section, change the decimal places to **zero**. The final histogram is shown in Figure 8.27.

The restaurant manager has determined that the target ticket price is $42. While the average of all ticket prices is higher than the target, the largest number of tickets still falls below this number. She may decide to raise prices or replace certain lower-priced menu items with higher-priced items.

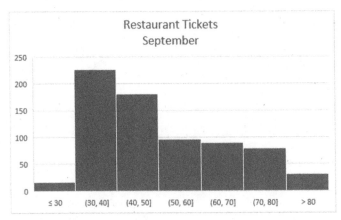

Figure 8.27: Custom bins on a histogram

Treemap Charts

Treemaps are logically similar to sunburst charts. They are used to plot hierarchical data. Where a sunburst chart shows the hierarchy radiating from a central point, the treemap uses rectangles. Larger rectangles are divided into smaller ones. Figure 8.28 shows an example of a treemap chart.

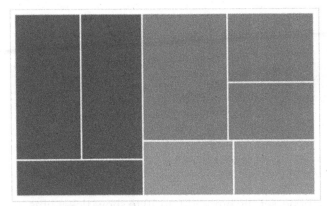

Figure 8.28: A treemap chart

Treemaps are useful for comparing how data points in a hierarchy contribute to each point's parent data point. They're not useful for comparing a data point to one of its peers. A column or bar chart is better suited to comparing peers because they start from a common place.

The data staging format for a treemap is identical to a sunburst chart. In fact, the data that drives the treemap in Figure 8.28 is the same data used for the sunburst chart in Figure 8.17. Some people believe that interpreting rectangles is easier than interpreting circles. You can compare these two figures to see if you agree.

Another trait common between treemaps and sunbursts is that the hierarchy doesn't have to be complete. That is, not every level of the hierarchy must have child data points. Figure 8.29 shows a treemap where only one of the top-level data points, the one labeled "b" in this example, has lower-level data points.

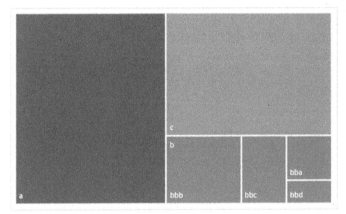

Figure 8.29: A treemap with an incomplete hierarchy

Treemaps have one additional series option that sunburst charts don't have. There are three options for displaying labels, as follows:

- **None:** If a data point has child data points, the label for the parent data point is not displayed. Only the lowest-level data points are displayed throughout the chart.

- **Overlapping:** The parent data point label is shown within one of the child data points. The treemap in Figure 8.29 displays both the "b" data point label and labels for all of its children.

- **Banner:** The parent data point label is shown in its own box that spans the child data point boxes, like a banner. The treemap in Figure 8.30 shows the "b" data point label in its own banner box above its children data points.

Case Study: Insurance Policy Averages

Your insurance company wants to see a breakdown of policies it has written in the last year. You compile the data shown in Figure 8.31 for all the policies written.

Treemaps are a built-in chart type in Excel, making them very easy to create. Simply select the data and choose Recommended Charts from the Insert tab on the Ribbon. If treemap is not one of the recommended chart types for your data set, select it from the All Charts tab.

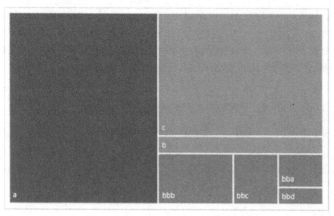

Figure 8.30: Displaying labels with the Banner option

▲	A	B	C	D
1	Class	Type	Premiums	
2	Health	High Deductible	$ 2,724,127	
3		Low Deductible	$ 4,171,177	
4	Life	Whole	$ 5,035,135	
5		Term	$ 1,140,959	
6		Universal	$ 3,137,519	
7	Disability	Long Term	$ 2,107,242	
8		Short Term	$ 1,011,074	
9				

Figure 8.31: Insurance policy data by class and type

NOTE   The workbook for this case study is `TreemapInsurancePolicies.xlsx` and can be found at www.wiley.com/go/datavizwithexcel.

To create the final treemap in Figure 8.32, add a chart title and remove the legend from Excel's default treemap chart. To add a chart title, click on the chart title and start typing. To remove the legend, click Chart Tools Design ⇨ Add Chart Element ⇨ Legend ⇨ None.

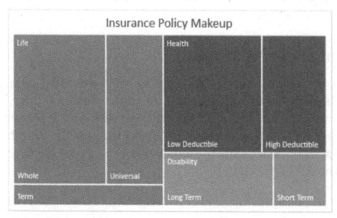

Figure 8.32: Insurance policy breakdown treemap

The treemap shows a lot of information in a compact space. You can see, among other things, that life insurance premiums are roughly half of all premiums and that whole life policies are the majority of those.

Waterfall Charts

Waterfall charts are an excellent way to show parts of a whole. They are particularly useful to show the cumulative effect of increases and decreases. Some of the other chart types discussed in this chapter use clever tricks to display negative values, but none of them compare to waterfall charts in this regard. Figure 8.33 shows a typical waterfall chart.

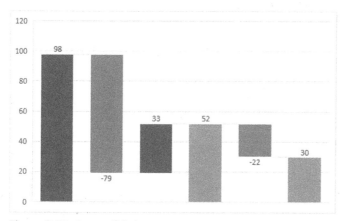

Figure 8.33: A waterfall chart

The first data point in a waterfall chart starts at zero and extends upward or downward depending on its value. You can designate certain data points as totals and they will start at zero also. Even if your data contains formulas, Excel will not automatically detect those data points as totals. Each of the other data points floats in the chart area extending from the data point on its left.

Most waterfall charts have connecting lines showing how the starting point of a data point relates to the ending point of the one to its left. You may find connecting lines unnecessary, particularly if you display values in the data labels.

Waterfall charts excel at showing how positive and negative data points contribute to the total. But they are also useful when most or all your data points go in the same direction. Figure 8.34 shows a waterfall chart that visualizes the change in sales from one year to the next by quarter. Figure 8.35 is a waterfall chart that shows how mortgage payments affect the balance over the life of the loan.

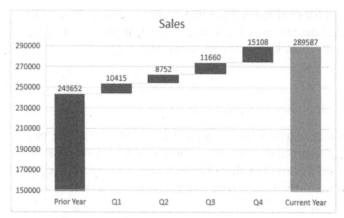

Figure 8.34: A waterfall chart to show the change in sales

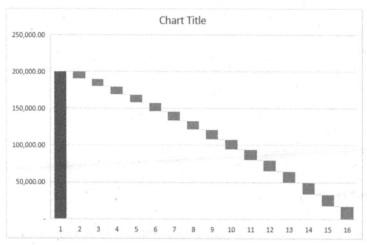

Figure 8.35: A waterfall chart of a mortgage loan

The waterfall chart type was introduced in Excel 2016. Prior to that, creating waterfall charts was a tedious process. They were made with a stacked column chart where some data points where hidden to create the floating column effect. While the built-in waterfall chart type has made creating these charts far simpler, they do have some limitations.

The most glaring limitation is that built-in waterfalls are always vertical. There is no way to show the data points as floating bars rather than floating columns. The data labels are also limited in that you can't display the value as a percentage. You can change your data to plot the percentages if you prefer that presentation, but you can't do both.

Case Study: Net Income

Management wants to include a visualization of the income statement in this year's annual report. The income statement data is shown in Figure 8.36.

	A	B
1	Sales	28,563,421
2	Cost of Sales	(17,423,687)
3	Gross Margin	11,139,734
4	Selling, General, and Admin	(8,283,392)
5	Operating Profit	2,856,342
6	Interest Expense	(1,258,769)
7	Misc. Income	623,487
8	Net Profit	2,221,060
9		

Figure 8.36: Income statement data

NOTE The workbook for this case study is `WaterfallNetIncome.xlsx` and can be found at www.wiley.com/go/datavizwithexcel.

To create the income statement waterfall chart, follow these steps:

1. Select the data and choose Insert ➪ Recommended Charts from the Ribbon.

2. From the All Charts tab, select Waterfall and click OK.

3. Select the Gross Margin data point. To select a single data point, click it once to select the whole series and click the same data point a second time to select only that data point.

4. Right-click the Gross Margin data point and choose Format Data Point to display the Format Data Point task pane.

5. Check the Set As Total check box.

6. Check the Set As Total check box for the Operating Profit and Net Profit data points. Once you have a single data point selected, you can select another data point and you don't have to select the whole series first. Figure 8.37 shows the chart at this stage.

7. Select any data label to show the Format Data Labels task pane. In the Label Options section, change the number format to * #,###,;* (#,###,).

8. Delete the vertical axis by selecting it and pressing the Delete key.

9. Delete the legend by selecting it and pressing the Delete key.

10. Change the title to **Income Statement (in thousands)**.

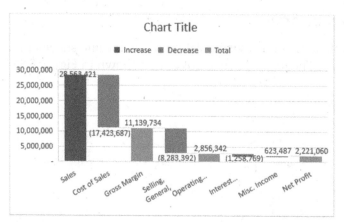

Figure 8.37: The waterfall chart with totals set

11. Add a line break to the Selling, General, and Admin label. In cell A4, place your cursor before **and** and press Alt+Enter.

12. Resize the chart so that the category axis labels are legible. The final chart is shown in Figure 8.38.

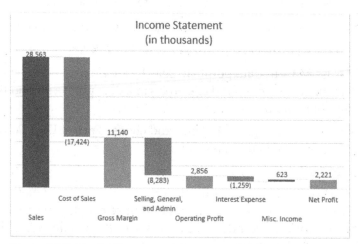

Figure 8.38: The final income statement waterfall chart

You want to present management with a second option that shows percentage data labels instead of dollars. Start by entering the formula =B1/$B$1 in cell C1 and fill down to cell C8. Format C1:C8 as a percentage with two decimal places.

To create the second chart, select the range A1:A8, hold down the Ctrl key, and select the range C1:C8, leaving column B unselected. Then insert a waterfall chart following the steps used to create the first chart. Format the chart to look like the first chart, including setting the Gross Margin, Operating Profit, and Net Profit data points as totals; deleting the vertical axis and legend; changing the chart's title; and resizing the chart to the same size. Figure 8.39 shows the income statement waterfall chart with percentage labels instead of dollars.

Figure 8.39: The income statement waterfall chart with percentage

Visualizing Changes Over Time

In This Chapter

- Line Charts
- Column Charts with Variances
- Combination Charts
- Line Charts with Differences
- Side-by-Side Box Plots
- Animated Charts
- Chart Automation

Visualizing changes over time is one of the most effective uses of charts. Almost any value that is interesting becomes more interesting when you show what happened to it over time. Plotting values on a time scale can show seasonality, growth, reductions, and trends to help predict the future. In addition to using time as the category axis, you can animate a chart to show how the data in an otherwise static chart changes over time.

Line Charts

Line charts are the most common way to show how a value changes over time. They are so closely associated with time that a reader will likely assume a line chart's category axis is time. Figure 9.1 shows an example of a line chart.

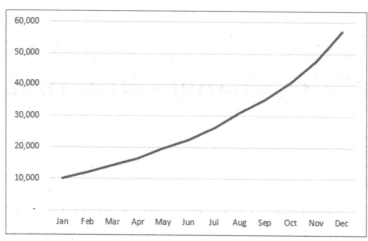

Figure 9.1: A line chart

As I described in Chapter 7, "Visualizing Performance Comparisons," line charts have a lot of the same characteristics as XY charts. They both can show lines, markers, both lines and markers, or neither. The category axis for a time-based line chart is ordered and at regular intervals. That is, time increases along the axis from left to right and each point along the axis represents the same amount of time (a week, a month, or a year, for example).

> **NOTE**   The charts in the figures for this chapter can be found on this book's companion website at www.wiley.com/go/datavizwithexcel. Each case study has its own file containing all its charts. You can find the names of those files in the sections containing the case studies..

Unlike some of the newer chart types Excel offers, line charts have a lot of configuration options. Figure 9.2 shows the line options in the Format Data Series task pane.

Most of the line options are self-explanatory. You can set the line to No Line and the markers to Solid to show only the data points. If you have multiple data series and you want to highlight one of them, you can increase the transparency of the other series. The line chart in Figure 9.3 has one series at zero transparency and all the others at 50%.

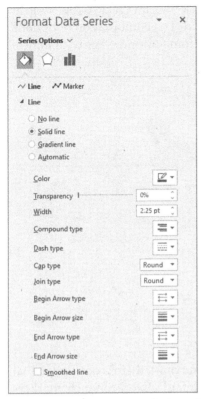

Figure 9.2: The Format Data Series task pane for a line chart

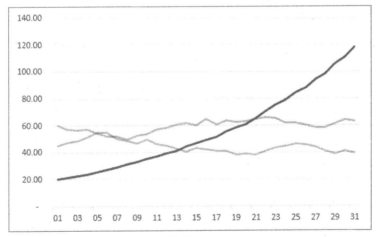

Figure 9.3: Use transparency to highlight a series.

By default, the lines are shown with rounded ends. You can change the ends to Square or Flat, but the difference is hard to detect when you use the standard line width. Another option is replacing the ends with one of several styles of arrows. Figure 9.4 shows a line chart with a thick line, an Oval Arrow style at the start of the line, and an Arrow style at the end. The combination of options seems endless, but make sure you don't detract from your message with unnecessary formatting.

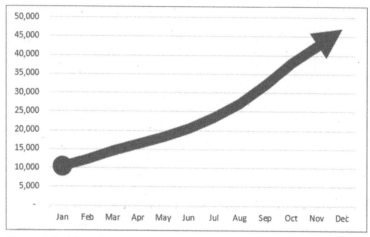

Figure 9.4: A line chart with arrows

While it's best to limit the line formatting in a line chart, there is one option that should always be avoided: Smoothed Line. By default, Excel connects markers with straight lines. If you check the Smoothed Line check box, Excel will change the line's direction more gradually. This makes for a visually appealing chart, but it can distort the display of your data.

Case Study: Sales by Product Category

Your company sells electronics in one of five main categories: Game Consoles, Audio Visual Equipment, Phones, Tablets, and Personal Computers. Your job is to create a visualization showing sales for each category over the first 10 months of the year. The accounting department has supplied the data in Figure 9.5.

	A	B	C	D	E	F	G	H	I	J	K
1		1	2	3	4	5	6	7	8	9	10
2	Game Consoles	358,798	423,423	356,213	437,382	398,090	455,477	476,674	476,674	393,437	496,837
3	Audio Visual	692,860	870,240	696,780	853,580	735,980	901,600	895,720	884,940	784,000	970,200
4	Phones	1,330,200	1,494,000	1,342,800	1,423,800	1,405,800	1,638,000	1,782,000	1,618,200	1,197,000	1,884,600
5	Tablets	202,720	239,120	234,080	228,480	186,760	256,480	281,960	293,720	229,040	298,760
6	Personal Computers	759,759	693,693	786,786	852,852	712,712	906,906	1,071,070	1,037,036	820,820	972,972

Figure 9.5: Sales data by product category

NOTE The workbook for this case study is `LineProductCategorySales.xlsx` and can be found at `www.wiley.com/go/datavizwithexcel`.

You know you want a line chart for this visualization, so you forego the Recommended Charts button and go straight to the Insert Line Or Area Chart drop-down on the Insert tab of the Ribbon and select the first line chart type, as shown in Figure 9.6.

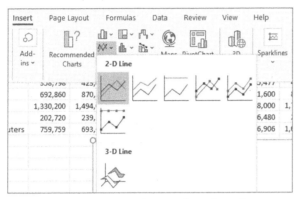

Figure 9.6: The Insert Line Or Area Chart drop-down

The initial chart, shown in Figure 9.7, shows the typical sales increase in late summer for back-to-school and another uptick for the start of the holiday shopping season. To format the chart, follow these steps:

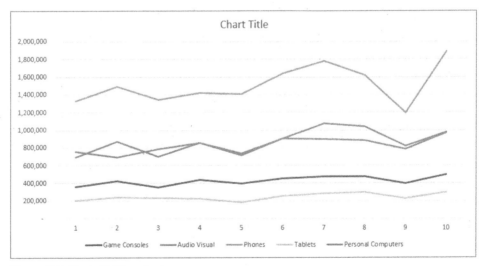

Figure 9.7: The initial line chart

1. Change the chart title to **Sales by Product Category**.

2. On the on-chart Chart Elements tool, choose Legend and Right to move the legend to the right side of the chart. Figure 9.8 shows the onscreen dialog.

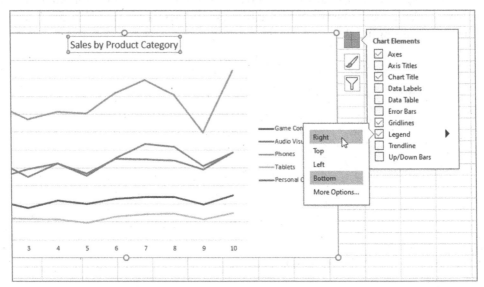

Figure 9.8: The onscreen dialog

3. Increase the width of the chart by dragging the left or right border to accommodate moving the legend.

4. On the on-chart Chart Elements tool, add Axis Titles. Change the value axis title to **Sales Dollars** and the category axis title to **Month**. Figure 9.9 shows the completed chart.

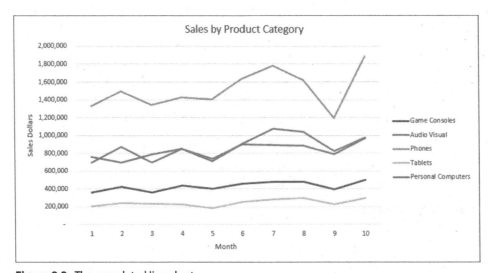

Figure 9.9: The completed line chart

The sales manager likes the chart but would like to see how November and December will look. You decide to include projections for the last two months of the year. You get prior year sales data from Accounting. To add projected sales for November and December based on prior year data, follow these steps:

1. Create a data area just below the current year actual data for the projected data, starting in cell A9. Include the same month headings in row 9 and category headings in column A as the current year data.

2. Paste the prior year data below the projected data. The three data staging areas should look like Figure 9.10.

	A	B	C	D	E	F	G	H	I	J	K	L	M
1	Actual	1	2	3	4	5	6	7	8	9	10	11	12
2	Game Consoles	358,798	423,423	356,213	437,382	398,090	455,477	476,674	476,674	393,437	496,837		
3	Audio Visual	692,860	870,240	696,780	853,580	735,980	901,600	895,720	884,940	784,000	970,200		
4	Phones	1,330,200	1,494,000	1,342,800	1,423,800	1,405,800	1,638,000	1,782,000	1,618,200	1,197,000	1,884,600		
5	Tablets	202,720	239,120	234,080	228,480	186,760	256,480	281,960	293,720	229,040	298,760		
6	Personal Computers	759,759	693,693	786,786	852,852	712,712	906,906	1,071,070	1,037,036	820,820	972,972		
7													
8													
9	Projected	1	2	3	4	5	6	7	8	9	10	11	12
10	Game Consoles										496,837	613,000	611,000
11	Audio Visual										970,200	1,079,000	1,116,000
12	Phones										1,884,600	2,416,000	2,437,000
13	Tablets										298,760	430,000	469,000
14	Personal Computers										972,972	1,211,000	1,394,000
15													
16													
17	Prior Year												
18	Product Category	1	2	3	4	5	6	7	8	9	10	11	12
19	Game Consoles	427,043	323,835	332,615	364,423	310,049	420,086	442,308	394,075	411,992	554,025	873,945	868,010
20	Audio Visual	807,892	490,568	640,347	723,661	484,012	773,254	868,282	782,216	615,236	1,083,079	1,598,485	1,726,670
21	Phones	1,261,152	833,715	1,402,796	1,259,712	1,122,077	1,530,817	1,541,689	1,550,016	1,172,621	1,933,339	3,131,096	3,171,861
22	Tablets	207,413	164,396	203,787	161,217	130,096	228,923	207,976	245,560	187,984	288,490	480,390	539,308
23	Personal Computers	918,089	545,078	565,416	589,741	516,142	811,411	840,128	900,323	797,762	967,779	1,427,540	1,783,806
24													

Figure 9.10: Date staging areas for projected line chart

3. Repeat the data for October in the new data area. In cell K10, enter the formula =K2 and fill down for all the categories.

4. In cell L10, enter the formula =ROUND(TREND($B2:$K2,$B19:$K19,L19),-3).

5. Fill the formula down and to the right to complete the projected sales for all categories for both months.

6. Select the projected data, A9:M14, and press Ctrl+C to copy.

7. Select the existing chart and choose Paste ⇨ Paste Special from the Home tab on the Ribbon to show the Paste Special dialog as shown in Figure 9.11.

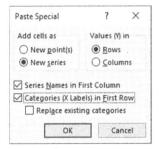

Figure 9.11: The chart's Paste Special dialog

8. Select New Series in the Add Cells As box, select Rows in the Values (Y) In box, check Series Names In First Column, and check Categories (X Labels) In First Row. Click OK to paste the new series. Figure 9.12 shows the resulting chart with the original series extended by the new series.

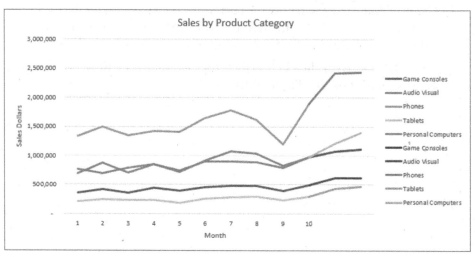

Figure 9.12: Newly pasted series on the line chart

9. For each new series, change the color to match the existing series and change the dash type to Dash. Start by selecting the first new series, right-click, and choose Format Series. The color and dash type properties are on the Fill & Line tab. In the color picker, the existing chart colors are in the top row.

10. Delete the individual legend entries for the new series. First select the legend, then click again to select an individual legend entry. Press the Delete key to remove it. Continue until only the original legend entries remain.

11. Right-click anywhere on the chart and choose Select Data. Edit the Horizontal Axis Labels option to extend the range to include the two new months.

12. Change the title to explain what the dashes mean. The final chart is shown in Figure 9.13.

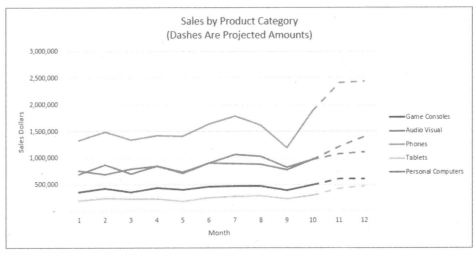

Figure 9.13: A line chart with projected sales

Column Charts with Variances

Column charts are a great way to show a single value by category. It's easy for a reader to compare one column with its neighbor. If you really want to highlight the changes between columns, you can add an additional series or two that helps the reader visualize the variances. Figure 9.14 shows an example of a column chart with variances.

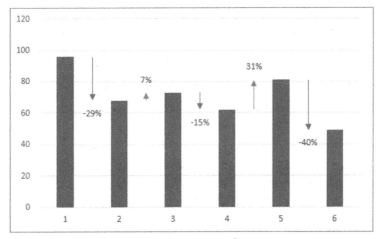

Figure 9.14: A column chart with variances

The two variance series, one for increases and one for decreases, make it easy to see the actual change beyond just a qualitative comparison. You can use arrows, colors, and data labels to enhance the readability. The data labels can show actual amounts or percentages.

Case Study: Houses Sold by Month

A realtor wants to see the total value of houses they closed last year, by month. The overall trend is important, but so are the month-to-month changes. You are provided with the data shown in Figure 9.15.

	A	B
1	Month	House Sales
2	Jan	1,189
3	Feb	2,158
4	Mar	2,086
5	Apr	5,674
6	May	4,600
7	Jun	9,516
8	Jul	4,022
9	Aug	3,927
10	Sep	5,790
11	Oct	2,934
12	Nov	3,077
13	Dec	1,730

Figure 9.15: House closings by month

NOTE The workbook for this case study is `ColumnHousesSoldbyMonth.xlsx` and can be found at www.wiley.com/go/datavizwithexcel.

You decide to create a column chart with variances. Start by setting up the data for the additional series. To stage the data, follow these steps:

1. In cell C2, enter the formula =B3-B2 and fill down to C12.

2. In cell E2, enter the formula =MONTH(A2)+0.5 and fill down to E12. Adding 0.5 to the month will place the variance series halfway between the sales data points.

3. In cell F2, enter the formula =IF(C2>0,B3,NA()). This defines the Y value for the increasing variance series. The NA() function returns the #N/A! error, which Excel will not plot on the chart.

4. In cell G2, enter the formula =IF(C2<0,B3,NA()). This defines the Y value for the decreasing variance series. Making the increasing and decreasing variances different series allows you to format them differently.

5. Fill F2:G2 down to the row 12. Format the number to the thousands. With F2:G12 selected, press Ctrl+1 to show the Format Cells dialog. On the

Number tab, choose Custom and enter **#,###,** in the Type text box. The first comma separates millions from thousands, and the second comma instructs Excel not to display the part of the number less than one thousand.

6. Add **Increase** and **Decrease** as column headings in F1 and G1, respectively. Your data staging area should look like Figure 9.16.

	A	B	C	D	E	F	G	H
1	Month	House Sales				Increase	Decrease	
2	Jan	1,189	969,715		1.5	2,158	#N/A	
3	Feb	2,158	(72,011)		2.5	#N/A	2,086	
4	Mar	2,086	3,587,245		3.5	5,674	#N/A	
5	Apr	5,674	(1,073,938)		4.5	#N/A	4,600	
6	May	4,600	4,916,113		5.5	9,516	#N/A	
7	Jun	9,516	(5,493,880)		6.5	#N/A	4,022	
8	Jul	4,022	(95,372)		7.5	#N/A	3,927	
9	Aug	3,927	1,862,907		8.5	5,790	#N/A	
10	Sep	5,790	(2,855,295)		9.5	#N/A	2,934	
11	Oct	2,934	142,914		10.5	3,077	#N/A	
12	Nov	3,077	(1,347,269)		11.5	#N/A	1,730	
13	Dec	1,730						
14								

Figure 9.16: Data staging area for a column chart with variances

With the data properly staged, you're ready to create the chart. Select the data in A1:B12 and choose Insert ➪ Recommended Charts from the Ribbon and choose the Clustered Column chart type. Before you add the variance series, format the sales data. For the Month column, apply a custom number format of mmm. For the House Sales column and the differences in column C, use the same custom number format you used for the variance data, that is, **#,###,**. Next, change the title to let the reader know the values are in thousands. Figure 9.17 shows the state of the chart at this point.

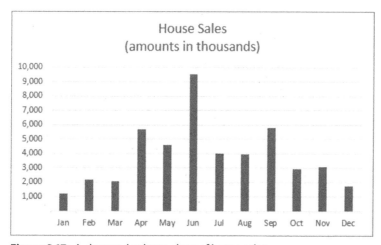

Figure 9.17: A clustered column chart of house sales

To add the variance series to the chart, follow these steps:

1. Copy the range E1:G12 by selecting it and pressing Ctrl+C.

2. Select the chart and choose Paste ⇨ Paste Special from the Home tab on the Ribbon to show the Paste Special dialog. Change the setting as shown in Figure 9.18 and click OK.

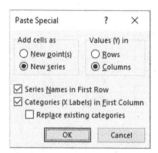

Figure 9.18: The Paste Special dialog for charts

3. By default, the new series chart type will match the existing series, a column chart. Right-click on any series and choose Change Series Chart Type to show the Change Chart Type dialog. Change the Increase and Decrease series to Scatter and leave them on the primary axis, as shown in Figure 9.19.

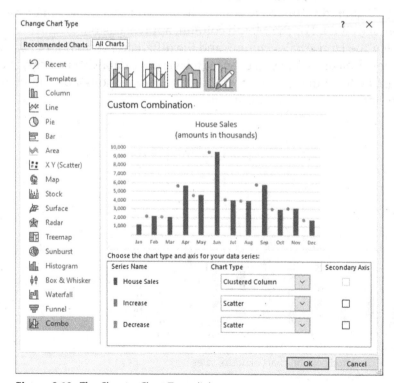

Figure 9.19: The Change Chart Type dialog

The resulting chart is shown in Figure 9.20. The new variance series is shown in between the existing sales series, and the Increase series is a different color from the Decrease series. Each Y value for the new series is at the same level of the following sales series data point.

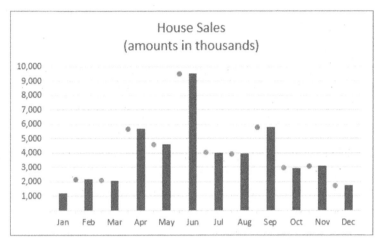

Figure 9.20: The variance series added to the column chart

Now you'll use error bars, color, arrows, and data labels to finish formatting the variance series. To complete the formatting, follow these steps:

1. Select the increase series and check Error Bars on the onchart Chart Elements tool. Excel will add both vertical and horizontal error bars as shown in Figure 9.21.

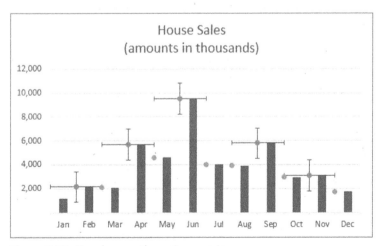

Figure 9.21: Error bars on the variance series

2. Select a horizontal error bar and press Delete to leave on the vertical error bars.

TIP   If you find it difficult to select small elements directly on the chart, use the drop-down box in the Current Selection group on the Chart Tool Format Ribbon.

3. Right-click a vertical error bar and choose Format Error Bars to show the Format Error Bars task pane.

4. Change End Style to No Cap.

5. Select Custom under Error Amount and click the Specify Value button to show the Custom Error Bars dialog. Change Positive Error Value to ={0} and Negative Error Value to the range C2:C12. Figure 9.22 shows the completed Custom Error Bars dialog. Click OK when you've made the changes.

TIP   The Custom Error Bars dialog doesn't give you much room and is particular about how you enter values. For a fixed value, like zero, you must put the value in curly braces. To select a range, delete what's in the error value box entirely, type an equal sign, and use the arrow keys to select the range you want.

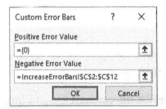

Figure 9.22: The Custom Error Bars dialog

6. Change the color of the error bars to green and set the width to **1.25 pt**. You can set the color and width properties to suit your taste.

7. Change the Begin Arrow type to Arrow.

8. Select the Increase series and set Marker Options to None to hide the markers. Figure 9.23 shows the chart after formatting the Increase series.

Repeat the preceding steps for the Decrease series, but choose a different color. The Custom Error Bars dialog is identical to the dialog for the Increase series. Both use only Negative Error Values and the sign of the number in column C determines which way they point. Because of this, you use the Begin Arrow type for both error bars also. Figure 9.24 shows the chart after formatting both variance series.

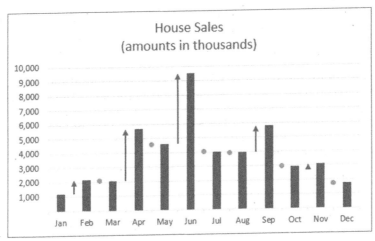

Figure 9.23: The formatted Increase series

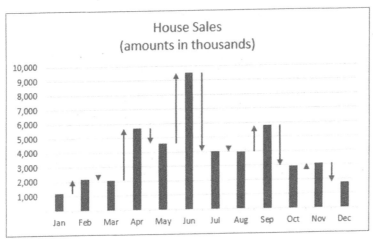

Figure 9.24: The formatted variance series

The last step is to add data labels. Follow these steps to add and format data labels:

1. Select the Increase series and add a data label from the on-chart Chart Elements tool.

2. Right-click a data label and choose Format Data Labels to show the Format Data Labels task pane.

3. Under Label Options, check Value From Cells and select C2:C12. Uncheck all other check boxes.

4. Change the label position to Above.

5. Change the color of the data label to match the error bar color by selecting the data label and using the Font Color tool on the Home tab of the Ribbon.

Repeat the process for the Decrease series but set the label position to Below. Increase the size of the chart so the data labels don't overlap the columns. The final chart is shown in Figure 9.25.

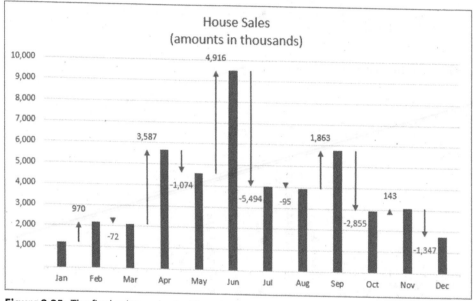

Figure 9.25: The final column chart with variances

Combination Charts

A combination chart, as you might expect from the name, is a combination of two or more chart types on a single chart. The most common combination is a column chart overlaid with a line chart, but combination charts are certainly not limited to that. Figure 9.26 shows an example of a combination chart.

Combination charts are useful when you have two or more data series that are related but are not at the same scale and you want to show that relationship over a continuous variable, like time. Figure 9.27 shows a chart with the same data as Figure 9.26, but with two line series instead of a combination. The second series values are so much lower than the first that it displays as an almost horizontal line at the bottom of the chart. Combination charts almost always use a secondary axis so that the relationship between the data is easier to see.

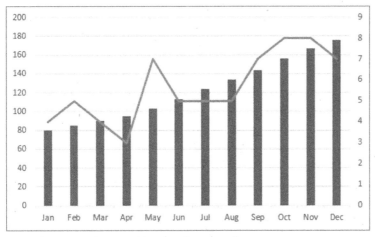

Figure 9.26: A column and line combination chart

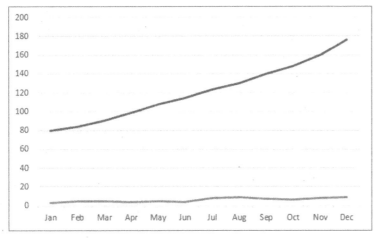

Figure 9.27: Related data at different scales on the same axis

You don't have to use different chart types in a combination chart. You could, for example, show two line charts on separate axes. The value in using different chart types is that it makes it clear to the reader that the data is at different scales. If you plot two line charts on different axes, for example, it would be difficult to know which line was on which axis.

Case Study: Freight Revenue vs. Miles

The management of a trucking company wants to know why September revenue was lower than expected. They ask you to investigate. The company charges their customers a rate per mile, so you start by comparing the revenue for each month to the miles driven. You compile the data shown in Figure 9.28.

◢	A	B	C	
1	Month	Revenue	Miles	
2	Jan	1,148,166	2,870	
3	Feb	1,222,498	3,056	
4	Mar	1,443,301	2,406	
5	Apr	1,139,507	1,899	
6	May	1,125,367	1,876	
7	Jun	1,135,223	1,892	
8	Jul	1,171,817	2,930	
9	Aug	1,402,942	2,806	
10	Sep	817,955	2,363	
11	Oct	1,243,113	3,108	
12	Nov	1,202,512	3,006	
13	Dec	1,200,681	2,001	
14				

Figure 9.28: Freight data by month

NOTE   The workbook for this case study is `CombinationFreight.xlsx` and can be found at `www.wiley.com/go/datavizwithexcel`.

To create the combination chart, select the data and choose Insert ⇨ Recommended Charts from the Ribbon. On the All Charts tab, choose Combo and change the Miles series to use a secondary axis as shown in Figure 9.29.

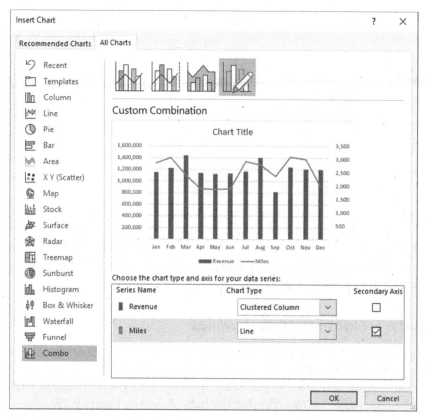

Figure 9.29: Insert a combination chart

The chart shows that while miles are down for September, it doesn't account for the drop in revenue. You know the Logistics department tries to keep trucks full on their return trips, but that it's not always possible. You decide to see how trips with no freight, also known as deadheads, looked during this period. You add deadhead miles to the data as shown in Figure 9.30.

	A	B	C	D
1	Month	Revenue	Miles	Deadhead Miles
2	Jan	1,148	2,870	344
3	Feb	1,222	3,056	458
4	Mar	1,443	2,406	361
5	Apr	1,140	1,899	285
6	May	1,125	1,876	281
7	Jun	1,135	1,892	208
8	Jul	1,172	2,930	440
9	Aug	1,403	2,806	281
10	Sep	818	2,363	912
11	Oct	1,243	3,108	466
12	Nov	1,203	3,006	421
13	Dec	1,201	2,001	300
14				

Figure 9.30: Deadhead miles added to the data

To add the new data to the chart, follow these steps:

1. Select the new data in D1:D13 and press Ctrl+C to copy it.
2. Select the chart and choose Paste Special from Home ⇨ Paste on the Ribbon.
3. On the Paste Special dialog, shown in Figure 9.31, choose New Series and click OK.

Figure 9.31: The Paste Special dialog

There is an unusual spike in deadhead miles in September that accounts for the drop in revenue. Complete the chart by adding axis titles and formatting the numbers in the revenue axis. The completed chart is shown in Figure 9.32.

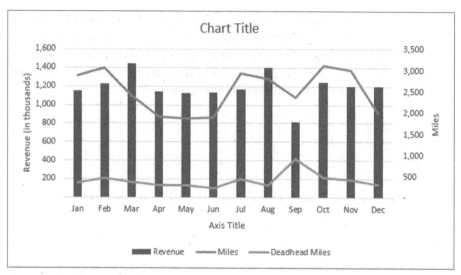

Figure 9.32: The completed combination chart

Line Charts with Differences

A line chart with two series is a great way to show how two variables change over time. When you want to highlight the differences between the data points in the series, you can add error bars to the chart. Figure 9.33 shows a typical line chart with differences.

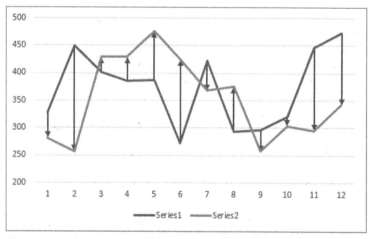

Figure 9.33: A Line chart with differences

Showing the differences between the data points is most useful when you have two lines that cross multiple times. It's easier for the reader to interpret the changes and to identify trends. Adding arrows to the error bars and using colors further the readability of the chart. This is also one of the few charts where the y-axis doesn't need to start at zero because the purpose of the chart is to highlight changes, not magnitude.

Case Study: Current vs. Prior Quarter Revenue

Management typically reviews revenue weekly. Due to volatility in the industry over the past year, they've asked to see how weekly revenue compares to the prior quarter. You compile the weekly revenue data as shown in Figure 9.34.

⊿	A	B	C	D
1	Week	Current	Prior	
2	1	74,566	80,002	
3	2	86,757	60,297	
4	3	70,094	94,183	
5	4	63,981	89,258	
6	5	64,864	91,952	
7	6	86,785	65,059	
8	7	82,070	93,887	
9	8	80,562	63,835	
10	9	65,534	86,495	
11	10	79,804	87,185	
12	11	73,758	86,042	
13	12	60,093	81,079	
14	13	76,976	97,327	

Figure 9.34: Weekly revenue data

NOTE   The workbook for this case study is `WeeklyRevenueComparison.xlsx` and can be found at `www.wiley.com/go/datavizwithexcel`.

Start by selecting the data and clicking Recommended Charts on the Insert tab of the Ribbon. On the Insert Chart dialog, select Line to insert the line chart. Figure 9.35 shows the initial chart Excel creates.

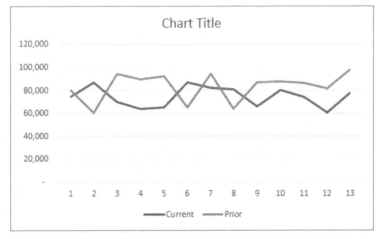

Figure 9.35: The initial line chart

Add two columns to the data to drive the error bars. In cell D2, add the formula =IF(B2-C2>0,B2-C2,NA()) and fill down to the end of the data. In cell E2, add the formula =IF(B2-C2<0,B2-C2,NA()) and fill down to the end of the data. Separating the positive and negative values into two columns allows you to apply separate formatting to each. To add the differences to the chart, follow these steps:

1. Select the Current series and add error bars using the on-chart Chart Elements tool. On the Error Bars submenu, choose More Options to show the Format Error Bars task pane. Figure 9.36 shows the on-chart Chart Elements tool.

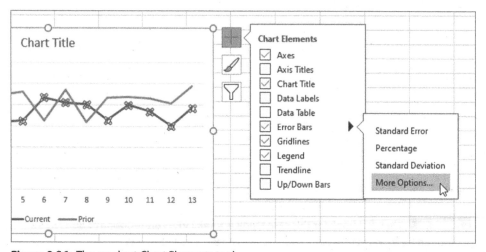

Figure 9.36: The on-chart Chart Elements tool

2. On the Format Error Bars task pane, set the End Style option to No Cap.

3. Under Error Amount, choose Custom and click the Specify Value button to show the Custom Error Bars dialog.

4. In the Custom Error Bars dialog, set Positive Error Value to ={0}.

5. Delete the text in the Negative Error Value text box and point to the range D2:D14. If you don't delete what's in the text box first, Excel attempts to add the range to whatever is in there.

6. On the Fill & Line tab of the Format Error Bars task pane, change Width to **1.25 pt**, change Begin Arrow Type to Arrow, and set Color to dark blue. Figure 9.37 shows the chart at this point in the process.

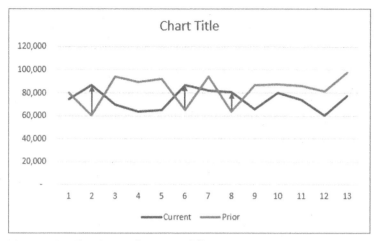

Figure 9.37: The chart with positive differences

7. Select the Prior series and add error bars as you did for the Current series.

8. On the Custom Error Bars dialog, set Positive Error Value to the data in column E and Negative Error Value to ={0}. Figure 9.38 shows the Custom Error Bars dialog for the Prior series.

Figure 9.38: The Custom Error Bars dialog for the Prior series

9. Set End Style to No Cap, Width to **1.25 pt**, End Arrow Type to Arrow, and Color to dark orange.

10. Change the Transparency of both series to **50%**. Making the series line more transparent will help the error bars stand out, highlighting the differences over the actual values.

11. Select the Value Axis and change the Minimum setting to **55000**. Normally it's best to start the axis at zero, but because we intend to highlight the change, this will increase the distance between the two series lines.

12. Change the chart title. The final chart is shown in Figure 9.39.

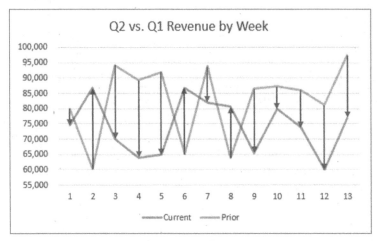

Figure 9.39: The Final Line Chart with Differences

Side-by-Side Box Plots

Box plots are called Box & Whisker in Excel. It is a visually interesting chart type used to compare the central tendency and the spread of two or more series. You can have only one box on your chart, but it's far more common to use it for comparison.

The data for a box plot consists of five measurements: the median, or middle value, the upper and lower quartiles, and the minimum and maximum values. Figure 9.40 shows a typical side-by-side box plot.

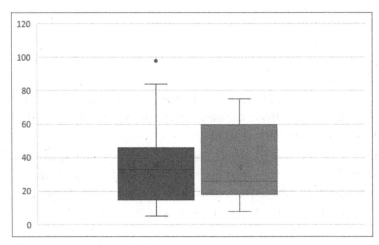

Figure 9.40: A side-by-side box plot

The box plot in Figure 9.40 shows the median as a horizontal line inside the box element. You can see that the median of the first series is higher than that of the second series. The box portion of the chart ranges from the first quartile to the third quartile, known as the *interquartile range*. The second series has a larger box because the data is more spread out than the first. The whisker elements extend downward to the minimum value and upward to the maximum value.

Both series show an X marker for the average (arithmetic mean). The first series also has an outlier, shown as a single dot near the 100 line. An outlier is any data point that is more than 1.5 times the interquartile range above or below the box.

As with most of Excel's newer chart types, there are limited options. Figure 9.41 shows the Series Option tab of the Format Data Series task pane for a box plot. The following options are available:

- **Gap Width:** A value between 0% and 500% that determines the width of the boxes.

- **Show Inner Points:** Checking this box shows a small circle for each data point, excluding outliers if they are shown separately.

- **Show Outlier Points:** Checking this box determines if any data points are outliers according to the calculation described earlier in this section and displays a filled circle for each data point. It also excludes outliers from the minimum and maximum calculations. Unchecking this box includes all data points in the minimum and maximum calculations.

- **Show Mean Markers:** Checking this box displays an X marker for the average of the series. Unchecking the box hides the marker.

- **Show Mean Line:** Microsoft claims this option displays a line connecting the mean markers for series, but checking or unchecking the box seems to have no effect.

- **Inclusive Median:** Includes the median value when calculating the quartiles.

- **Exclusive Median:** Excludes the median value when calculating the quartiles.

NOTE   There are several methods for calculating quartiles. The benefits of each method are beyond the scope of this book. Excel provides an option for two methods: including or excluding the median in the quartile calculation. Whichever you choose, use it consistently in your chart.

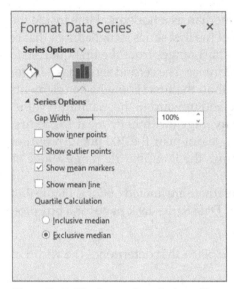

Figure 9.41: The Format Data Series task pane for a box plot

Case Study: Salaries by Department

Management wants to analyze salaries by department to see where they are spending labor dollars. Rather than simply compare total salaries expense by department, you decide to do a deeper analysis using box plots. You start with salaries data, a portion of which is shown in Figure 9.42.

▲	A	B	C	D	E
1		Administration	Marketing	Accounting	Production
2		145,075	232,288	290,917	45,768
3		88,045	170,295	211,248	61,340
4		73,146	144,739	188,669	39,604
5		127,089	236,622	443,845	39,194
6		109,442	164,006	281,232	72,734
7		142,404	171,975	353,147	102,935
8		117,913	226,129	344,004	34,184
9		55,026	131,843	264,051	43,765
10		98,537	80,990	298,507	94,500
11		96,801	169,790	203,195	49,149
12		134,644	134,468	258,408	85,371
13		138,796	147,538	252,928	63,634
14		126,409	177,445	327,329	47,579
15		98,773	128,863	280,460	81,071
16		77,531	231,118		103,371
17		124,068	90,928		102,085
18		114,405	117,000		115,507
19		81,293	228,975		82,160
20		93,031			98,611

Figure 9.42: Salaries data

NOTE   The workbook for this case study is `BoxPlotSalaries.xlsx` and can be found at www.wiley.com/go/datavizwithexcel.

To create the box plot, select the data and choose Recommended Charts from the Insert tab on the Ribbon. Don't worry if some of the columns contain blank cells. Excel will ignore the blanks. From the Insert Chart dialog's All Charts tab, choose Box & Whisker. The initial chart is shown in Figure 9.43.

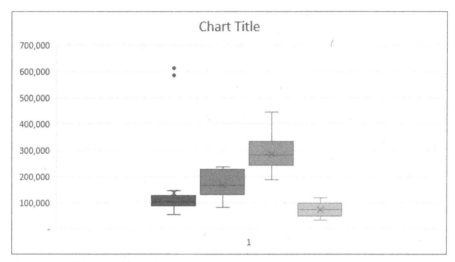

Figure 9.43: The initial box plot

Had you simply compared total amounts, the Administration department would show the largest total salaries. But the initial box plot shows us that there is more to the story. There are two outliers that drive up the total, and when they are excluded, the Administration department's salaries appear reasonable.

To finish formatting the chart, follow these steps:

1. Right-click the chart and choose Select Data.

2. For each series, click Edit and point to the first row for that column to name the series. Figure 9.44 shows an example of renaming a series.

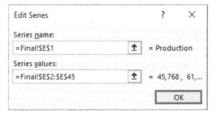

Figure 9.44: Renaming a series

3. Change the chart title to Salaries by Department.

4. Select the x-axis and press the Delete key to delete it.

5. Add a legend to the bottom of the chart.

6. Optionally, delete the y-axis. The final chart is shown in Figure 9.45.

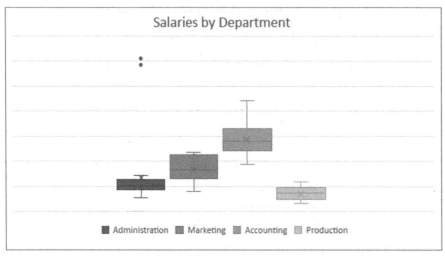

Figure 9.45: The final box plot

Animated Charts

There are three main reasons to add motion to a chart: to fit more data into a smaller space, to change the chart to follow a presentation, and to give the user control over the chart. It's easy to abuse chart animations, so use them sparingly and with a purpose.

To fit more data in a smaller space, you can change the data that is presented in your chart. For example, you could create a column chart showing revenue by department. If you want to show the same chart for the past three years, you may find that you have too many data points and your chart is cluttered and hard to read. By cycling through each year's chart, you can present all the data with less clutter.

Another common animation technique is adding data series as you present the information in the chart. You can start with a line chart that only shows one line, such as, for example, unit sales for one product category. As your presentation shifts to talking about the next product category, you add a new series to the chart. For each product category you discuss, you continue to add series.

Sometimes you can't predict what the user will want to see. You can build animations to allow the user to have some control. You could, for example, connect a scroll bar to a chart that allows the user to control the date range displayed.

PivotCharts

A chart connected to a PivotTable is called a PivotChart. It's the simplest way to give a user control over a chart. In older versions of Excel, PivotCharts had many more limitations than regular charts. Microsoft has been removing those limitations in more recent versions. The biggest remaining limitation is that only certain chart types can be used with a PivotChart. If you want to use a scatter plot, for example, you won't be able to with a PivotChart.

To create a PivotChart, start with a data set like the one shown in Figure 9.46. Highlight the data and choose PivotCharts from the Insert tab of the Ribbon.

	A	B	C	
1	Date	Region	Units	
2	1/1/2021	West	971	
3	7/6/2021	Midwest	1,042	
4	7/20/2021	Southeast	856	
5	1/20/2021	Southeast	1,060	
6	8/16/2021	Northeast	1,123	
7	12/9/2021	Northeast	1,060	
8	2/21/2021	Midwest	1,198	
9	5/24/2021	Midwest	1,137	
10	6/22/2021	Midwest	1,036	
11	5/5/2021	Midwest	1,141	
12	1/31/2021	West	1,126	
13	1/13/2021	Midwest	1,085	
14	8/2/2021	Southeast	1,138	
15	7/8/2021	Northeast	1,114	
16	11/12/2021	Midwest	1,146	
17	12/5/2021	Midwest	983	
18	4/28/2021	West	955	
19	2/1/2021	West	1,151	
20	8/30/2021	Northeast	863	
21	1/4/2021	Northeast	1,107	
22	2/17/2021	West	1,177	
23	1/18/2021	Northeast	1,108	

Figure 9.46: A partial data set for a PivotChart

Excel displays the Create PivotChart dialog box, which will look familiar to anyone who's created a PivotTable. The dialog allows you to confirm or change your data range and choose where to place the PivotChart. When you click OK, Excel puts the outline of a PivotTable and a PivotChart on your worksheet and displays the PivotTable Fields task pane, as shown in Figure 9.47.

To build the PivotChart, drag the Date field to the Axis area of the task pane, drag the Units field to the Values area, and drag the Region field to the Legend area. Excel will automatically group the dates into months. Figure 9.48 shows the PivotChart after these few simple steps.

The first thing you'll notice is that the PivotChart has field buttons displayed on it. The user can click on a field button to sort and filter the data. Figure 9.49 shows the options if you click the Region field button.

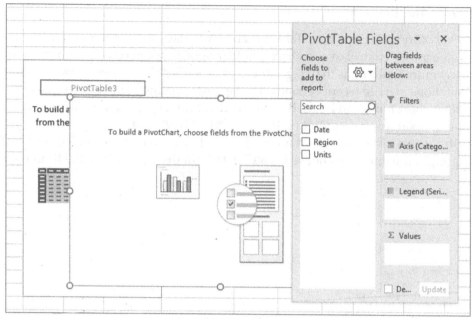

Figure 9.47: A PivotChart with no data

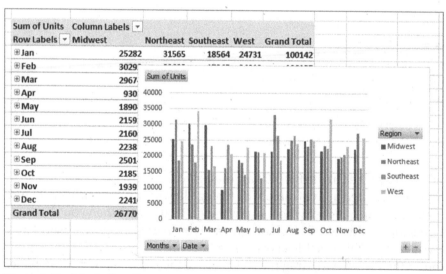

Figure 9.48: A basic PivotChart

TIP   To show or hide the field buttons on a PivotChart, use the Field Buttons tool on the PivotChart Tools Analyze tab of the Ribbon.

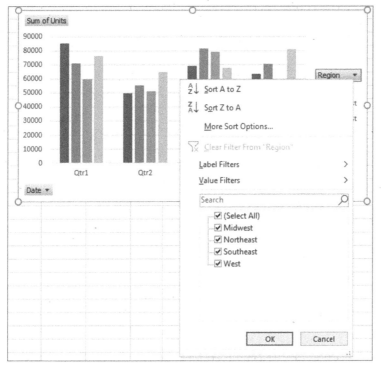

Figure 9.49: Field button options

If you prefer a different grouping of the date field, you can change the underlying PivotTable. For example, right-click on a date in the PivotTable and choose Group to display the Grouping dialog box. Change the grouping to Quarters and click OK. The PivotChart redraws to reflect the new grouping as shown in Figure 9.50.

> **TIP**   You can add Slicers to PivotTables to allow users to filter the data in the table. A Slicer is an attractive user-interface control. If you hide the field buttons and add Slicers, it makes for a pleasant user experience.

Staging Area Formulas

Another way to animate charts is to stage the data using formulas that change based on a control, such as a slider control or a drop-down. This technique can be used to allow the user to change the chart by manipulating the controls or to follow along with a live presentation where the presenter manipulates the controls.

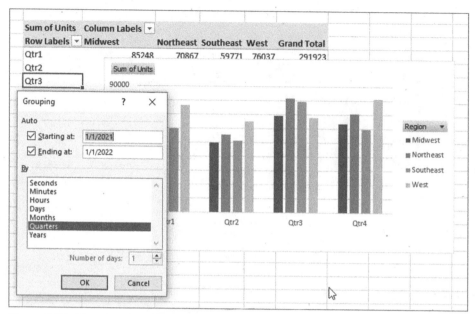

Figure 9.50: Changing how dates are grouped in a PivotChart

A slider control that changes the timeline of a chart is the classic example of using staged formulas for animation. A portion of some annual revenue data is shown in Figure 9.51. For this example, you'll create a chart that shows five years of data and a slider control to determine which five years are shown.

	A	B
1	Year	Revenue
2	1993	612,543
3	1994	600,292
4	1995	636,310
5	1996	661,762
6	1997	668,380
7	1998	701,799
8	1999	750,925
9	2000	720,888
10	2001	756,932
11	2002	825,056
12	2003	907,562
13	2004	980,167
14	2005	989,969
15	2006	980,069
16	2007	1,068,275
17	2008	1,143,054
18	2009	1,108,762

Figure 9.51: Annual revenue data

The first step is to create a staging area with formulas. Follow these steps to create the staging area:

1. In cells D1 and E1, repeat the header from cells A1 and B1.

2. Cell D2 will contain the first year that the chart displays. For now, type **1993** into cell D2.

3. Enter the formula `=D2+1` into cell D2 and fill it down to cell D6. The range D2:D6 now contain the five years the chart will display.

4. In cell E2, enter the formula `=VLOOKUP(D2,$A$2:$B$31,2,FALSE)` and fill it down to cell E6. The completed staging area is shown in Figure 9.52.

D	E
Year	Revenue
1993	612,543
1994	600,292
1995	636,310
1996	661,762
1997	668,380

Figure 9.52: The staging area for five years of data

With the staging area complete, select the data and insert a line chart. By changing the value in cell D2, you change what data the chart displays. Figure 9.53 shows the chart after you entered 2001 into cell D2.

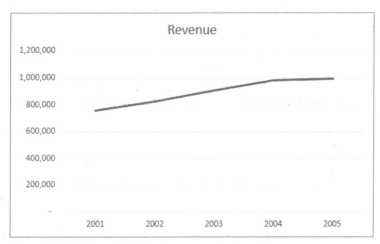

Figure 9.53: A dynamic chart changes as the data changes.

When animating a line chart, it's usually a good idea to fix the value axis. Right-click on the value axis and choose Format Axis to show the Format Axis task pane. Set Minimum to **0** and Maximum to **1800000**. The buttons next to Minimum and Maximum will change from Auto to Reset. When the axis is set to Auto, the chart moves around during animation and some of the effect is lost.

The next step is to create a control to change the starting value in the staging area. Entering a new value in cell D2 changes the chart, but a control makes it easier and makes sure that the year entered is within the source data. To add a slider control, follow these steps:

1. From the Developer tab on the Ribbon, choose Insert ⇨ Form Controls ⇨ Scroll Bar and click anywhere on the worksheet to place the control.

TIP   If you don't see the Developer tab, right-click on the Ribbon and choose Customize The Ribbon. In the Excel Options dialog, check the box next to Developer to show that tab.

2. Right-click the control and choose Format Control to display the Format Control dialog.

3. On the size tab, change Height to **0.2** and Width to **5**.

4. On the Control tab, change Minimum Value to **1993**, Maximum Value to **2017**, Page Change to **1**, and Cell Link to **D2**. Figure 9.54 shows the Format Control dialog.

5. Move the control below the chart.

Figure 9.54: The Format Control dialog for a scroll bar

TIP   When you make a scroll bar control wider than it is tall, it turns into a slider. The control is still called a scroll bar, it's just oriented horizontally instead of vertically.

When you click the slider, the value is stored in cell D2, which drives the staging area formulas and changes the chart. When you set the Minimum Value and Maximum Value properties, you ensured that the number in cell D2 would always be within the source data range. Figure 9.55 shows the chart and slider combination.

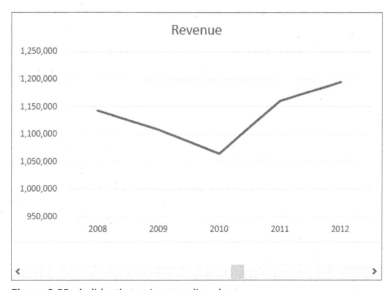

Figure 9.55: A slider that animates a line chart

You have a lot of options when setting up staging areas and controls. If you prefer to show 10 years of data, you simply fill your formulas down further. If you have a lot more source data, you may want the option of scrolling through it faster. In that case, you can set the Page Change property to something higher.

Chart Animation Macros

You can use the Visual Basic for Applications (VBA) programming language that's built into Excel to animate your chart with no user interaction. A piece of VBA code is commonly called a macro.

NOTE   The workbook for this section is `LineChartAutomation.xlsm` and can be found at www.wiley.com/go/datavizwithexcel.

In the example from the previous section, the user clicks the slider to change where the chart starts. A macro could change the value in cell D2 automatically. Writing a macro to automate a chart that uses formulas in a staging area is a great way to get started with chart automation. The macros are easy to understand because the formulas are doing most of the work. To add a macro to the line chart showing five years of revenue data, follow these steps:

1. Click Visual Basic from the Developer tab on the Ribbon to open the Visual Basic Editor (VBE).

2. Press Ctrl+R to show the Project Explorer.

3. Locate the workbook in the Project Explorer. A new, unsaved workbook will have a name like VBAProject (Book1).

4. Right-click anywhere on the project and choose Insert ⇨ Module. A new code window will appear as shown in Figure 9.56.

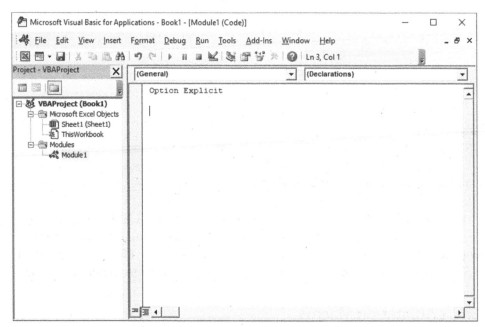

Figure 9.56: A new code window in the Visual Basic Editor

5. Type the following code into the code window:

```
Option Explicit

Sub AnimateChart()

    Dim counter As Long
```

```
For counter = 1993 To 2017
    Sheet1.Range("D2").Value = counter
    Sheet1.ChartObjects(1).Chart.Refresh
    DoEvents: DoEvents
    Application.Wait Now + TimeSerial(0, 0, 1)
    DoEvents: DoEvents
Next counter

End Sub
```

To run the code, choose Close And Return To Microsoft Excel from the File menu. When you're back in Excel, click Macros from the Developer tab on the Ribbon. In the Macro dialog, choose AnimateChart and click Run. The value in cell D2 will change every second and the chart will update.

The macro, AnimateChart, is part of the workbook. If you save the workbook as a macro-enabled workbook, the code will be saved and will be available whenever you open the workbook. VBA is a very big subject, and this book only focuses on interacting with charts. But the following is a brief description of the AnimateChart code.

The keyword `Option Explicit` tells VBA that when you use a variable, like `counter`, you will first declare the variable with a `Dim` statement. Requiring variable declaration helps prevent typos. The next line, `Sub AnimateChart()`, defines the start of a macro. Macros are also known as *subprocedures,* which is where the `Sub` keyword comes from. For every `Sub` keyword that defines the start of the macro, there's an `End Sub` keyword that defines the end of it.

The first line inside the macro, `Dim counter As Long`, tells VBA that you intend to use a variable named `counter` and that it will hold a Long Integer data type. Using the `Dim` statement is known as declaring a variable.

The main part of the macro is a *For loop*. A For Loop starts with a `For` keyword and ends with a `Next` keyword. The statements between `For` and `Next` are executed once every time it loops. In this case, it will loop 25 times. The counter variable is first set to 1993, and all the statements inside the loop are executed. When it gets to the `Next` keyword, it increases `counter` by one and executes all the statements again. This continues until `counter` is set to 2018, one more than the `For` statement's upper limit. At that point, the loop is done and the statement after the `Next` statement is run. In this case, the statement after `Next` is `End Sub`, and the macro completes.

Inside the loop are five lines that are run 25 times. The first line sets the value of cell D2 to 1993 on the first loop, 1994 on the second loop, and so on. Next, the chart is refreshed. Excel doesn't always do a great job of updating the screen while a macro is running, so the code contains two `DoEvents` statements to give Excel a chance to catch up. Next, a `Wait` statement is executed so the user has a chance to see the chart change. Without the `Wait` statement, it would execute too fast. Finally, another set of `DoEvents` statements lets Excel catch back up redrawing the screen.

Chart Automation

You can use VBA to help you construct charts as well as animate them. With animation, the VBA code usually manipulates the data and Excel's charting engine responds accordingly. With automation, the VBA manipulates the chart itself. Generally, you use chart automation when you're designing and creating charts, not when you're presenting them.

Manipulating Chart Objects

Earlier in this chapter, you created a line chart titled Sales by Product Category and added some new series to show the projected sales amounts for the last two months of the year. Part of that process was pasting in new series and changing the projected series to look like an extension of the actual series.

> **NOTE**   The workbook for this section is `FormatDataSeries.xlsm` and can be found at `www.wiley.com/go/datavizwithexcel`.

Whenever you have to do tedious tasks, like changing the colors of individual series, it's a good opportunity to automate the process. Sometimes writing the VBA code takes as long as doing it manually, but if you ever have to do it again, you'll be glad you took the time to automate it. Figure 9.57 shows the chart after pasting the new series.

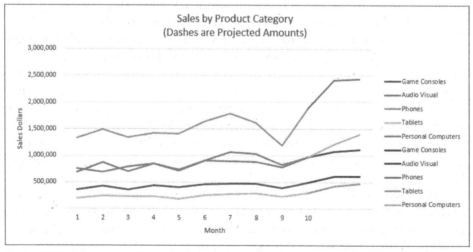

Figure 9.57: A line chart with newly pasted series

The first step in automating a chart is learning which objects you need to manipulate. VBA for Excel uses an object model, a hierarchy of objects representing elements on the screen. Excel's object model is large, but the parts relating to charting are a smaller subset, so it's more manageable. The good news is that for the most part, Excel's object model is well organized and uses meaningful names.

If you're new to VBA or the Excel object model, start by recording a macro. The generated code won't be exactly what you want, but it will give you the names of the objects you need to manipulate. To record a macro that changes one series, follow these steps:

1. Click Record Macro on the Developer tab of the Ribbon.

2. Accept the defaults and click OK on the Record Macro dialog box.

3. Right-click one of the new series and choose Format Data Series to show the Format Data Series task pane.

4. Modify the data series as you did earlier in this chapter to match the color and change the line to dashes.

5. Select the legend entry for that series and press Delete to remove it.

6. Click Stop Recording on the Developer tab.

To see the recorded macro, click Visual Basic on the Developer tab to open the VBE. Press Ctrl+R to show the Project Explorer if it's not already visible. Find your project in the Project Explorer and open the Modules folder. Double-click the module named Module1 to view the code shown below:

```
Sub Macro1()
'
' Macro1 Macro
'

'
    ActiveSheet.ChartObjects("Chart 1").Activate
    ActiveChart.FullSeriesCollection(13).Select
    With Selection.Format.Line
        .Visible = msoTrue
        .ForeColor.ObjectThemeColor = msoThemeColorAccent3
        .ForeColor.TintAndShade = 0
        .ForeColor.Brightness = 0
        .Transparency = 0
    End With
    ActiveChart.Legend.Select
    With Selection.Format.Line
        .Visible = msoTrue
        .DashStyle = msoLineDash
```

Continues

(continued)

```
        End With
        ActiveChart.Legend.LegendEntries(8).Select
        Selection.Delete
    End Sub
```

Don't worry if your recorded macro looks slightly different. The macro recorder records almost every action you take. Sometimes when you're recording a macro, you click the wrong thing or select the wrong color and correct it. The recorder dutifully records all the mistakes too. The recorder is great for giving you hints on what your code should look like, not for creating code to use.

The objects we're interested in are FullSeriesCollection and LegendEntries. The references to these objects in the code are followed by numbers. The code manipulates the 13th series and the 8th legend entry. These objects are known as *collection objects* because they contain a collection of similar objects.

You know there aren't 13 series on the chart, only 10; the original 5 actual series and the new 5 projected series. The FullSeriesCollection object may contain series that have been filtered out. All your series are visible, so you don't need the FullSeriesCollection object. You can use the more straightforward SeriesCollection object instead.

Create a new macro after the End Sub statement of the recorded macro. On a new line, type **Sub FormatProjections** and press Enter. The VBE will add parentheses after the Sub statement line and add an End Sub line. Your code will go between these two lines. Start with the simplest code you can and build on it from there. You may have to makes some copies of your chart to practice on until the code is complete. The following code does the same thing as the recorded code; that is, it formats one series and deletes its legend entry:

```
Sub FormatProjections()

    With ActiveChart
        .SeriesCollection(6).Format.Line.ForeColor.RGB = _
            .SeriesCollection(1).Format.Line.ForeColor.RGB
        .SeriesCollection(6).Format.Line.DashStyle = msoLineDash
        .Legend.LegendEntries(6).Delete
    End With

End Sub
```

Everything that happens between the With and End With statements is acting on the ActiveChart. *With blocks* help keep your code clean and save you from having to type objects like ActiveChart over and over. Another aspect of VBA to note is the *line continuation character*. The character combination of a space followed by an underscore indicates that the next line is a continuation of the current line.

The first line inside the With block set the RGB of the sixth series to the same values as the RBG of the first series. Series 1 through 5 are the actual data series and series 6 through 10 are the projections. Because of how Excel numbers series (more or less in the order they were added), series 6 corresponds to series 1, series 7 corresponds to series 2, and so on.

TIP The *dot operator* is an important concept in VBA. When you manipulate an object, you start with the object's name followed by a period. What comes after the period is either a property or method of the object. For example, the code `ActiveChart.Name` works with the `Name` property of the `ActiveChart` object.

In many cases, a property returns another object that has its own properties and methods. When you have multiple dot operators on one line, it's because you are calling properties that return other objects. The code `ActiveChart.Legend.LegendEntries(6).Delete` has three dot operators. It calls the `Delete` method of the `LegendEntry` object. The property `LegendEntries(6)` of the `Legend` object returns a `LegendEntry` object. The `Legend` property of the `ActiveChart` object returns a `Legend` object.

The second line in the With block formats the line as a dash. The constant `msoLineDash` was lifted from the recorded macro. The last line deletes the sixth legend entry. As you probably guessed, the legend entries are numbered the same as the series. Figure 9.58 shows the chart with two series formatted. One series was formatted manually when you recorded the macro and the other when you ran the new FormatProjections macro.

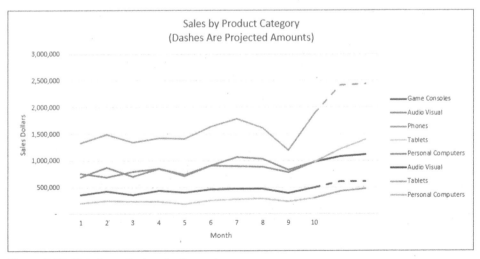

Figure 9.58: Two formatted projection series

Now that you have code to format one series, you can modify the code to loop through all the series and change them. One important point is the collection objects renumber their child objects when something is deleted. If you delete the first of 10 legend entries, there's still a 1st legend entry but here is no longer a 10th entry. The objects in the collection get renumbered one through nine. Whenever you delete in VBA, it's best to loop backwards to avoid renumbering.

The following code loops through the projection series, formats each series, and deletes the legend entry:

```
Sub FormatProjections()

    Dim lCount As Long
    Dim Actual As LineFormat
    Dim Projection As LineFormat

    For lCount = 10 To 6 Step -1
        With ActiveChart
            Set Actual = .SeriesCollection(lCount - 5).Format.Line
            Set Projection = .SeriesCollection(lCount).Format.Line
            Projection.ForeColor.RGB = Actual.ForeColor.RGB
            Projection.DashStyle = msoLineDash
            .Legend.LegendEntries(lCount).Delete
        End With
    Next lCount

End Sub
```

The code starts by defining three variables using the Dim statement. The first variable, lCount, is a counter variable that's used in the For Loop that comes later. The other two variables are LineFormat objects. By storing the objects you want to manipulate in well-named variables, you write code that's easier to read and maintain.

The main block of code is a For Loop that loops backward from 10 to 6. The Step statement tells the code to reduce the variable lCount by 1 every time it loops. Inside the loop, a With block is used just like in the previous iteration of this macro.

The first two lines in the With block store objects in variables. In the first pass of the For Loop, when lCount is 10, the LineFormat of the 5th series is stored in the Actual variable, and the LineFormat of the 10th series is stored in the Projection variable. These variables make the next two lines easy to interpret. The color of the projection line is set to the same value as the actual line, and the projection line changed to a dash. The final piece of code deletes the legend entry.

Creating Panel Charts

Using panel charts is a great way, maybe the only way, to show many series at one time. Figure 9.59 shows a line chart with too many series on the left and a panel chart breaking the series apart on the right.

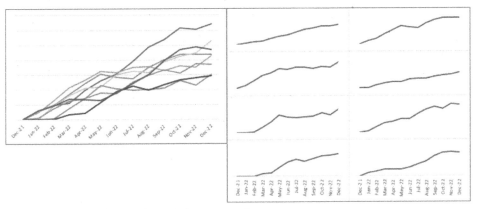

Figure 9.59: A line chart and panel chart comparison

> **NOTE** The workbook for this section is `PanelChartAutomation.xlsm` and can be found at `www.wiley.com/go/datavizwithexcel`.

Placing the panels of the panel chart manually is a tedious process. It takes about the same amount of time to write a macro to place the panels as it does to do it by hand. But there are other advantages to using a macro. With a macro, you get exact placement of the charts, so you know everything is not even one pixel off. The other advantage is dealing with changes. If you change something about your chart, repositioning everything by hand takes as long as doing it the first time. Repositioning with a macro usually means changing a few numbers and rerunning it.

As with the previous example, start by recording a macro to give you the names of the objects you need to manipulate. To record a macro that creates a chart, follow these steps:

1. Click Record Macro on the Developer tab of the Ribbon and click OK on the Record Macro dialog.

2. Select A1:B14 on the worksheet.

3. Click Recommended Charts on the Insert tab of the Ribbon and select Line.

4. Select the chart's title and press the Delete key.

5. Select the vertical axis and press the Delete key.

6. Resize the chart by dragging the corner to make it larger or smaller.

7. Move the chart to a different location on the worksheet by dragging the edge of the chart. It doesn't matter where you move it, you only want to see the code responsible for positioning a chart.

8. Click Stop Recording on the Developer tab of the Ribbon.

The preceding steps generate the following VBA code. To see the VBA code in your workbook, click Visual Basic on the Developer tab of the Ribbon:

```
Sub Macro2()
'
' Macro2 Macro
'

'
    Range("A1:B14").Select
    ActiveSheet.Shapes.AddChart2(227, xlLineMarkers).Select
    ActiveChart.SetSourceData Source:=Range("Sheet4!$A$1:$B$14")
    ActiveChart.ChartTitle.Select
    Selection.Delete
    ActiveChart.Axes(xlValue).Select
    Selection.Delete
    ActiveSheet.ChartObjects("Chart 3").Activate
    ActiveSheet.Shapes("Chart 3").ScaleWidth 0.7229166667, msoFalse, _
        msoScaleFromTopLeft
    ActiveSheet.Shapes("Chart 3").ScaleHeight 0.6736111111, msoFalse, _
        msoScaleFromTopLeft
    ActiveSheet.ChartObjects("Chart 3").Activate
    ActiveSheet.Shapes("Chart 3").IncrementLeft 15
    ActiveSheet.Shapes("Chart 3").IncrementTop -84.75
End Sub
```

When you record a macro, Excel generates a line of code for every step you take. The first line was generated when you selected a range, the second line was generated when you added a chart, and so on. The value of recording a macro is to learn the objects and syntax you'll need to write your own code. In this case, you can see you'll need AddChart2, SetSourceData, ActiveChart, and ChartObjects. Don't worry if you don't understand all the code, just keep it handy as a reference.

The first thing you might notice about recorded macros is that Excel selects or activates objects, then does something with the selection or the active object. The macro recorder has to do it that way, because it doesn't know if you intend to do something when you select an object or not. But for your own code, avoid selecting objects. The example in the rest of this section will show you how.

To start writing your own macro, type **Sub MakeSinglePanel** below the recorded macro and press Enter. VBA will automatically add parentheses and an `End Sub` statement. The `Sub` and `End Sub` statements are the starting and ending points for your macro.

Next create a variable to hold your chart. Instead of creating a chart and manipulating the `ActiveChart`, you'll create a chart, assign it to a variable, and manipulate the variable. Type the following two lines between the `Sub` and `End Sub` statements:

```
Sub MakeSinglePanel()

    Dim cht As Chart

    Set cht = ActiveSheet.Shapes.AddChart2(227, xlLine).Chart

End Sub
```

The `Dim` statement creates the variable, and the `Set` statement assigns a new chart to it. The recorded macro creates the chart using `xlLineMarkers` but doesn't display markers. Use `xlLine` to make sure there are no markers displayed. The first argument, `227`, is not well documented, so just accept what the macro recorder provides.

If you run this code, you get a blank chart on your worksheets. We'll need to manipulate the chart variable, `cht`, to add elements to it. Start by setting the range you want to drive the chart. Use `With` and `End With` statements to save yourself some typing and organize your code. Make your code look like the following:

```
Sub MakeSinglePanel()

    Dim cht As Chart

    Set cht = ActiveSheet.Shapes.AddChart2(227, xlLine).Chart

    With cht
        .SetSourceData ActiveSheet.Range("A1:B14")
    End With

End Sub
```

If you run this code, you'll get a chart with something in it. Figure 9.60 shows the chart the code creates. It's already close to what you want. You just need to clean up some of the elements and size and position it. Start by removing the chart title and value axis. The code should now look like the following:

```
Sub MakeSinglePanel()

    Dim cht As Chart
```

Continues

(continued)

```
    Set cht = ActiveSheet.Shapes.AddChart2(227, xlLine).Chart

With cht
    .SetSourceData ActiveSheet.Range("A1:B14")
    .ChartTitle.Delete
    .Axes(xlSecondary).Delete
End With

End Sub
```

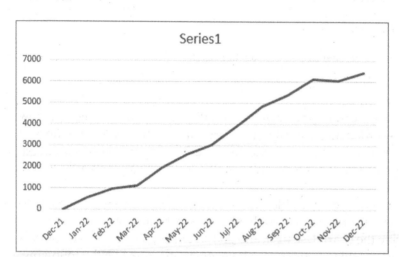

Figure 9.60: A chart with source data

The final step to replicate the recorded macro is to resize and reposition the chart. The recorded code manipulates the shape object using properties that change the scale and that increment from its current position. I'm not sure why Excel chooses those properties, but there is a simpler way. So far, you've been manipulating a Chart object. One level up in the object model hierarchy, the parent of the Chart object, is the ChartObject object. It has properties like Top and Height that you can set directly. The following code adds another With block acting on the Parent object and sets its properties to position and size the chart:

```
Sub MakeSinglePanel()

    Dim cht As Chart

    Set cht = ActiveSheet.Shapes.AddChart2(227, xlLine).Chart

    With cht
        .SetSourceData ActiveSheet.Range("A1:B14")
        .ChartTitle.Delete
```

```
        .Axes(xlSecondary).Delete
    With .Parent
        .Top = 107
        .Left = 580
        .Height = 145
        .Width = 260
    End With
    End With

End Sub
```

That code replicates the recorded macro. You could run this code over and over to make new charts and they would end up right on top of each other. For this data set, you want to make eight charts, not one. You can use the `MakeSinglePanel` macro to do that, but you'll have to change it so that each chart uses different data and ends up in a different place. To do that, you add arguments to the code. The new macro, `MakeSinglePanel2`, follows and shows how to add arguments to a macro:

```
Sub MakeSinglePanel2(rSource As Range, _
    dTop As Double, dLeft As Double, _
    dHeight As Double, dWidth As Double)

    Dim cht As Chart

    Set cht = ActiveSheet.Shapes.AddChart2(227, xlLine).Chart

    With cht
        .SetSourceData rSource
        .ChartTitle.Delete
        .Axes(xlSecondary).Delete

    With .Parent
        .Top = dTop
        .Left = dLeft
        .Height = dHeight
        .Width = dWidth
    End With
    End With

End Sub
```

When you created the first `Sub` statement, VBA added parentheses at the end. Anything you put between those parentheses are the arguments that you pass into the sub. Arguments act just like variables in your macro, only their values are set in a different macro. In this example, you're passing in a `Range` object that will be the source of the chart and four `Double` values that will determine the chart's position and size. You can call `MakeSinglePanel2` from another macro and pass in arguments like in the following example:

```
MakeSinglePanel2 ActiveSheet.Range("A1:B14"), 107, 580, 145, 260
```

Instead of those values being part of the macro, they are passed in. You can pass in different values to get a different chart. The next step is to create the macro that calls `MakeSinglePanel2` eight times with different values. Figure 9.61 shows the output of this macro.

```
Sub MakeAllPanels()

    With ActiveSheet
        MakeSinglePanel2 .Range("A1:B14"), 255, 746, 100, 200
        MakeSinglePanel2 .Range("A1:A14, C1:C14"), 255, 946, 100, 200
        MakeSinglePanel2 .Range("A1:A14, D1:D14"), 355, 746, 100, 200
        MakeSinglePanel2 .Range("A1:A14, E1:E14"), 355, 946, 100, 200
        MakeSinglePanel2 .Range("A1:A14, F1:F14"), 455, 746, 100, 200
        MakeSinglePanel2 .Range("A1:A14, G1:G14"), 455, 946, 100, 200
        MakeSinglePanel2 .Range("A1:A14, H1:H14"), 555, 746, 100, 200
        MakeSinglePanel2 .Range("A1:A14, I1:I14"), 555, 946, 100, 200
    End With

End Sub
```

You'll probably notice the pattern in all those calls. The top keeps increasing, the left alternates between 746 and 946, and the height and width stay constant. When you see patterns in your code, you can usually create a loop to give you more flexibility. In the next iteration, shown below, `MakeSinglePanel2` is called from within two For loops. This gives you the flexibility of changing the layout of your panel charts. For example, you could lay them out four wide and two deep just by changing the values of the loops. If your source data changes, it's easier to modify this code to accommodate it:

```
Sub MakeAllPanels2()

    Dim rAxis As Range
    Dim i As Long, j As Long
    Dim lCnt As Long
    Dim dWidth As Double, dHeight As Double

    Set rAxis = ActiveSheet.Range("A1:A14")

    dWidth = 200
    dHeight = 100

    For i = 1 To 4
        For j = 1 To 2
            lCnt = lCnt + 1
```

```
                MakeSinglePanel2 _
                    rSource:=Union(rAxis, rAxis.Offset(0, lCnt)), _
                    dTop:=255 + ((i - 1) * dHeight), _
                    dLeft:=746 + ((j - 1) * dWidth), _
                    dHeight:=dHeight, _
                    dWidth:=dWidth
            Next j
        Next i

    End Sub
```

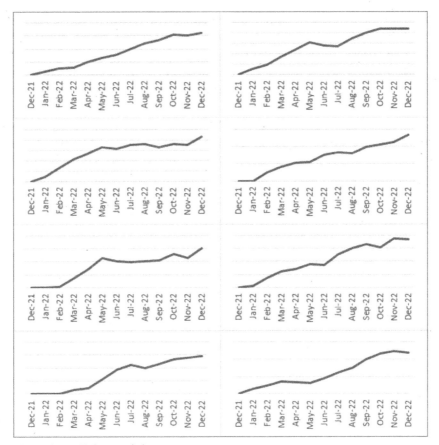

Figure 9.61: Eight panel charts

The main part of this macro is two For loops. The first loop determines how tall the panel is and the second how wide. Because the range A1:A14 was the same for all eight calls, a variable is created to store that range. Then the `Union` statement is used to combine that range with each value range as it loops through, incrementing one column at a time.

The top and left start at 255 and 746 respectively. Each time the outer loop is executed, it adds the height to the previous top so that chart is just below the previous one. Similarly, each time the inner loop is executed, it adds the width to the previous left so the chart is placed just to the previous chart's right.

The `MakeAllPanels2` macro produces the same charts as `MakeAllPanels`. If you wanted to make the panel 4x2, you simply change the out loop to `For i = 1 to 2` and the inner loop to `For j = 1 to 4`.

The final adjustment to make to the code is to only show the axis on the bottom charts. Repeating the axis for all charts is a waste of space. The problem with deleting the axis on some, but not all, charts is that the plot area of the chart with no axis will be bigger than those with an axis. The plot area will increase to fill the chart area. The trick is to make the `PlotArea.InsideHeight` property the same for all charts.

If you set the `PlotArea.InsideHeight` property directly, your charts will scale the same, but the `ChartArea.Height` property won't change, and you'll be left with white space where the axis would normally be.

The new code, `MakeSinglePanel3`, is shown below. Instead of being a subprocedure, it's now a function. A function can return a value or an object back to the procedure that called it. This function will return the chart that it creates so you can store the `PlotArea.InsideHeight` value for later. The function also has two new arguments: `dInsideHeight` and `bHideAxis`:

```
Function MakeSinglePanel3(rSource As Range, _
    dTop As Double, dLeft As Double, _
    dHeight As Double, dWidth As Double, _
    dInsideHeight As Double, bHideAxis As Boolean) As Chart

    Dim i As Long
    Dim cht As Chart

    Set cht = ActiveSheet.Shapes.AddChart2(227, xlLine).Chart

    With cht
        .SetSourceData rSource
        .ChartTitle.Delete
        With .Axes(xlSecondary)
            .Delete
            .HasMajorGridlines = False
        End With
        If bHideAxis Then
            With .Axes(xlPrimary)
                .Delete
                .HasMajorGridlines = False
            End With
            .Parent.Height = dHeight
        Else
            .Parent.Height = dHeight
            Do Until .PlotArea.InsideHeight > dInsideHeight
                .Parent.Height = .Parent.Height + 1
```

```
            Loop
        End If

        With .Parent
            .Top = dTop
            .Left = dLeft
            .Width = dWidth
        End With
    End With

    Set MakeSinglePanel3 = cht

End Function
```

Just as in the previous iteration, this creates the chart, deletes the title, and deletes the secondary axis. It also deletes the gridlines, but this is optional. You want to hide the axis for all charts except the bottom row. The bHideAxis argument determines whether the axis will be hidden. When it's True, the primary axis is deleted. When it's False, it's a chart on the bottom row and the height is increased until the plot area is the same size as the other charts. In the last line, the chart is returned to the calling procedure by assigning it to the name of the function.

The calling procedure has to change also. You need to determine when you're on the bottom row of charts so you can set the bHideAxis argument appropriately. The new procedure, MakeAllPanels3, is shown below:

```
Sub MakeAllPanels3()

    Dim rAxis As Range
    Dim i As Long, j As Long
    Dim lCnt As Long
    Dim dWidth As Double, dHeight As Double
    Dim dInsideHeight As Double
    Dim cht As Chart

    Const lHigh As Long = 4
    Const lWide As Long = 2

    Set rAxis = ActiveSheet.Range("A1:A14")

    dWidth = 200
    dHeight = 100

    For i = 1 To lHigh
        For j = 1 To lWide

            lCnt = lCnt + 1
            Set cht = MakeSinglePanel3( _
                rSource:=Union(rAxis, rAxis.Offset(0, lCnt)), _
                dTop:=255 + ((i - 1) * dHeight), _
```

Continues

(continued)

```
                        dLeft:=746 + ((j - 1) * dWidth), _
                        dHeight:=dHeight, _
                        dWidth:=dWidth, _
                        dInsideHeight:=dInsideHeight, _
                        bHideAxis:=i < lHigh)

                If i = 1 And j = 1 Then
                        dInsideHeight = cht.PlotArea.InsideHeight
                End If
            Next j
        Next i

    End Sub
```

This procedure contains two new variables to hold the plot area's height and the chart object we're returning from the function. There are also two constants added that will determine how tall and wide the panel is. Instead of hard-coding the numbers in the `For Next` statements, you can set them at the top of the procedure in a constant. If you want to change the orientation, you only have to change the numbers in one place.

Instead of calling the procedure to make the single panel, the code now sets the chart object variable, `cht`, to a function that makes the panel. When you call a function like this, the arguments must be in parentheses. Below the function call, the code stores the `PlotArea.InsideHeight` value of the first chart made so when it gets to the bottom row, the function will know how tall to make those charts. The final panel chart is shown in Figure 9.62.

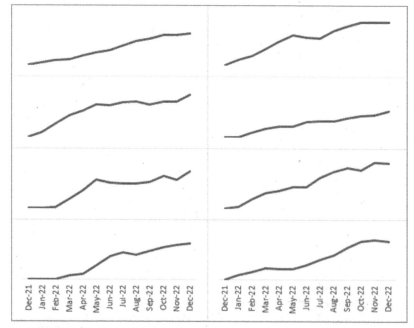

Figure 9.62: The final panel chart

Index